Cultural Hybridity and the Environment

Kirsten Maclean

Cultural Hybridity and the Environment

Strategies to celebrate local and Indigenous knowledge

Springer

Kirsten Maclean
CSIRO (Adaptive Social and Economic
Systems Program)
Dutton Park, Australia

ISBN 978-981-10-1213-6 ISBN 978-981-287-323-1 (eBook)
DOI 10.1007/978-981-287-323-1

Springer Singapore Heidelberg New York Dordrecht London

Softcover reprint of the hardcover 1st edition 2015

Printed on acid-free paper

Springer Science+Business Media Singapore Pte Ltd. is part of Springer Science+Business Media
(www.springer.com)

I dedicate this book to my wonderful family who continue to provide me with endless intellectual and emotional support. In no particular order: the Hambleys – Tom, Hannah and Happy; Anne Warren; and the Macleans – Rupert, Michiko, Lisa, Amie-Anne, Janelle, Joan and Donald.

Preface

David Harvey has proclaimed, "The geography we make must be a peoples' geography" (1984, p. 7). This clarion call challenges geographers everywhere to consider the power and potential of geographic knowledge as basis for social action. This book answers Harvey's call. It provides its readers tools to understand the social world and empowers them to mobilize social change.

Maclean has achieved this tremendous feat through a sophisticated distillation of relevant theory and an eloquent presentation of two rich empirical case studies from local environmental management and community development.

The theoretical analysis is built on a brilliant critique of western scientific views of the natural world to reveal how understandings of nature are a social construction. By documenting how knowledge generation is "essentially locally situated and socially derived", Maclean charts a path to move to beyond what Vandana Shiva so aptly describes as "monocultures of the mind".

Maclean moves beyond seeing local knowledge in opposition to scientific knowledge. She demonstrates that neither local and indigenous knowledge nor contemporary western scientific knowledge hold all the answers to localised socio-environmental problems. However as she shows when these respective knowledge systems learn to speak to each other we do have powerful tools to move towards more sustainable outcomes.

It is the successful deconstruction of knowledge dichotomies that makes the book "practical" and allows Maclean to demonstrate how "ESD" can become more than an empty slogan. The case studies examined reveal in the starkest terms how existing resource management polices and programs do not acknowledge local environmental and cultural diversity.

Through her analysis, Maclean demonstrates the importance of understanding scale in natural resource management. She argues "environmental governance consists of locally situated environmental management actions that have ramifications for regional, national and global environments". Maclean concludes by arguing that best practice environmental management must include best practice social processes. This is a simple but crucial message, and is brilliantly made.

This is a book that everyone involved with environmental policy, planning and politics needs to read and learn from. It is indispensable to anyone wanting to make this planet a more sustainable and just place.

The Australian National University
Canberra, Australia

Richard Baker

Acknowledgements

I wish to acknowledge Professors Richard Baker and Valerie Brown from the Fenner School of Environment and Society, The Australian National University, for their enthusiasm for this study. I thank the Fenner School for providing support during the research study, in particular I am grateful for the creative direction of Mr. Clive Hilliker and sincere thanks to Drs. Sue Feary, Stefan Kaufman, and David Eastburn; also Mr. Charles Tambiah and Mrs. Bronwyn Battison. I also wish to acknowledge Dr. Simon Naylor, The University of Glasgow, and Professor Marcus Power, Durham University, for their involvement in early research discussions.

The case studies that bring the research alive reflect the passion, dedication and energy of the many people involved in environmental management and community development in Victoria and the Northern Territory, Australia. I am indebted to the numerous people who spent time speaking of their personal experiences and showing me their land and their country. In Victoria, members of local landcare, field naturalist and environment groups, community facilitators and project officers from the catchment management authority, researchers, government officers from the then Department of Sustainability and Environment, the local shire council and Parks Victoria as well as the Melbourne office of the Worldwide Fund for Nature provided insight into the workings of the threatened species project. In particular I wish to thank Ms. Jenni Thomas, Mr. Geoff Park and Ms. Julie Kirkwood for their initial enthusiasm and ongoing support and interest in the research. In the Northern Territory, the experiences shared by many Aboriginal people from the communities of Willowra, Nyirippi, Yuendumu and Lajamanu form a fundamental part of the research study as do those of pastoralists and conservation land managers from the region and government officers based in Alice Springs.

Research affiliation and the associated financial support from the Desert Knowledge Cooperative Research Centre greatly assisted the research work in the Northern Territory. I am particularly grateful to Dr. Craig James, Dr. Glenn Edwards, Dr. Alicia Boyle and Mrs. Ruth Brown for their assistance in galvanising the affiliation and ongoing support. Much of the fieldwork conducted in the Northern Territory was generously facilitated by members of the then Desert Fire project, in particular: Dr. Grant Allan, Mr. Richard Tuckwell, Ms. Kasia Gabrys, Mr. Angus

Duguid, Ms. Andrea Johnson and Mr. Chris Materne. I also acknowledge Mr. Jamie Moore, Dr. Rachel Paltridge and Mr. Shane Brumby.

I acknowledge support from the Commonwealth Scientific Industrial and Research Organisation (CSIRO) that enabled the final manuscript editorial. In particular I thank Dr. Rosemary Hill and Dr. Andrew Shephard and the Building Resilient Australian Biodiversity Assets research theme.

Thank you to Professor Ritchie Howitt, Macquaire University; Dr Will Allen, Landcare Research NZ; and Dr Karen Fisher, Auckland University, for reviews of an earlier draft. I also acknowledge the editorial team at Springer Singapore for their excellent support in the development of this book: Mr. Lawrence Liu, Ms. Jayanthie Krishnan, Ms. Kanako Tanaka, Mr. Vishal Daryanomel and Ms. Chitra Sundarajan.

Contents

Acronyms and Abbreviations

ABS	Australian Bureau of Statistics
AIATSIS	Australian Institute of Aboriginal and Torres Strait Islander Studies
BFC	Bushfires Council (Northern Territory)
CLC	Central Land Council (Northern Territory)
CLMA	Centralian Land Management Association (Northern Territory)
CRC	Cooperative Research Centre
CSIRO	Commonwealth Scientific and Industrial Research Organisation (Australia)
DCM	Department of the Chief Minister (Northern Territory)
DDT	Dichlorodiphenyltrichloroethane
DEH	Department of Environment and Heritage (Federal)
DEST	Department of Education, Science and Training (Federal)
DIPE	Department of Infrastructure and Planning (Northern Territory)
DKCRC	Desert Knowledge Cooperative Research Centre
DNRE	Department of Natural Resources and Environment (Victoria)
DPI	Department of Planning and Infrastructure (Victoria)
DPIFM	Department of Primary Industries, Fisheries and Mines (Northern Territory)
DSE	Department of Sustainability and Environment (Victoria)
ECC	Environment Conservation Council (Victoria)
EM&CD	Environmental management and community development
EPBC	Environment Protection and Biodiversity Conservation Act, 1999 (Federal)
ESD	Ecologically sustainable development
ESDSC	Ecologically Sustainable Development Working Group (Federal)
FFG	Flora and Fauna Guarantee Act, 1988 (Victoria)
IBRA	Interim Biogeographic Regionalisation for Australia
LCNT	Landcare Council of the Northern Territory
NHMRC	National Health and Medical Research Council
NHT	Natural Heritage Trust

NHT2	Natural Heritage Trust phase 2
NLC	Northern Land Council
NMR	Natural Resource Management
NRETA	Department of Natural Resources, Environment and the Arts (Northern Territory)
TSN	Threatened Species Network (a program of the Worldwide Fund for Nature, Australia)
WSSD	World Summit on Sustainable Development, Johannesburg 2002
WWF	Worldwide Fund for Nature

List of Figures

List of Tables

Chapter 1
Introduction

Abstract There are ongoing debates in the contemporary environment and development literature regarding the role of scientific, local and Indigenous participation in sustainable development initiatives. The debates have been critical of the supremacy of western scientific knowledge in such initiatives, with some academics asserting that science can be imperialistic, and its application can sometimes lead to social inequity and exclusion. In response, local and Indigenous knowledges have been offered as providing a panacea for all environment and development problems. This book offers a new conceptual framework to provide a way to move beyond these unhelpful dichtomies towards the notion of cultural hybridity (cf Bhabha, The third space: interview with Homi Bhabha. In: Rutherford J (ed) Identity: community, culture, difference. Lawrence & Wishart, London, pp 207–221, 1990). The framework provides a way to consider what lies between the complex sets of knowledge of best practice environmental management at the local environmental management and community development interface. By recognising the hybrid knowledge spaces that exist between the different ontologies of multiple and diverse actors, we can work towards the creation of new spaces of representation, with the potential of enabling a third cultural space, a space that exists beyond the dichotomy of self/other. The *very process of working towards* this third cultural space and the pathway of cultural hybridity may give 'rise to something different, something new and unrecognisable, a new area of negotiation of meaning and representation' (Bhabha, The third space: interview with Homi Bhabha. In: Rutherford J (ed) Identity: community, culture, difference. Lawrence & Wishart, London, p 211, 1990).

This chapter provides an overview of the book with an introduction of the new conceptual framework that is advocated to enable cultural hybridity. The epistemological tools that form the basis of this framework are also introduced. The chapter provides an overview of how the rich empirical insights gleaned from the two local environmental management and community development case studies used in this study demonstrate how this conceptual framework can provide a way to move beyond dominant discourses that are comprised of knowledge binaries (e.g. scientific knowledge/local and Indigenous knowledge), to a pluralised and scaled frame for understanding place-based knowledges, and the claims these knowledges make on governance and management of environmental systems. These empirical studies provide a way to engage with local geopolitics. They show the local and place-based dimensions of the complexities of moving towards a narrative of ecologically sustainable development premised upon the notion of cultural hybridity.

K. Maclean, *Cultural Hybridity and the Environment*,
DOI 10.1007/978-981-287-323-1_1

1.1 A Framework for Cultural Hybridity

This book considers ways to alleviate the contemporary challenges of environmental and social degradation. The framework to enable cultural hybridity consists of an epistemological tool, a conceptual tool, a set of guiding questions that, when used to understand any social ecological situation, provide the way to open spaces for cultural hybridity and a set of suggested strategies to enable cultural hybridity within environmental management and community development projects and settings. The epistemological tool – an 'applied peoples' geography' (after Harvey 1984, explored in more detail later) – is used in the book to engage, unpack and unpick the complex sets of knowledge of best practice environmental management that are active in any environmental management and community development project. This is complemented by the conceptual tool – an 'edge politics' (after Howitt 2001a explored in more detail later) – that enables a critique of the nation state's commitment to the global dimensions of sustainable development and provides a way to explore how the metanarrative of ecologically sustainable development can influence local environmental governance and management in any nation. Part I presents *the foundations for this new conceptual framework for cultural hybridity*. Chapter 2 locates the research within the contemporary environment and development literature and thereby presents the argument for why we need this new conceptual framework, and Chap. 3 provides the epistemological tools of the framework.

The framework offers a way to explore the tensions that exist at the nexus between environmental governance and environmental management. This includes what I call the environment and development interface where environmental governance is formalised in policy and articulated in government strategies and then enacted via government-funded programs. It also includes what I call the environmental management and community development interface where community groups carry out environmental management at the local scale. On-ground environmental management projects are facilitated and funded through programs and projects that also advocate community development. The tensions between these two interfaces appear when we consider the rhetoric of environment and development policy and the reality of lived local experience as exemplified at the environmental management and community development interface. Part II puts *the edge politics* of the framework into action by highlighting the tensions that exist at the nexus between environmental governance and environmental management. It provides a way to critique and thus understand the political and cultural landscapes (Chaps. 4 and 5) in which any environmental management and community development project is located.

The framework is founded upon a set of guiding questions that both explore the tensions that exist at the nexus between environmental governance and environmental management and provide a way to open the space for cultural hybridity. How do knowledges of best practice environmental management move across and between international, national and local scales of governance and community advocacy? What is the role of community stakeholder groups and their knowledge in the networks surrounding environmental governance and management? How can greater knowledge sharing between the many interest groups involved in environmental management and community development projects be devised? The first question provides the basis of the critique and exploration conducted in Part III: *local voices in the landscape* (Chaps. 6 and 7). The second question is then explored in Part IV: *knowledge networks across the landscape* (Chaps. 8 and 9). Part V (Chaps. 10 and 11) draws on the lessons, insights and conclusions presented in Parts III and IV and provides a discussion into the final question by presenting suggested *strategies for cultural hybridity*.

This enquiry acknowledges that equitable and ecologically sustainable development is dependent upon moving beyond dichotomies that position western scientific knowledge of best practice environmental management as universal and thus more powerful than local and Indigenous knowledges of best practice environmental management. The book confronts and considers ways to move beyond these dichotomies by first delivering a critique of environmental governance and management. Second, it considers what it means to move beyond the knowledge dichotomies that are highlighted in Chap. 2 as central to the metanarrative of ecologically sustainable development (hereon referred to as ESD). A research praxis that integrates theoretical and empirical investigations is used to provide insight into the contemporary challenges of environmental and social degradation.

1.2 Epistemological Tools

A framework to enable cultural hybridity is grounded in an ontology that celebrates the existence of a biophysical world that is composed of dynamic biological, chemical and physical processes. These biophysical processes support a great diversity of life. These biophysical processes and life forms are interdependent. They develop, evolve and destruct in ongoing cycles and exist independent of social epistemologies. The framework is also grounded in an epistemology that acknowledges the many social understandings, interpretations and qualifications of this biophysical world. This epistemology holds that human beings belong to particular cultures that ascribe different meanings to the biophysical world. Some of these cultures understand the world according to binaries. The framework engages with various theoretical and philosophical conceptualisations of social process to argue that genuine ESD can only occur through the celebration of diversity. Celebrating diversity means moving beyond binaries that carve the biophysical and social world into unhelpful dichotomies of 'them and us' (Murdoch 1997a).

In this book I propose that these binaries and dichotomies evolve from social conceptualisations of power as static, knowledge as hierarchical, governance scale as hierarchical and the denial that what constitutes the natural world is based on social constructs. Following Harvey (1984) I engage with an epistemology that celebrates an 'applied peoples' geography'. This applied peoples' geography provides tools to describe, analyse and understand the social world that are empowering and create the basis for social action (Harvey 1984). This geography is based upon the fluid and entangled realities of knowledge, power, governance scale and nature. As such it provides a way to open up the local spaces of environmental governance and management, that is, the spaces of knowing and acting in the world that celebrate diversity and as such provide a basis for social action.

In the following discussion, I briefly define these epistemological tools (these tools are explored in more detail in Chap. 3). I engage with postcolonial (e.g. Said 1979; Guha and Spivak 1988; Bhabha 1994), political ecology (e.g. Bryant 1997, 2001; Peet and Watts 1996; Forsyth 2003; Biersack and Greenberg 2006) and cultural and political geography (e.g. Sharp et al. 2000) literatures to conceive of power as entangled. I delve into the history and philosophy of science (e.g. Latour 1987; Golinski 1998; Kendall and Wickham 1999) and cultural geography literatures (e.g. Haraway 1991; Murdoch 1997a, b) to develop a critique of knowledge as situated, tied to place, networked and associated across time and space. I use the work of cultural and political geographers (e.g. McGuirk 1997; Swyngedouw 1997; Howitt 1998, 2003) to conceive of governance scale as relational, networked and associated across time and space. Finally, I critique western scientific constructions of the so-called natural world to develop an understanding of nature as a social construction.

When I refer to 'local knowledge', I speak first of the knowledge that is juxtaposed with scientific knowledge and understood in relation to its connection to the place where it evolved. As the book progresses, the complexity of this term is revealed as I explore how knowledges of best practice environmental management move between different governance arenas and different geographical places. All knowledges are revealed to be in some sense local. The success of, for example, specific threatened species management techniques depends upon how appropriate these techniques are to the demands of different geographical places. The success of such techniques also depends upon the interest and skills of local actors and the extent to which local actors can adapt such techniques to local circumstances. In Chap. 7 the notion of 'place-based knowledge' is proposed and used to refer to local knowledge that is confined to knowledge of a specific geographical place.

When I refer to 'knowledges of best practice environmental management', I speak of the complex sets of knowledge active at any environmental management and community development interface. These knowledges that are explained visually in Fig. 1.1 encompass the many different ways to govern and manage specific places. When I refer to 'knowledge networks', I speak of the networks of individuals located in various geographical places and governance arenas across the landscape. I argue that what might be conceived of as a bounded and ordered environmental management and community development project actually represents a point of intersection of these networks that make up entangled and very local worlds.

When I refer to 'environmental governance scale', I speak of the various arenas, international, national, regional and local where individuals, political institutions and governments articulate best practice environmental management. I argue that each of these arenas is located in specific geographical places. Accordingly, environmental governance scale is enacted similarly at any one geographical place

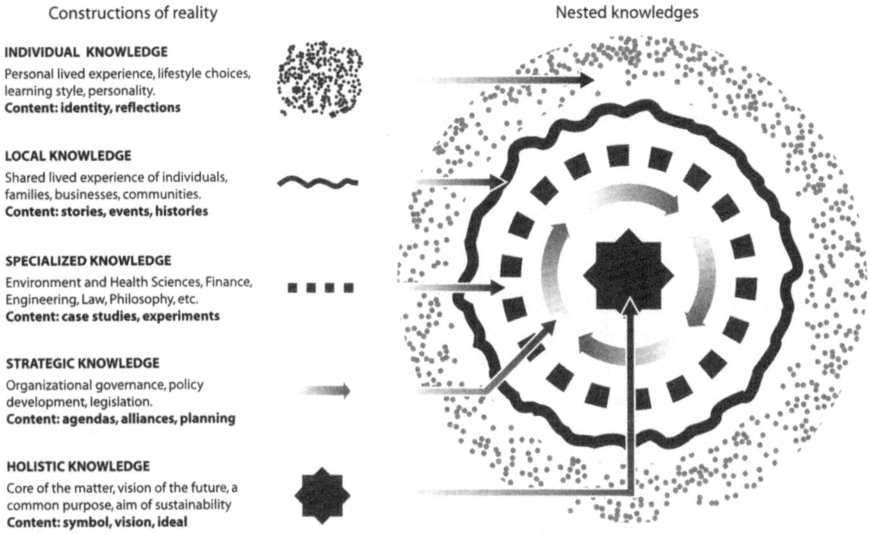

Fig. 1.1 Knowledge cultures in western decision-making systems. In this figure, the shapes of the knowledge diagrams represent the different structures of these diverse knowledge systems. For example, local knowledge is diverse and loosely connected; specialist knowledge is tightly specified within the different frameworks; strategic knowledge is organised and directional; and holistic knowledge is considered the core focus of decision-making systems (See Aslin and Brown 2004. Source: Brown 2001a)

through multiple, networked and entangled local spaces of environmental governance and management. As such environmental knowledge moves differently through local spaces of environmental management and community development than through the metanarratives of policy and political agendas.

1.3 Empirical Case Studies Show Local Dimensions of the Wider Complexities of 'Ecologically Sustainable Development'

Working towards ecologically sustainable development that is premised on and celebrates hybridity requires detailed local-scale empirical studies that enable an investigation into the role of local knowledge and the local in community development and environmental management. Such empirical studies allow an engagement with local geopolitics in a way that reflects the wider national and global issues of ecologically sustainable development. These studies provide a way to illustrate how an applied peoples' geography, an edge politics and related questions form the basis of the new conceptual framework for hybridity. They enable a 'real-world' discussion about the wider conceptual, political and practical significance of the new conceptual framework for hybridity, by highlighting the significance of the lived local experience.

The two environmental management and community development projects that are used here as case studies are derived from the Australian context: they show how any such project can provide a lens through which to understand the theoretical complexities as well as the practical realities at the local environmental management and community development interface. Further, the two case studies provide insights into the phenomenon of community involvement in environmental governance and management relevant to any nation. They provide insight into the wider conceptual, political and practical significance of local experiences.

As with any community development and environmental management project across the world, these projects are afforded boundaries by government process and project demarcation. They have been captured within project documentation and funding regimes. But they are in fact without boundaries because, as I argue here, the projects are created by social relations and social processes. These relations and processes are constantly negotiated and renegotiated as individuals learn, adapt and evolve within the project boundaries, as voices become stronger or are silenced. The case studies show how any community development and environmental management project is a product of a geographic place. Important to note is that any such place is unique and understood in many ways by diverse and multiple actors. The actual physical and material existence of these places is also dynamic, for example, animal species reproduce and migrate; plant species flower and die back; rain falls or indeed does not; spinifex grasslands reach their optimum burning, or cure rate and carry fire long distances, or burn out in localised patches; and winds rise and fall.

A participatory research and action approach was used to drive the empirical research (see Maclean 2007 for details of the methods used). This approach questions how seemingly devolved environmental governance structures look from the local point of view. In doing so it questions the capacity of devolution to strengthen grass-roots social and political participation (Gaventa and Valderrama 1999; Gaventa 2001). Similarly, following the postcolonial critique (see Sylvester 1999), it investigates the embedded power dynamics inherent to environment and development initiatives. It questions whose knowledge is privileged and whose knowledge is silenced by these initiatives. Participatory research and action approach uses qualitative research methodologies that are *participatory* in nature that work to reveal power relationships between project members. These methodologies then take the research practice one step further to consider locally derived *actions* necessary for improved knowledge sharing for ecologically sustainable development at the local environmental management and community development interface. These methodologies are based upon the philosophy of 'participatory rural appraisal' (see Chambers 1994a, b; Mosse 1994; IDS 1998; Cleaver 1999; Campbell 2002; David 2002) and resonate strongly with the role of participatory approaches to 'social impact assessment' for local community empowerment (see Craig 1990; Rickson et al. 1990; Ross 1990; Gagnon et al. 1993; Howitt 1993).

Participatory research and action approach complements the epistemological tools used as the basis of the framework to enable hybridity. This is because it supports a conceptualisation of knowledge generation as essentially locally situated and socially derived. This approach provides a means to engage with the many voices of environmental governance and management in any nation. It also opens the space and the potential for greater interfacing between different kinds of knowledge, in working towards environmental governance and management. The participatory research and action approach acknowledges that social research does not occur within a vacuum of time, space and social and political contexts. Engaging with social and cultural processes is not about control and attempting to prove or disprove a particular hypothesis, but about interpreting the processes in light of the research aim. As such the research engaged with people connected to two specific community development and environmental management projects and worked with them to tap into their perspectives, attitudes and hopes relating to the themes of this research. Thus, the research was grounded in the local and involved two-way research relationships, transparency, mutual participation and evolving processes. This qualitative approach assumes a dynamic and negotiated reality as opposed to more positivist quantitative methods (Furze et al. 1996).

It is important to note that this research and the supporting methodological tools used to gather empirical data continue the unsettling practiced by some contemporary human geographers and anthropologists. These researchers work to confront the postmodern challenge of moving beyond positivist social research practice and embracing polyvocality (Clifford 1997: 194) attests that 'fieldwork has become a problem because of its positivist and colonial associations – the field as 'laboratory', the field as place of 'discovery''.). Their work seeks to unsettle such discourses through practices and writings (e.g. Davies 1995; Smith 1999; Howitt 1999, 2001a, b; Young 1995, 1999; Rose 1996, 2004; Baker 1999; Baker et al. 2001; Brown 2001b; Howitt and Suchet-Pearson 2003; Brown and Pitcher 2005; Maclean 2009; Maclean and Cullen 2009; Maclean and Woodward 2013).

The epistemological stance of this research stems from the critique of scientific knowledge claims to objectivity (outlined in Chap. 3). The intention of this critique is not to undervalue scientific knowledge generation nor is it to further dichotomise scientific knowledge against other knowledge systems. Rather it is to conceptualise knowledge generation as essentially locally situated and socially derived. This provides a means to engage with the many voices of environmental governance and management in any nation. It also opens the space and the potential for greater interfacing between different kinds of knowledge, in working towards environmental governance and management. The approach used in this research complements this epistemology. It acknowledges that social research does not occur within a vacuum of time, space and social and political contexts. Engaging with social and cultural processes is not about control and attempting to prove or disprove a particular hypothesis, but about interpreting the processes in light of the research aim. As such the research engaged with people connected to two specific community development and environmental management projects and worked with them to tap into their perspectives, attitudes and hopes relating to the themes of this research.

Thus, the research was grounded in the local and involves two-way research relationships, transparency, mutual participation and evolving processes. This qualitative approach assumes a dynamic and negotiated reality as opposed to more positivist quantitative methods (Furze et al. 1996).

1.3.1 Empirical Case Studies

The two case studies that bring this research alive are located in the state of Victoria in southeast Australia and the Northern Territory, located, as its name suggests, in northern Australia (see Fig. 1.2). The case studies are located in specific geographical places and act as points of access into the localised knowledge networks

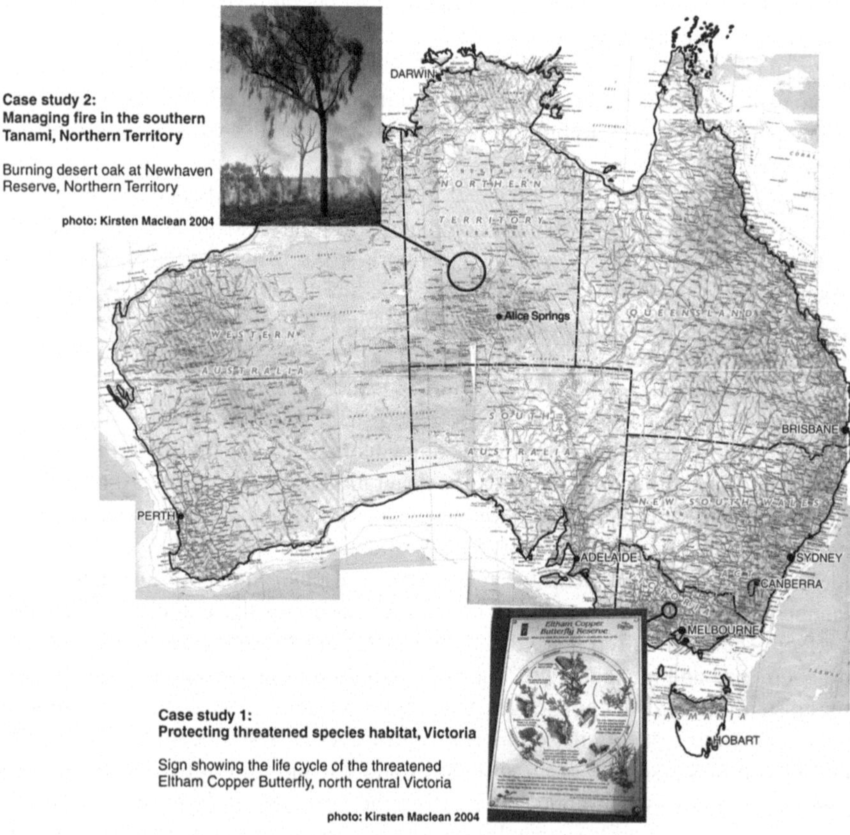

Fig. 1.2 Map of Australia showing the location of the two case study projects

surrounding environmental governance and management in Australia. They are introduced in detail in Chaps. 4 and 5, and in the following chapters, I apply the previously mentioned applied peoples' geography and edge politics to the two case studies as a means of opening the local spaces for social action and developing strategies for cultural hybridity that are central to Bhabha's (1990) third cultural space.

Case Study 1 Protecting Threatened Species Habitat, Victoria was a project of the World Wide Fund for Nature (WWF) Threatened Species Network. The aim of the Threatened Species Network – which ceased to exist in 2006 when the Australian Federal Government no longer provided relevant funding – was to work with the community to protect threatened plant and animal species and to stop them from disappearing from their natural habitats. The aim of the case study project was 'to promote and enhance native biodiversity by facilitating movement of native fauna and flora between [a specific] Bushland Reserve and the [a specific] State Forest' (Bushland Link-up Project 2002: 1). Interviews, participant observation and transect walks were conducted with project members (individuals from volunteer environmental conservation groups, Victorian Government agencies and non-government environmental agencies). *Case Study 2 Managing Fire in the Southern Tanami, Northern Territory* was a project of the Desert Knowledge Cooperative Research Centre (DKCRC). The DKCRC was a program of the Australian Federal Government's 'Cooperative Research Centres' program that supports 'industry led research partnerships between publically funded researchers, business and the community to address major long term challenges' (CRC Program 2014: 1). The aim of this case study project was to collate existing knowledge, develop new knowledge and disseminate knowledge for improved management of fire in the southern Tanami desert where frequent, large, uncontrolled wildfires are common. Interviews, participant observation and transect walks were conducted with project members (Aboriginal people, pastoralists and conservationists from the region, individuals from a variety of government agencies). Background information of both case studies is provided in more detail in Chap. 4.

As this research investigates the ways in which environmental governance and management are played out at the local, these two case studies form the basis to examine and critique the metanarrative ESD. Throughout the book I draw upon the experiences of individuals working at the local environmental management and community development interface of two very different projects in Australia. I engage with these local experiences to demonstrate and celebrate the diversity of local voices working at the environmental management and community development interface in Australia and across the world. I conclude that valuing pluralism across the Australian landscape engages the potential to both maintain diversity and create a diversity of approaches for ESD. Following Gunderson and Holling (2002), this diversity is a key part of the resilience of any system. My particular focus is upon the processes whereby different interest groups work together to govern and manage the natural environment.

1.4 Book Structure

The book is structured around five parts. Part I provides the *foundations for a new conceptual framework for cultural hybridity*. Chapter 2 locates the book within the contemporary environment and development literature and thus argues why we need this new conceptual framework. Chapter 3 develops the epistemological tools that are the basis of the framework. In Part II the *edge politics* of the framework is practised. Chapters 4 and 5 highlight the tensions that exist at the nexus between environmental governance and environmental management that are embodied in any environmental management and community development project. The critique of the political, cultural, knowledge and social landscapes in which the two case studies are embedded provides both an approach and a way to understand the wider complexities that are articulated in the lived local experiences of individuals involved with any environmental management and community development project. The applied peoples' geography is put into action in Parts III and IV. In Part III *local voices in the landscape*, Chaps. 6 and 7 respond to the first part of the research enquiry: they unpack the place-based spaces of environmental governance and environmental management at each case study locale. In Part IV *knowledge networks across the landscape*, Chaps. 8 and 9 address the second part of the research enquiry. These chapters consider the politics of knowledge at each of the two project case study interfaces. Part V *strategies for cultural hybridity* (Chaps. 10 and 11) synthesises the applied peoples' geography and the edge politics practised throughout the research with models from the social learning and community development literatures. Theoretical and practical strategies for hybridity are explored in this final part of the book. These strategies celebrate diversity and provide ways to open up the creative space necessary for cultural hybridity. This part also highlights the methodological, empirical and theoretical significance that this research has for future ESD.

References

Aslin HJ, Brown VA (2004) Towards whole of community engagement: a practical toolkit. Murray-Darling Basin Commission, Canberra

Baker R (1999) Land is life. From bush to town: the story of the Yanyuwa people. Allen & Unwin, St. Leonards

Baker R, Davies J, Young E (2001) Managing country: an overview of the prime issues. In: Baker R, Davies J, Young E (eds) Working on country: contemporary indigenous management of Australia's Lands and Coastal Regions. Oxford University Press, Melbourne, pp 3–19

Bhabha HK (1990) The third space: interview with Homi Bhabha. In: Rutherford J (ed) Identity: community, culture, difference. Lawrence & Wishart, London, pp 207–221

Bhabha HK (1994) The location of culture. Routledge, London

Biersack A, Greenberg JB (2006) Reimagining political ecology. Duke University Press, Durham

Brown VA (2001a) Monitoring changing environments in environmental health. Environ Health 1:20–31

Brown VA (2001b) Planners and the planet. Aust Plan 38(2):63–67

Brown VA, Pitcher J (2005) Linking community and government: islands and beaches. In: Keen M, Brown VA, Dyball R (eds) Social learning in environmental management. Towards a sustainable future. Earthscan, London, pp 123–145

Bryant RL (1997) Beyond the impasse: the power of political ecology in third world environmental research. Area 29(1):5–19

Bryant RL (2001) Political ecology: a critical agenda for change? In: Castree N, Braun B (eds) Social nature: theory. Practice and politics. Blackwell, Oxford, pp 151–169

Bushland Link-up Project (2002) Draft action plan: threatened species Bushland Link-up Project. Taradale & District Walking and Landcare Group, Taradale

Campbell J (2002) A critical appraisal of participatory methods in development research. Int J Soc Res Methodol 5(1):19–29

Chambers R (1994a) Participatory Rural Appraisal (PRA): challenges, potentials, paradigm. World Dev 22(10):1437–1454

Chambers R (1994b) The origins and practice of participatory rural appraisal. World Dev 22(7):953–969

Cleaver F (1999) Paradoxes of participation: questioning participatory approaches to development. J Int Dev 11:597–612

Clifford J (1997) Spatial practices: fieldwork, travel and the disciplining of anthropology. In: Gupta A, Ferguson J (eds) Anthropological locations: boundaries and grounds of a field science. University of California Press, California, pp 185–222

Craig D (1990) Social impact assessment: politically oriented approaches and applications. Environ Impact Assess Rev 10:37–54

CRC Program (2014) About the program http://www.crc.gov.au/About-the-program/Pages/default.aspx. Accessed 16 Jun 2014

David M (2002) Problems of participation: the limits of action research. Int J Soc Res Methodol 5(1):11–17

Davies J (1995) Appropriate planning for aboriginal self determination. Department of Geography and Oceanography. University of New South Wales, Sydney. Unpublished Doctor of Philosophy thesis

Forsyth T (2003) Critical political ecology. The politics of environmental science. Routledge, Abingdon

Furze B, De Lacy T, Birchhead J (1996) Using methods from the social sciences. In: Furze B, De Lacy T, Birchhead J (eds) Culture, conservation and biodiversity: the social dimension of linking local level development and conservation through protected areas. Wiley, England, pp 48–92

Gagnon C, Hirsch P, Howitt P (1993) Can SIA empower communities? Environ Impact Assess Rev 13(4):229–253

Gaventa J (2001) Towards participatory local governance: six propositions for discussion, Institute of Development Studies, http://www.ids.ac.uk. 20 July 2006

Gaventa J, Valderrama C, (1999) Participation, citizenship and local governance, Institute of Development Studies, http://www.ids.ac.uk. 20 Jul 2006

Golinski J (1998) Making natural knowledge: constructivism and the history of science. Cambridge University Press, Cambridge

Guha R, Spivak GC (eds) (1988) Selected subaltern studies. Oxford University Press, Oxford

Gunderson LH, Holling CS (eds) (2002) Panarchy: understanding transformations in human and natural systems. Island Press, Washington, DC

Haraway D (1991) Simians, cyborgs and women. Routledge, London

Harvey D (1984) On the history and present condition of geography: an historical materialist manifesto. Prof Geogr 36(1):1–11

Howitt R (1993) Social impact assessment as 'applied peoples' geography'. Aust Geogr Stud 31(2):127–140

Howitt R (1998) Scale as relations: musical metaphors of geographical scale. Area 30(1):49–58

Howitt R (1999) Opening the margins: nurturing discursive spaces in fieldwork, writing and teaching. In: Howitt R (ed) Institute of Australian Geographers Conference, University of Sydney
Howitt R (2001a) Frontiers, borders, edges: liminal challenges to the hegemony of exclusion. Aust Geogr Stud 39(2):233–245
Howitt R (2001b) Rethinking resource management: sustainability, justice and indigenous peoples. Routledge, London
Howitt R (2003) Scale. In: Agnew J, Mitchell K, Tuathail GO (eds) A companion to political geography. Blackwell, Oxford, pp 138–157
Howitt R, Suchet-Pearson S (2003) Spaces of knowledge: ontological pluralism in contested cultural landscapes. In: Anderson K, Domosh M, Pile S, Thrift N (eds) Handbook of cultural geography. Sage Publications, London
IDS (Institute of Development Studies) (1998) Participatory monitoring and evaluation: learning from change, Institute of Development Studies, http://www.ids.ac.uk. 16 June 2006
Kendall G, Wickham G (1999) Using Foucault's methods. Sage Publications, London
Latour B (1987) Science in action: how to follow scientists and engineers through society. Harvard University Press, Cambridge
Maclean K (2007) Creating spaces for negotiation at the environmental management and community development interface in Australia, The Fenner School of Environment and Society. The Australian National University, Canberra
Maclean K (2009) Reconceptualising desert landscapes: unpacking historical narratives and contemporary realities for sustainable livelihood development in Central Australia. GeoJournal 74(5):451–463
Maclean K, Cullen L (2009) Research methodologies for the co-production of knowledge for environmental management in Australia. J R Soc N Z 39(4):205–208
Maclean K, Woodward E (2013) Photovoice evaluated: an appropriate visual methodology for aboriginal water resource research. Geogr Res 51(1):94–105
McGuirk P (1997) Multiscaled interpretations of urban change: the federal, the state, and the local in the Western Area Strategy of Adelaide. Environ Plan D Soc Space 15:481–498
Mosse D (1994) Authority, gender and knowledge: theoretical reflections on the practice of participatory rural appraisal. Dev Chang 25:497–526
Murdoch J (1997a) Towards a geography of heterogeneous associations. Prog Hum Geogr 21(3):321–337
Murdoch J (1997b) Inhuman/nonhuman/human: actor-network theory and the prospects for a nondualistic and symmetrical perspective on nature and society. Environ Plann D 15:731–756
Peet R, Watts M (1996) Liberation ecology, development, sustainability, and environment in an age of market triumphalism. In: Peet R, Watts M (eds) Liberation ecologies, environment, development, social movement. Routledge, London, pp 1–45
Rickson RE, Western JS, Burdge RJ (1990) Social impact assessment: knowledge and development. Environ Impact Assess Rev 10(1–2):1–10
Rose DB (1996) Nourishing terrains: Australian aboriginal views of landscape. Australia Heritage Commission, Canberra
Rose DB (2004) Reports from a wild country: ethics for decolonisation. University of NSW Press Ltd, Sydney
Ross H (1990) Community social impact assessment: a framework for indigenous peoples. Environ Impact Assess Rev 10:185–193
Said E (1979) Orientalism. Routledge, London
Sharp J, Routledge P, Philo C, Paddison R (2000) Entanglements of power: geographies of domination/resistance. In: Sharp J, Routledge P, Philo C, Paddison R (eds) Entanglements of power: geographies of domination/resistance. Routledge, London, pp 1–42
Smith L (1999) Decolonizing methodologies: research and indigenous peoples. University of Otago Press, Dunedin

Swyngedouw E (1997) Neither global nor local: 'glocalization' and the politics of scale. In: Cox KR (ed) Spaces of globalization: reasserting the power of the local. The Guilford Press, New York, pp 137–166

Sylvester C (1999) Development studies and postcolonial studies: disparate tales of the 'Third World'. Third World Q 20(4):703–721

Young E (1995) Third world in the first: development and indigenous peoples. Routledge, London

Young E (1999) Hunter-gather concepts of land and its ownership in remote Australia and North America. In: Anderson K, Gale F (eds) Cultural geographies. Longman, Australia, pp 319–339

Part I
The Foundations for a New Conceptual Framework for Cultural Hybridity

Chapter 2
An Environmental and Social Crisis?

Abstract The aim of this chapter is to locate this research within the contemporary field of environment and development and thus provide the basis for why there is a need for a new conceptual framework for cultural hybridity. First, it traces a trajectory through contemporary development theory and considering the role that community participation and local knowledge can have in meeting the goals of sustainable development. Next, it considers how international environmental governance processes inform environmental governance policy and practice in any nation. Australia is used as a case study to provide focus to this critique. The chapter ends by highlighting why a new conceptual framework for cultural hybridity is necessary in this space.

2.1 Is There a Crisis?

After the Rio Earth Summit in 1992, Brown (1992)[1] called for an Environmental Revolution. An environmentally sustainable future, he said, depended on a restructuring of the global economy, major shifts in human reproductive behaviour and dramatic changes in values and lifestyles. How does the world look from this meta-perspective now: do we still face global ecological and social crisis? Perhaps we can find an answer to this question in the recent United Nations Millennium Declaration, 2000. The United Nations Millennium Development Goals are part of the road map to the implementation of the Millennium Declaration (MDG 2004). The 191 Member States have pledged to meet these goals by the year 2015. They fit under the broad themes of poverty eradication, education, gender equality, health, environmental stability and the evolution of a global partnership for development (UN 2003).[2] These development goals were declared at the turn of the twenty-first

[1] Brown (1992) founded the Worldwatch Institute in 1974; 10 years later he launched the State of the World reports and is winner of the United Nations 1989 environment prize.

[2] The eight goals are to eradicate extreme poverty and hunger; achieve universal primary education; promote gender equality and empower women; reduce child mortality; improve maternal health; combat HIV/AIDS, malaria and other major diseases; ensure environmental stability (important to this discussion) to integrate the principles of sustainable development into country policies and programs; reverse the loss of environmental resources; and develop a global partnership for development (UN 2003). The goals were to be reassessed by Member States in 2005. To date, progress

K. Maclean, *Cultural Hybridity and the Environment*,
DOI 10.1007/978-981-287-323-1_2

century as the building blocks for a more equitable and sustainable world. Perhaps not the revolution that Brown called for, they certainly signify a global commitment to overcome the previously mentioned ecological and social crisis. However, the significance of an international commitment is lost if there is no follow-up by member nations to institutionalise these goals and if positive actions already occurring on the ground are not acknowledged and reinforced in this process.

2.2 A Critique of Contemporary Development Theory

In this section I trace a trajectory through contemporary development theory. Important to this research is an awareness of how this theory informs the metanarrative of ecologically sustainable development (ESD). A reading of this section will reveal the imperative to critique whose notion of development is privileged in environmental governance policy and resulting programs in any nation state. This critique is premised on the idea that knowledge does not simply reflect but also constructs reality, and as such, it is political. Considering the trajectory is my take on development, it must be remembered that 'the map should not be mistaken for the territory' (Pieterse 2001: 13).

It is often argued that the contemporary development era began with the American President Truman's inaugural address in 1949. Truman stated that it was the responsibility of the western world to aid the poorer nations to achieve increased economic development because 'their economic life is primitive and stagnant' and 'for the first time in history humanity possesses the knowledge and the skill to relieve the suffering of these people' (Truman 1949 as cited by Esteva 1992: 6). Many policymakers heralded these words as signalling the end of the colonial white man's burden, but in reality they echoed the myriad power dynamics at play during colonial times (Kothari 1988). Truman's depiction of a dichotomy equating 'the west' with all that was positive and advanced versus 'the rest' as undeveloped and backward was dubbed by Said (1979) as a form of cultural imperialism and is argued by some to be the basis for contemporary development discourse (Sachs 1992; Escobar 1995; Doty 1996; Adams and Mulligan 2003; McGregor 2009). Words like modernisation and westernisation that are stated as synonymous with development reinforce this metanarrative.

In the 1970s it was argued that far from alleviating the poverty of individuals living in the 'third world',[3] economic growth had compounded their continued

has not been very successful. Anti-development theorists see these goals as a perpetuation of the development industry, whereby the management and decisions about development are made by development professionals 'whose specialised knowledge allegedly qualifies them for the task' (Escobar 1995: 52).

[3]There are many ways in which the developing nations of the world are classed. This is always done in relation to the developed world (e.g. the use of signifiers such as North/South, first world/third world). The 'second world' was used to denote the socialist revolutionary regimes, which some researchers believe no longer exist; the 'fourth world' is sometimes used to refer to minority

marginalisation and poverty. Increased environmental destruction and degradation were also by-products of this economic development. Coupled with these self-evident truths was a growing body of literature critical of the hegemonic discourse of development ideology and practice. The supposed linear course of development as advocated in Rostow's (1960) five-stage model of development was questioned. For example, Bernstein (1979) noted that the developed world may once have been undeveloped but has never passed through a stage of underdevelopment. Wallerstein's world systems theory based upon the dependency theory and spurred by the occurrences of what were termed the 'newly industrialised countries' suggested an interdependence of the first, second and third worlds. This suggests that underdevelopment occurs because countries are subject to inequitable trade regimes and the production of goods and services for the world market (Schuurman 1993).

Following from this, anti-development theorists state that a developed state necessitates an underdeveloped other (Sachs 1992; Escobar 1995). This dichotomy has been further perpetuated by past development practices that condone top-down, prescriptive or directed development (McGregor 2009). For example, the problem of underdevelopment was seen partially to be due to a science and technology gap between the more and less developed nations (Cohen and Uphoff 1980); it was believed this could be alleviated by the transfer of science and technology. Implicit within the discourse and praxis of technology transfer is the assumption of a passive, ignorant populous waiting for help to improve their livelihoods. Indeed it assumes a linear continuum of development where 'underdevelopment' is just one stage. Shiva (1993a, b), Crewe and Harrison (1998) and Chambers (1999) condemn what they see as an attempt to define the reality of the rural poor in the South by taking control of their means of production and adjusting it to suit Northern ideas of development in terms of sustained economic growth. Such technology is often viewed as inappropriate, and its dissemination may be gendered in its dispersal, invention, use, production and distribution (Crewe and Harrison 1998).

This technology transfer is inherently based upon knowledge transfer which Shiva (1993a) describes as the creation of 'monocultures of the mind', a form of intellectual imperialism which will inevitably lead to 'intellectual and cultural impoverishment since it would displace other ways of knowing, other objectives for knowledge creation, and other modes of knowledge sharing' (Shiva 1993b: 32). This discourse and resulting practice homogenises all remaining knowledge as primitive, unscientific and wrong (Nygen 1999). It also advocates that development efforts must seek to educate, direct and transform the minds of those who maintain these adverse knowledge bases (Scoones and Thompson 1994; Nygen 1999). At the same time there has been an increasing interest in the development literature regarding the social dimension of development (Cernea 1991). This is seen as a means of promoting equality, fostering freedom and engendering a sense of belonging and

indigenous nations living in the 'first world', whose experiences of development – marginalisation, colonialism and underdevelopment – are said to be analogous to their 'third world peers' (Young 1995). These signifiers are part of development discourse and have changed over time accordingly.

social purpose (Midgley et al. 1986). Without direct participation in environmental management projects, for example, people may benefit but not develop from a project (Finsterbusch and Van Wicken 1987). This participation takes various guises as described in more detail in Sect. 2.5. There has been a radical change in the way in which development has been theorised from the economic growth of Truman's era to the understanding of development in the mid-1980s as the 'enlargement of people's choices' (UNDP 2004a: 1). To post- or anti-development theorists who advocate for alternatives to development (rather than development alternatives) that include: the 'unmaking of the third world' which is stated to be a construct of the development era (Sachs 1992; Escobar 1995); and 'hopeful geographies' (see Gibson-Graham 2008) that seek to empower alternative voices, world views and processes that are often obscured in development research and practice. These theorists call for an encouragement of new spaces and re-imagined places thought of in relation to 'capacity and opportunity', rather than in terms of 'needs and limitations' (McGregor 2009) and to give consideration to what local groups may already be doing to embrace opportunities as they arise (see Ireland and Mckinnon 2013). There are also alternative development theorists who aver the importance of the spiritual dimension in socioeconomic regeneration (Rahnema 1997). As a result of the many critiques of the development process and the evolution of ideologies such as sustainable development, there has been a shift from structuralism, that social realities are determined and patterned by macrostructures, to constructivism, that social realities are socially constructed (McGregor 2009). The emphasis on agency has resulted in development thinking becoming more spatialised in the fact that it is taking more account of the local or regional and is starting to embrace diversity and differentiation (Pieterse 2001). Pieterse (2001) argues that there are no more recipes for development, no blue print for development, but rather the singular is making way for a more plural, multidimensional, interdisciplinary holistic approach.

Gender, ecology, good governance, capacity building, empowerment and participation are now prominent in development discourse and resultant agendas; however, some researchers question the reality of these ideologies positing them instead as buzzwords of development (see Cornwall 2007; Eade 2007; Leal 2007). Buzzwords are words that have 'lost their moorings and become depoliticised' (Smyth 2007: 582). But buzzwords or not, these words still have very real impact on people's lives. These words echo the main themes of the Millennium Development Goals mentioned at the start of this chapter and are seen as central to sustainable development. Of particular interest to this research is the seventh goal of the Millennium Development Goals: to ensure environmental stability to integrate the principles of sustainable development into country policies and programs and reverse loss of environmental resources. But how does one reconcile environmental protection and management with poverty, arguably the two most pressing issues to face humanity at the present time?

The first international environment conference that was held in Stockholm in 1972 placed environmental issues on the world's agenda and resulted in the establishment of the United Nations Environment Program. This conference clearly highlighted the multiple attitudes concerning the environment across the developed and developing nations of the world: 'the rich world had to face up to the effluence of affluence' (Sandbrook 1992: 15) contrasted with the situation in the developing world where 'of all the pollutants we face, the worst is poverty – we want more development' (I. Ghandi cited in Sandbrook 1992: 16).

Conversely, there is the argument that it is the poor who actually suffer more from environmental degradation. There are many examples of environmental stewardship and activism among poorer people in developing nations around the world. A pertinent example is the work of the first African woman Peace Prize Laureate. Wangari Maathai was awarded the 2004 Nobel Peace Prize for her work in promoting ecologically viable social, economic and cultural development in Kenya and Africa. Her work with the grass-roots organisation the Green Belt Movement empowers women to conserve their environment and quality of life through education, nutrition, family planning and planting trees. This work is based upon engendering a secure and strong base for ESD that embraces democracy, human rights and in particular, women's rights (Nobel Prize 2004).

Ecologically sustainable development clearly has different definitions depending upon the world view: for example, sustainable development as an enabling, empowering practice that embraces the local or as a principle of economic globalisation. What are the arguments put forward for sustainable development?

2.3 The Sustainable Development Era

The World Conservation Strategy in 1980 (published by the World Conservation Union and the World Wide Fund for Nature International) first coined the term 'sustainable development' as a means of drawing attention to the environmental limits to economic growth. The World Commission on Environment and Development adopted this term in 1987 with a very different meaning. It has gained greater international currency with the United Nations Convention on Environment and Development (1992) and the more recent Johannesburg World Summit on Sustainable Development (2002).

The Brundtland Report (1987: 5) *Our Common Future* states that

> [w]e have in the past been concerned about the impacts of economic growth upon the environment. We are now forced to concern ourselves with the impacts of ecological stress – degradation of soils, water regimes, atmosphere and, forests – upon our economic prospects.

As such it can be argued that the ideology of sustainable development (declared by some as an oxymoron) first advocated as a counter to the environmental degradation resulting from economic development perpetuates that very same development. Adams (1990) suggests this economic dimension of sustainable development makes it more achievable and realistic considering we live in a world driven by world markets. The Brundtland Report defines sustainable development as 'development that meets the needs of the present without compromising the ability of future generations to meet their own needs' (Brundtland 1987: 87). These words are argued by many as being overly simplistic with no suggestion of what sustainable development actually means in practice (Beder 1993; Reid 1995).

A central tenet of sustainable development is inter- and intra-generational equity. It must be questioned how this responsibility to future generations (itself a contested idea) can be met when there persists great inequity between current generations between and within different nations. As such critics continue to question the utility of sustainable development as a tool for change, questioning instead if it continues more imperial, anthropocentric and utilitarian attitudes towards development and, in particular, nature (Adams and Mulligan 2003).

It is essential to recognise the different agendas of nations, and indeed it cannot be denied that the number of people enjoying 'the most basic capacities for human development' (UNDP 2004a: 1)[4] is far greater in more developed nations. But when one considers the social development aspects of sustainable development, certain similarities appear. These are related to the previously mentioned buzzwords: gender, good governance, empowerment and participation. It is interesting to consider how this plays out in, for example, the developed nation of Australia particularly in relation to minority groups such as indigenous Australians. For example, Langton (2003) points out that there was a cut to the very productive ethnobiology program in the Northern Territory despite a recognition in the *National Strategy for the Conservation of Australia's Biological Diversity (1992)* of 'the contribution of the ethnobiological knowledge of Australia's Indigenous peoples to the conservation of Australia's biological diversity' (DEST 1996: 14). This in an area where many indigenous languages and knowledge systems are in danger of being lost and where it can be argued indigenous Australians community empowerment and participation is much lower than in other parts of Australia.

2.4 Sustainable Development as Participation

The following discussion critiques the notion that community participation can deliver equitable and sustainable ESD. This critique provides the basis for the investigation of this research into the role of local environmental management and community development projects as the location where cultural hybridity can be fostered

[4]The Human Development Report states that development is about enlarging people's choices. Fundamental to this is the building of people's capabilities: 'the most basic capabilities for human development are to lead long and healthy lives, to be knowledgeable, to have access to the resources needed for a decent standard of living and to be able to participate in the life of the community' (UNDP 2004a: 1). Human development is measured using a series of indexes; these include human development index, the gender-related development index, gender empowerment measure, the human poverty index and the technological achievement index. The Human Development Report was launched in 1990 and releases a report each year. It is an independent report commissioned by the United Nations Development Program authored by leading researchers, development practitioners and members of the United Nations Development Program Human Development Office (UNDP 2004b: 1).

and form the basis for ESD in any nation. Dovers (1999, 2003) states that sustainability and sustainable development are not the same thing: the first is a goal, the latter a process. The philosophy of participation (one of the base tenets of sustainable development) could also be described as a process. That is community participation as an ends to sustainable development rather than a means, although as will be discussed in the following section of this chapter, there are multiple definitions and expectations of participation, ranging from passive participation to self-mobilisation (Pretty 1995) (see Table 2.1). Ross et al. (2002) see participation as embedded in

Table 2.1 Typology of participation

Type of participation	Description
Passive participation	People participate by being told what is going to happen or has already happened. It is a unilateral announcement by administration or project management without any listening to people's responses. The information being shared belongs only to external professionals
Participation in information giving	People participate by answering questions posed by extractive researchers using questionnaire surveys or similar approaches. People do not have the opportunity to influence proceedings, as the findings are neither shared nor checked for accuracy
Participation by consultation	People participate by being consulted and external agents listen to views. These external agents define both problems and solutions and may modify these in light of people's responses. Such a consultative process does not concede any share in decision making, and professionals are under no obligation to take on people's views
Participation for material incentives	People participate by providing resources, for example, farm labour, in return for food, cash or other material incentives. Much on-farm research falls into this category, as farmers provide the fields but are not involved in experimentation or the process of learning. It is very common to see this called participation, yet people have no stake in prolonging activities when the incentives end
Functional participation	People participate by forming groups to meet predetermined objectives related to the project, which can involve the development or promotion of externally initiated social organisation. Such involvement does not tend to be at the early stages of project cycles or planning but rather after major decisions have been made. These institutions tend to be dependent on external initiators and facilitators but may become self-dependent
Interactive participation	People participate in joint analysis, which leads to action plans and the formation of new local institutions or the strengthening of existing ones. It tends to involve interdisciplinary methodologies that seek multiple perspectives and make use of systematic and structured learning processes. These groups take control over local decisions and so people have a stake in maintaining structures or practices
Self-mobilisation	People participate by taking initiatives independent of external institutions to change systems. They develop contacts with external institutions for resources and technical advice that they need but retain control over how resources are used. Such self-initiated mobilisation and collective action may or may not challenge existing inequitable distributions of wealth or power

Source: Adapted from Pretty (1995: 1252) and Jeffery and Vira (2001: 3)

natural resource management; varieties of participation range from community-based management to agency and corporation management. For the purposes of this research, the ideology of participation is inextricably entwined with other concepts such as power, empowerment, community and local knowledge (the way in which the concepts of power and local knowledge are defined in this research is discussed in Chap. 3, Sects. 3.2 and 3.3, respectively).

The discourse of a harmonious community has ingrained gender inequality and marginalised minority groups in the development process. This discourse has often resulted in elite capture (Corbridge 2003) and accentuated local hierarchy and inequality (Ghimire and Pimbert 1997). With the advent of critiques such as gender and development (Moser 1989), this is beginning to change (see also Boserup 1970; Jahan and Papenek 1979; Shiva 1989; Antrobus 1991; Hays-Mitchell 1995; Rathgeber 1995; Williams et al. 1995; Burgess and Beilstein 1996; Rocheleau et al. 1996; Fierlbeck 1997; Goetz 1997; Razavi 1997; Afshar 1998; Ahmed and Laarman 2000). Communities are anything but homogenous: they are made up of diverse and dynamic individuals who are working out ongoing power struggles and negotiations (Eyben and Ladbury 1997). The discourse of participation has been mainstreamed in development theory by development practitioners such as Chambers who advocated this in the early 1980s in his work entitled *Rural Development: Putting the Last First* (Chambers 1983). His later works, which include *Whose Reality Counts? Putting the First Last* (Chambers 1999), speak of valuing local knowledge in environment and development initiatives. The phrase 'handing over the stick' encapsulates a philosophy of working with local people to assess their needs and to develop relevant environment and development programs. Estrella and Gaventa (2003) develop this concept further. They argue that the monitoring and evaluation of development and other community-based initiatives should be conducted by local people. They advocate that questioning 'who counts reality?' may prove as significant as asking 'whose reality counts?' These approaches clearly condemn prescriptive development initiatives that marginalise local knowledge and minority groups.

The World Bank devotes a section of their website to issues of participation and civic engagement (see World Bank 2013); however, many researchers critique the extent to which this rhetoric is actually put into practice (Power 2003). Indeed, there is a significant body of literature that critiques the tyranny of participation (Williams 2004). This is regarded as having resulted from 'frenzied levels of global interest in participatory methodologies' whereby participatory processes became a condition for funding approval from agencies (Guijt 1996: 53). Cleaver (1999) suggests this is a problem if participation is considered a necessary good regardless of circumstance. Cooke and Kothari (2001) further this argument by describing the three tyrannies of participation. These are the tyranny of decision making and control, the tyranny of the group and the tyranny of method.

The critiques of participation are based mainly around the idea that participation is about power where empowerment is about the redistribution of power and really listening to the local is about handing over the power. Critics argue that under this guise, participation continues to operate within a prescriptive development paradigm (Mayoux 1995; Rahnema 1997; Rowlands 1998; Cleaver 1999) whereby the participant is brought into the process and empowered to act within the structures of society. Bryant (1997) states that even in the most generous of participatory schemes, the ultimate authority and control remains with the state. This statement has particular connotations for environmental management and community development initiatives where the survival of the resource in question often depends upon the involvement of local people in establishing and maintaining institutions and rules for environmental governance. What is the role of the local and local knowledge in environmental management and community development initiatives?

2.5 Sustainable Development as Knowledge(s)

The following section critiques how local knowledge is constructed within the sustainable development metanarrative. This critique provides the basis for the investigation of this research that considers the role of local knowledge in environmental management and community development projects and what this means for cultural hybridity and ESD in any nation. This research works from the perspective that local participation in any development initiative is integral to local sustainable development because it enables people to make decisions about resource use and management that directly impact upon their welfare and livelihoods (see Maclean 2001). In order for environmental management to be sustainable, it must engage local people (Brandon and Wells 1992; Sillitoe 2007) since exclusion can cause problems such as lack of ownership of the environment and development initiative resulting in resistance to change and even sabotage of the resource itself.

I have already mentioned above the role of technology and knowledge transfer in past development practice and the criticism this has received from many researchers (see Shiva 1993a; Crewe and Harrison 1998; Chambers 1999). In response there has been a tendency for some advocates of local and indigenous knowledge to reinvent the resulting dichotomy. The result has been the conception of local and indigenous knowledge as providing a panacea for all environment and development problems caused by science (Bebbington 1993; de Walt 1994; Gubbels 1994; Nygen 1999). This is problematic because it homogenises local knowledge, and in relation to local indigenous knowledge, it works to reiterate romantic images of the noble savage existing in a pristine and sustainable state. In addition it places local knowledge in opposition to scientific knowledge. This perspective does not acknowledge that local and indigenous knowledge may not necessarily hold all the answers to localised socio-environmental problems because they occur within a global setting (Bebbington 1993). It also fails to address the critical role of knowledge synergy and exchange as a possible way out of this divide.

Local and indigenous knowledges are not necessarily unscientific (Murdoch and Clark 1994; Sillitoe 2007), but neither are they necessarily in harmony with their natural and social environments; some local practices may be environmentally degrading. Equally, scientific knowledge is not necessarily asocial, but it does often advocate a technocratic fix that is often devised in isolation from the local situation

(Pretty and Scoones 1997). What place is there, then, for knowledge interfacing between these knowledge bases? The generation and utilisation of knowledge involves all aspects of power and control inherent in social interaction (Long and Villareal 1994). Is a 'knowledge in action' (Blaike et al. 1997) and resultant situated knowledge discourse a viable mechanism for knowledge exchange at the environment and development interface and a way out of the polemic debate that surrounds local versus scientific knowledge?

This research engages with the work of the following researchers to consider what it means to move beyond this divide. For example, Hajer (1995) speaks of the importance of developing 'discourse coalitions' between different stakeholders. These coalitions are not necessarily based on shared interests and goals but upon shared terms and concepts that give meaning to social and physical processes and the nature of the (policy) problem under consideration. In this way interdependencies are not only based on power and material gain but also on resources such as legitimacy, knowledge, meaning and argument. Murdoch and Clarke (1994) call for 'sustainable knowledge', the synergy between local knowledge bases (of which science is one) in working towards equitable knowledge exchange at the environment and development interface. They stress an approach to nature and culture, the local and the universal that stresses hybridity. This approach is based upon considering the extent to which these categories are inextricably mixed. Knorr-Cetina (1983) writes about 'transepistemic communities' where different groups such as academics, activists, specialists, scientists and indigenous peoples enter into resource relationships and knowledge is shared and transmitted between different agents. Finally, Brown (2001, 2006) identifies five constructions of knowledge necessary for the governance of sustainable futures. She speaks of the importance of social processes to bring all knowledge constructions together 'in making collective decisions and taking collective action' (Brown 2006: 1). These approaches can be used as a means of understanding the complexities and overcoming the tensions surrounding the role of local, indigenous and scientific knowledge in environmental governance and management.

Holling et al. (1998) state that the phrase sustainable development is not an oxymoron. They state that it only appears as such from a conventional western resource management stance based upon reductionism and exploitative development, where natural resources are managed for sustainable yield. Such a stance does not include the integration of ecological, social and economic objectives of sustainable development nor does it allow for the unpredictability, complexities and dynamisms inherent to ecological, social and economic worlds. These features of economic, social and ecological behaviours are argued to be non-linear cross-scale in time and space and have an evolutionary character. As such the only means for planning or managing for sustainable development is cross-scale in time and space, takes an interdisciplinary or holistic approach and acknowledges great creative potential of unpredictability in 'opportunities for novel co-operation and feedback management' (Holling et al. 1998: 357). Gunderson and Holling (2002) speak of 'panarchies' to describe the evolutionary nature of the adaptive cycles of social and ecological systems that are nested one within the other across time and space scale.

Collectively the system for managing for sustainable development that these authors and others (e.g. Dovers and Wild River 2003; Sayer and Campbell 2004) call for is one of adaptive management.

2.6 Social and Institutional Learning for Ecologically Sustainable Development

Adaptive management is based upon the premise that the only condition that is constant is change. It is built upon the recognition of the multiple realities as espoused by constructivism. As such it recognises that there is no single sustainable development because of the multiplicity of players, locations, scales (both temporal and spatial) and complexities inherent to social and ecological systems. It works from the ecological standpoint that the more flexible a system or the more resilient a system is to disturbance, the more sustainable it will be. This system embraces change, because it recognises the unpredictability inherent in the numerous systems of this world. The only way to plan or manage or institutionalise for this dynamism is to be adaptive, interdisciplinary and inclusive of it. Adaptive management celebrates the local and acknowledges the situatedness of sustainable development. As such community participation is central to successful adaptive management of natural resources.

Following from the principles of adaptive management, Dovers (2003) calls for more adaptive policy processes and institutional arrangements. He believes this would offer a more flexible, informed and inclusive approach to ESD. He lists the following features of such an approach (2003: 4): respect for and combination of perspectives from the natural and social sciences; recognition of uncertainty, complexity and long timescales; construing policy and management interventions as driven by a defined purpose but explicitly experimental, consistently testing understanding and capabilities along the way; wide inclusion of stakeholders in a purposeful and structured fashion; and design and maintenance of sophisticated mechanisms of feedback and communication between policy and practice and across different situations.

Work by other researchers (Dietz et al. 2003; Schultz et al. 2004) make similar assertions. Indeed, Dietz et al. (2003) embrace strategies that realise the agency of local regulatory institutions in the context of cross issues such as climate change. They encourage approaches that facilitate 'dialogue among interested parties, officials, and scientists; complex, redundant and layered institutions; a mix of institutional types and designs that facilitate experimentation, learning and change' (p1907). Schultz et al. (2004) speak of institutional arrangements that enable self-organisation at the local level, provide funding and 'create arenas for collaborative learning'. They argue that arrangements which encourage creativity have enormous potential to reinforce localised adaptive management resulting in diverse and resilient systems.

Such institutional arrangements would not only encourage rich and diverse social learning but would be constantly undergoing sustained social learning as part of the adaptive management process. McCool and Guthrie (2001) advocate social learning as crucial to addressing environment and development issues. This is because learning can only result when we understand the consequences of taking a particular action. Such social learning can take place in many arenas, not least the local environmental management and community development interface. At the local interface, Fien and Skoien (2002: 281) identify that action competence (knowledge of the particular skills and learning needed to facilitate action), good social capital (relationship building based on trust, reciprocity and shared norms) and access to information (extended knowledge and communication networks and participatory democracy) are important in community action projects because they provide the supportive and informative social conditions that can maximise social learning.

The work of these researchers and others interested in social learning for ESD (Parson and Clark 1995; Schusler et al. 2003; Keen et al. 2005) emphasises the importance of co-learning between groups, which may be in conflict, to develop collaborative working relationships for improved environmental management and governance. Of central importance to this approach is the recognition of the potential and the importance of knowledge sharing and co-learning for future ESD. This sharing and co-learning can occur in many arenas. There is a wealth of literature advocating that successful planning for environmental management and governance is about much more than simply producing, for example, the final planning document. It is about social learning, relationship building, ownership and improved social and political acceptability (McCool and Guthrie 2001). Indeed, the actual process itself can be as important, if not more so, than the outcome. Schusler et al. (2003: 317) identify eight process characteristics that foster social learning in deliberate planning processes. These are depicted in Fig. 2.1.

2.7 Environmental Governance in Australia

Central to environmental governance decisions are those who make them. In the following discussion I critique how international environmental governance conventions and agendas inform national environmental governance policies and resulting programs in Australia. Australia is used as a case study to consider how the metanarrative of ESD that is embedded within governance policies and programs privileges specific discourses of development, and of environment, that do not celebrate local diversity. I end this discussion by highlighting the importance of local diversity for equitable and sustained ESD. This discussion also presents the impetus for the investigation into the role of local and indigenous knowledge as central to the processes for cultural hybridity for ESD.

The World Resources Institute (2002: 3) publication (complied by the United Nations Development Program, the United Nations Environment Program, the World Bank and the World Resources Institute) defines environmental governance as being:

> about decisions and how we make them… about the exercise of power, about being in charge. It relates to decision-makers at all levels – government managers and ministers, business people, property owners, farmers and consumers. In short, governance deals with who is responsible and how they wield their power, and how they are held accountable.

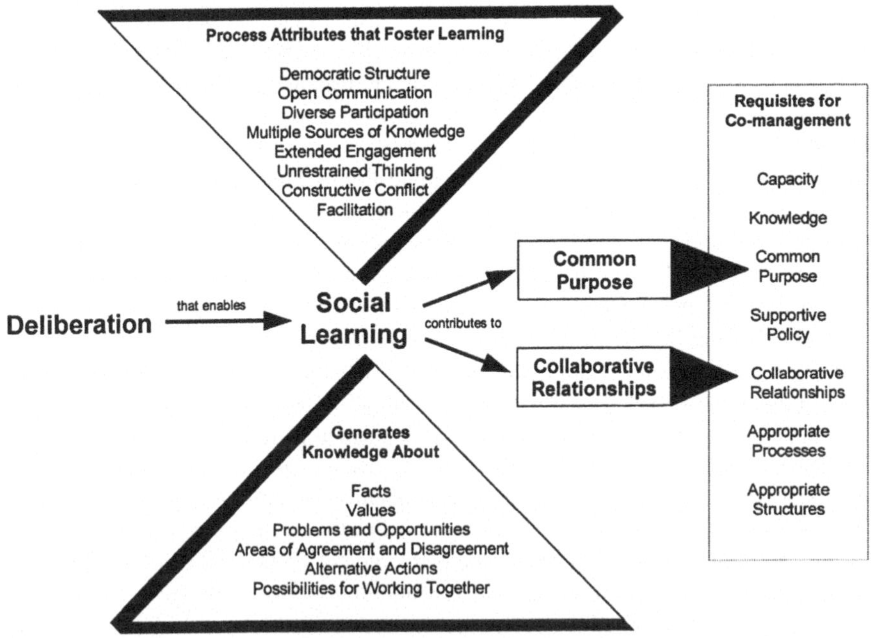

Fig. 2.1 Eight process characteristics to foster social learning in deliberate planning processes (Source: Schusler et al. 2003: 317)

The United Nations Conference on Environment and Development held in Rio in June 1992 that reaffirmed the Declaration of the United Nations Conference on the Human Environment adopted in Stockholm (1972) resulted in the international Rio Declaration on Environment and Development. This declaration defined the rights and responsibilities of states to combat the growing environmental and social degradation. This conference also generated Agenda 21, described as the 'blue print for global actions to affect the transition to sustainable development' (Strong 1992: 9), the Framework Convention on Climate Change and the Convention on Biological Diversity. The World Summit on Sustainable Development (WSSD) held in Johannesburg in 2002 did not attempt to renegotiate Agenda 21 but developed a Political Declaration and a Plan of Implementation to fill 'key gaps that have impeded its implementation' (UN 2002: 2). This summit also reinforced the importance of developing and strengthening global partnerships as a means to transition to more sustainable development.

The effect these conferences have had on international and national policies cannot be understated: the harsh reality that the current systems of development have led to poverty, environmental destruction and social inequity has been acknowledged at the global scale. But as Speth (2003) points out, at Johannesburg as at Rio, the difficult issue of assuring accountability in the implementation process was largely ignored. In addition, he remarks that governments were more willing to discuss the social and economic elements of sustainable development than the environmental, and this is reflected in the weakness of the Plan of Implementation to address environmental issues. As such the environmental community has much work to do to bring attention to global and local environmental governance. The World Wide Fund for Nature called the WSSD, the World Summit of Shameful Deals (WWF 2002), and Greenpeace Climate Policy Director, Sawyer, states that the energy section of the Plan of Action 'is not much of a plan and it contains almost no action' (Greenpeace 2002: 1). Despite the recent ratification of the Kyoto protocol by the Russian Parliament (October 2004), the Australian Federal Government (alongside the United States of America) still remains resolute not to ratify the protocol. Bearing this in mind, what is the Australian Federal Government's commitment to sustainable development and what impact have these World Summits on Environment and Development had on environmental governance in Australia?

The governance of Australia's natural environment is multifaceted and complex. It involves relationships between the Commonwealth government, state, territory and local governments, nongovernment organisations, community groups and individuals. In the following section I touch very briefly on the process engaged in to develop relevant policies that reflect the principles of ESD to consider the impacts of the earth summits on formalised environmental governance in Australia.

The concept of sustainable development was not new to Australia[5] where fulfilling a more international grand plan for the environment began with the *National Conservation Strategy of Australia* as a result of the Brundtland Report in 1987. But the response of the Australian Federal Government to Agenda 21 was the most intensive and broad policy process concerning the environment ever to be conducted in Australia (Dovers 2003). In response to the statement of Agenda 21 (UNCED 1992: 47) that 'reflects a global consensus and political commitment at the highest level on development and environment cooperation [and] its successful implementation is first and foremost the responsibility of governments', the national government of Australia initiated a series of processes and public policy related to ESD. ESD is defined within these processes as 'development that improves the total quality of life, both now and in the future, in a way that maintains the ecological processes on which life depends' (ESDSC 1992). Two main features distinguish this approach to development: the need to consider an integrated approach to the wider economic, social and environmental implications of decisions and actions and the need to take a long-term rather than short-term view in regard to those decisions and actions.

[5]The final report of the Ecologically Sustainable Development Working Group (ESDWG) (1991: v) states 'although the idea of ecologically sustainable development has come to international prominence only in recent years, the concept has been around somewhat longer. As early as 1961, Rachel Carson's *Silent Spring* had highlighted the need for more concern to be shown regarding the effects that humankind was having on the environment'. It is interesting that the ESDWG refers back to work of an American ecologist rather than acknowledging Australia's own ecological pioneers (Mulligan and Hill 2001).

The main outcomes of this ESD process were (after Dovers and Gullett 1999: 112) the *Intergovernmental Agreement on the Environment (1992)* and the *National Strategy for Ecologically Sustainable Development (1992)*; a range of national macro-policies dealing with problems such as land degradation (building upon the Decade of Landcare), biodiversity (*National Strategy for the Conservation of Australia's Biological Diversity, 1992*), rangelands (*National Strategy for Rangeland Management, 1999*) and so on; a complex array of policies, programs dealing with 'various "meso" and "micro" policy problems'; active Local Agenda 21 initiatives across local government; a national state of the environment reporting process; and some codification of ESD principles as statutory objects.

The ESD process in Australia was exemplified internationally as a key national response to the global sustainable development agenda (Dovers 2003). The draft National Strategy for ESD was prepared by the ESD steering committee (comprising senior officials from the Commonwealth, state, territory and local governments) and was the response to over 500 recommendations that arose from the ESD working group process that began in 1990 (ESDSC 1992). This process involved nine sectoral working groups (non-government organisations, community groups, government, unions, industry). Although this whole-of-government and cross-sectoral approach certainly enriched the process with information from different perspectives, local government was not explicitly represented, nor were indigenous people; in addition general community input was too limited and too late to be properly effective (Dovers 2003).

Dovers and Gullett (1999) assert that although stated as an international exemplar, ESD lacked sustained implementation, adequate resourcing and institutionalisation (lack of greater status and permanence through process, law, organisational capacity and so on) necessary for the long-term commitment it advocates. In addition, the whole-of-government and cross-sectoral approach advocated in the ESD policy process has not been complemented with continued practice in its implementation: this fails the modern idea of sustainability as being about an intended and integrated policy agenda. In fact the policy resulting from the ESD process could be argued to have succumbed to the policy ad hocery and amnesia pattern of another resource and environmental policy and management in Australia, that is, what is done at any given time often appears uninformed by previous experiences and often previous policy and management attempts are not even recognised (Dovers 2003). In addition, Dovers questioned the bad timing of the very collective, long-term, holistic concept of sustainable development into a world dominated by world markets and neo-liberal ideals that sees the individual competing for the maximisation of profit in the short term. Market mechanisms of freer trade certainly have not eventuated in the development of green technologies.

The essential tension in environmental governance is that between top-down state-initiated practices and those of more localised, grass-roots groups. For example, the *National Strategy for Ecologically Sustainable Development (1992)* and resultant government strategies in Australia work to include the local, but with whose discourse? Carr (2002) points out that grass-roots environmental stewardship occurs because of the onset of complex environmental problems, rather than due to state policy development. Self-mobilisation, self-governance and resistance to institutional governance are essential driving forces in bottom-up environmental governance. As Proctor (1996: 296) puts it, 'nature is a contested terrain'; there are certainly many varieties of environmentalism (Guha and Martinez-Alier 1997), so whose nature should be protected? Whose management ethos should be advocated? In response to certain kinds of environmental governance, many social movements have emerged articulating struggles for cultural, ecological and economic survival (Routledge 2002). The multidimensional aspects of these struggles are indicative of 'an alternative politics seeking to create autonomous spaces of action outside of the state arena' (Peet and Watts 1996: 33). These social movements are in no way homogenous. They include, for example, international pressure groups such as Greenpeace and more regional Aboriginal groups struggling against uranium mining in Australia.

Some researchers speak of environmental racism (Langton 2003) when environmental governance policy favours the nature of the majority. The ethos of environmental justice (Deutsch Lynch 1993; di Chiro 1996; Proctor 1996) works to move beyond this divide, by bringing humans back into environmental discourse. This once again begs the question not only of how knowledge about the environment is constructed but, equally, how is it disseminated, legitimated and contested (Eden 1998)? How does it move and how is it transferred? This research attempts to answer these rhetorical questions by conducting an investigation into the role of local, indigenous and scientific knowledge in environmental governance and management. The conceptual framework for cultural hybridity is grounded in the three questions posed in this book. These questions explore, firstly, how knowledges of best practice environmental management move across and between international, national and local scales of environmental governance and community-based environmental management; secondly, the role of community stakeholder groups and their knowledge in the networks surrounding environmental management; and thirdly, how greater knowledge sharing between the many interest groups involved in environmental management can be devised. The discussions articulated in the following chapters bring the research full circle to the notion of ESD as knowledge and thus the need for a new conceptual framework for cultural hybridity.

2.8 Conclusion

The purpose of this chapter has been to locate this research within the contemporary environment and development literature. It develops a critique that emphasises the importance of knowledge for ESD. The premise of this chapter suggests that the lack of genuine knowledge sharing between interest groups involved in environmental governance and management in any nation undermines the potential of local projects to overcome current levels of environmental and social degradation. Inherent to this premise is the idea that increased knowledge sharing between local, indigenous and scientific knowledge cultures is integral to equitable and sustainable

ESD. As will be presented in the following chapter, a conceptual framework that provides the way to open up the creative spaces necessary to enable cultural hybridity can provide a way to foster such knowledge sharing for sustainable ESD.

References

Adams WM (1990) Green development: environmental sustainability in the third world. Routledge, London

Adams WM, Mulligan M (2003) Introduction. In: Adams WM, Mulligan M (eds) Decolonizing nature: strategies for conservation in a post-colonial era. Earthscan Publications Ltd, London, pp 1–15

Afshar H (1998) Introduction: women and empowerment, some illustrations. In: Afshar H (ed) Women and empowerment: illustrations from the third world. Macmillan Press Ltd, London, pp 1–10

Ahmed MR, Laarman JG (2000) Gender equity in social forestry programs in Bangladesh. Hum Ecol 28(3):433–450

Antrobus P (1991) Women in development. In: Wallace T, March C (eds) Changing perceptions: writings on gender and development. Oxfam, Oxford, pp 245–252

Bebbington A (1993) Modernisation from below: an alternative indigenous development. Econ Geogr 69:274–293

Beder S (1993) The nature of sustainable development. Scribe Publications, Newham

Bernstein H (1979) Sociology of underdevelopment versus sociology of development. In: Seers D (ed) Development theory. Franklass Ltd, England

Blaike P, Brown K, Stocking M, Tang L, Dixon P, Sillitoe P (1997) Knowledge in action: local knowledge as a development resource and barriers to its incorporation in natural resource research and development. Agric Syst 55(2):217–237

Boserup E (1970) Women's role in economic development. George Allen and Unwin Ltd, London

Brandon KE, Wells M (1992) Planning for people and parks: design dilemmas. World Dev 20(4):557–570

Brown LR (1992) An environmental revolution. In: UNCED (United Nations Conference on Environment and Development) (ed) Earth summit '92. The United Nations conference on environment and development: Rio de Janeiro. The Regency Press, London, pp 18–21

Brown VA (2001) Monitoring changing environments in environmental health. Environ Heal 1:20–31

Brown VA (2006) Collective decision-making between public health, sustainability governance and environmental management. In: Soskolne C (ed) Sustaining life on earth: environmental and human health through global governance. Lexington Books, New York

Brundtland H (1987) Our common future. Oxford University Press, Oxford

Bryant RL (1997) Beyond the impasse: the power of political ecology in third world environmental research. Area 29(1):5–19

Burgess SF, Beilstein JC (1996) Women's voices and agency in rural Africa: small-scale communal farmers in Zimbabwe. Women Polit 16(2):19–43

Carr A (2002) Grass roots and green tape: principles and practices of environmental stewardship. The Federation Press, Sydney

Cernea M (1991) Putting people first. Oxford University Press, New York

Chambers R (1983) Rural development: putting the last first. Longman, London

Chambers R (1999) Whose reality counts? Putting the first last. Intermediate Technology Publications, London

Cleaver F (1999) Paradoxes of participation: questioning participatory approaches to development. J Int Dev 11:597–612

Cohen JM, Uphoff NT (1980) Participation's place in rural development: seeking clarity through specificity. World Dev 8:213–235
Cooke B, Kothari U (2001) The case for participation as tyranny. In: Cooke B, Kothari U (eds) Participation: the new tyranny? Zed Books, London, pp 1–15
Corbridge S (2003) Elite capture seminar. School of Geographical Sciences, Bristol
Cornwall A (2007) Buzzwords and fuzzwords: deconstructing development discourse. Dev Pract 17(4–5):471–484
Crewe E, Harrison E (1998) Whose development: an ethnography of aid. Zed Books Ltd, London
de Walt BR (1994) Using indigenous knowledge to improve agriculture and natural resource management. Hum Organ 53(2):123–131
DEST (Department of Environment Sport and Territories) (1996) National strategy for the conservation of Australia's biological diversity. Commonwealth of Australia, Canberra
Deutsch Lynch B (1993) The garden and the sea: U.S. ladino environmental discourses and mainstream environmentalism. Soc Probl 40(1):108–124
Di Chiro G (1996) Nature as community: the convergence of environment and social justice. In: Cronon W (ed) Uncommon ground: rethinking the human place in nature. W.W. Norton & Company, London, pp 298–320
Dietz T, Ostrom E, Stern PC (2003) The struggle to govern the commons. Science 302:1907–1912
Doty L (1996) Imperial encounters: the politics of representation in N-S relations. University of Minneapolis Press, Minneapolis
Dovers S (1999) Institutionalising ecologically sustainable development: promises, problems and prospects. In: Walker KJ, Crowley K (eds) Australian environmental policy 2. University of New South Wales Press, Sydney, pp 204–223
Dovers S (2003) Processes and institutions for resource and environmental management: why and how to analyse. In: Dovers S, Wild River S (eds) Managing Australia's environment. Federation, Sydney, pp 3–14
Dovers S, Gullett W (1999) Policy choice for sustainability: marketization, law and institutions. In: Bosselmann K, Richardson BJ (eds) Environmental justice and market mechanisms: key challenges for environmental law and policy. Kluwer Law International, The Hague, pp 110–128
Dovers S, Wild River S (eds) (2003) Managing Australia's environment. Federation Press, Sydney
Eade D (2007) Capacity building: who builds whose capacity? Dev Pract 17(4–5):630–639
Eden S (1998) Environmental issues: knowledge, uncertainly and the environment. Prog Hum Geogr 22(3):425–432
Escobar A (1995) Encountering development: the making and unmaking of the third world. Princeton University Press, Princeton
ESDSC (Ecologically Sustainable Development Steering Committee) (1992) National strategy for ecologically sustainable development. Australian Government Publishing Service, Canberra
ESDWG (Ecologically Sustainable Development Working Group) (1991) Final report: executive summaries. Australian Government Publishing Service, Canberra
Esteva G (1992) Development. In: Sachs W (ed) The development dictionary. Zed Books Ltd, London, pp 6–25
Estrella M, Gaventa J (2003) Who counts reality? Participatory monitoring and evaluation: a literature review, IDS development studies, http://ww.ids.ac.uk. 20 July 2006
Eyben R, Ladbury S (1997) Popular participation in aid-assisted projects: why more in theory than practice? In: Nelson N, Wright S (eds) Power and participatory development: theory and practice. Intermediate Technology Publications, London, pp 192–200
Fien J, Skoien P (2002) "I'm learning…how you go about stirring things up – in a consultative manner": social capital and action competence in two community catchment groups. Local Environ 7(3):269–282
Fierlbeck K (1997) Getting representation right for women in development: accountability, consent and the articulation of women's interests. In: Goetz AM (ed) Getting institutions right for women in development. Zed Books, London, pp 31–44
Finsterbusch K, Van Wicken WA (1987) The contribution of beneficiary participation to development project effectiveness. Public Adm Dev 7:1–23

Ghimire K, Pimbert M (1997) Social change and conservation: an overview of issues and concepts. In: Pimbert M, Ghimire K (eds) Social change and conservation. Earthscan Publications Ltd, London, pp 1–45

Gibson-Graham JK (2008) Diverse economies: performative practices for 'other worlds'. Prog Hum Geogr 32(5):613–632

Goetz AM (1997) Getting institutions right for women in development. Zed Books Ltd, London

Greenpeace (2002) Axis of oil, www.greenpeace.org. 13 July 2006

Gubbels P (1994) Populist pipedream or practical paradigm? Farmer-driven research and the project agro-forester in Burkina Faso. In: Scoones I, Thompson J, Chambers R (eds) Beyond farmer first. Intermediate Technology Publications, London, pp 233–243

Guha R, Martinez-Alier J (eds) (1997) Varieties of environmentalism: essays north and south. Earthscan Publications, London

Guijt I (1996) Participation in natural resource management: blemished past and hopeful future? Making Forest Policy Work, Oxford

Gunderson LH, Holling CS (eds) (2002) Panarchy: understanding transformations in human and natural systems. Island Press, Washington, DC

Hajer M (1995) The politics of environmental discourse: ecological modernization and the policy process. Clarendon, Oxford

Hays-Mitchell M (1995) Voices and visions from the streets: gender interests and political participation among women informal traders in Latin America. Environ Plan D Soc Space 13:445–469

Holling CS, Berkes F, Folke C (1998) Science, sustainability and resource management. In: Berkes F, Folke C (eds) Linking social and ecological systems: management practices and social mechanisms for building resilience. Cambridge University Press, Cambridge, pp 342–362

Ireland P, McKinnon K (2013) Strategic localism for an uncertain world: a postdevelopment approach to climate change adaptation. Geoforum 47:158–166

Jahan R, Papenek H (1979) Women and development: perspectives from south and southeast Asia. Darim International, Dacca

Jeffery R, Vira B (eds) (2001) Conflict and cooperation in participatory natural resource management. Palgrave Macmillan Press, London

Keen M, Brown VA, Dyball R (2005) Social learning: a new approach to environmental management. In: Keen M, Brown VA, Dyball R (eds) Social learning in environmental management. Towards a sustainable future. Earthscan, London, pp 3–21

Knorr-Cetina KD (1983) The ethnographic study of scientific work: towards a constructivist interpretation of science. In: Knorr-Cetina KD, Mulkay M (eds) Science observed. Sage Publications, London, pp 115–140

Kothari R (1988) Rethinking development: in search of humane alternatives. Ajanta, Delhi

Langton M (2003) The 'wild", the market and the native: indigenous people face new forms of global colonization. In: Adams WM, Mulligan M (eds) Decolonizing nature: strategies for conservation in a post-colonial era. Earthscan Publications, London, pp 79–107

Leal P (2007) Participation: the ascendancy of a buzzword in the neo-liberal era. Dev Pract 17(4–5):539–548

Long N, Villareal M (1994) The interweaving of knowledge and power in development interfaces. In: Scoones I, Thompson J, Chambers R (eds) Beyond farmer first. Intermediate Technology Publications, London

Maclean K (2001) The role of local knowledge in participatory natural resource management: practice or rhetoric? Department of Geography. University of Cambridge, Cambridge. Unpublished Master of Philosophy dissertation

Mayoux L (1995) Beyond naivety: women, gender inequality and participatory development. Dev Chang 26:235–258

McCool SF, Guthrie K (2001) Mapping the dimensions of successful public participation in messy natural resource management situations. Soc Nat Resour 14:309–323

McGregor A (2009) New possibilities? Shifts in post-development theory and practice. Geogr Compass 3(5):1688–1702

MDG (Millennium Development Goals) (2004) Millennium development goals. www.developmentgoals.org. 15 Aug 2006
Midgley J, Hall A, Hardiman M, Narine D (1986) Community participation, social development and the state. Methuen, London
Moser C (1989) Gender planning in the third world: meeting practical and strategic gender needs. World Dev 17(11):1799–1825
Mulligan M, Hill S (2001) Ecological pioneers: a social history of Australian ecological thought and action. Cambridge University Press, Cambridge/New York
Murdoch J, Clark J (1994) Sustainable knowledge. Geoforum 25(2):115–132
Nobel Prize (2004) www.nobelprize.org. 26 Oct 2004
Nygen A (1999) Local knowledge in the environment-development discourse: from dichotomies to situated knowledges. Crit Anthropol 19(3):267–288
Parson EA, Clark WC (1995) Sustainable development as social learning: theoretical perspectives and practical challenges for the design of a research program. In: Gunderson L, Holling CS, Light S (eds) Barriers and bridges to the renewal of ecosystems and institutions. Columbia University Press, New York, pp 428–460
Peet R, Watts M (1996) Liberation ecology, development, sustainability, and environment in an age of market triumphalism. In: Peet R, Watts M (eds) Liberation ecologies, environment, development, social movement. Routledge, London, pp 1–45
Pieterse NJ (2001) Development theory: deconstructions/reconstructions. Sage Publications, London
Power M (2003) Rethinking development geographies. Routledge, London
Pretty J (1995) Participatory learning for sustainable agriculture. World Dev 23(8):1247–1263
Pretty J, Scoones I (1997) Institutionalising adaptive planning and local-level concerns: looking to the future. In: Nelson N, Wright S (eds) Power and participatory development. Intermediate Technology Publications, London, pp 157–169
Proctor J (1996) Whose nature? The contested moral terrain of ancient forests. In: Cronon W (ed) Uncommon ground: rethinking the human place in nature. W.W. Norton & Company, London, pp 269–297
Rahnema M (1997) Signposts for post-development: in search of a different language and new paradigms. ReVision 19(4):4–12
Rathgeber EM (1995) Gender and development in action. In: Marchand MH, Parpart JL (eds) Feminism/postmodernism/development. Routledge, London, pp 204–220
Razavi S (1997) Fitting gender into development institutions. World Dev 25(7):1111–1125
Reid D (1995) Sustainable development: an introductory guide. Earthscan Publications LTD, London
Rocheleau D, Thomas-Slayter B, Wangari E (1996) Gender and environment. A feminist political ecology perspective. In: Rocheleau D, Thamas-Slayter B, Wangari E (eds) Feminist political ecology, global issues and local experiences. Routledge, London
Ross H, Buchy M, Proctor W (2002) Laying down the ladder: a typology of public participation in Australian natural resource management. Aust J Environ Manag 9:205–217
Rostow W (1960) The stages of economic growth: a non-communist manifesto. Cambridge University Press, Cambridge
Routledge P (2002) Resisting and reshaping destructive development: social movements and globalizing networks. In: Johnston RJ, Taylor PJ, Watts M (eds) Geographies of global change: remapping the world. Blackwell Publishers Ltd, Oxford, pp 310–327
Rowlands J (1998) A word of the times, but what does it mean? Empowerment discourse and practice of development. In: Afshar H (ed) Women and empowerment: illustrations from the third world. Macmillan Press, London, pp 11–33
Sachs W (ed) (1992) The development dictionary: a guide to knowledge as power. Zed Books Ltd, London
Said E (1979) Orientalism. Routledge, London

Sandbrook R (1992) From Stockholm to Rio. In: UNCED (United Nations Conference on Environment and Development) (ed) Earth summit '92. The United Nations conference on environment and development: Rio de Janeiro. The Regency Press, London, pp 15–17
Sayer J, Campbell B (2004) The science of sustainable development: local livelihoods and the global environment. Cambridge University Press, Cambridge
Schultz L, Olsson P, Johannessen A, Folke C (2004) Ecosystem management by local steward associations. A case study from "Kristianstads Vattenrike", the Swedish MA. Bridging Scales and Epistemologies, Alexandria
Schusler TM, Decker DJ, Pfeffer MJ (2003) Social learning for collaborative natural resource management. Soc Nat Resour 15:309–326
Schuurman F (1993) Beyond the impasse. Zed Books Ltd, London
Scoones I, Thompson J (1994) Knowledge, power and agriculture: towards a theoretical understanding. In: Scoones I, Thompson J, Chambers R (eds) Beyond farmer first. Intermediate Technology Publications, London, pp 17–32
Shiva V (1989) Staying alive: women, ecology and development. Zed Books Ltd, London
Shiva V (1993a) Monocultures of the mind: perspectives on biodiversity and biotechnology. Zed Books LTD, London
Shiva V (1993b) Why we should say 'no' to GATT-TRIPs. Third World Resurgence 39:32–34
Sillitoe P (2007) Local science vs global science. Approaches to Indigenous knowledge in international development. Berghahn Books, New York
Smyth I (2007) Talking of gender: words and meanings in development organisations. Dev Pract 17(4–5):582–588
Speth JG (2003) Environment and globalization after Johannesburg. In: Speth JG (ed) Worlds apart. Island Press, Washington, DC, pp 155–165
Strong M (1992) Foreword. In: UNCED (United Nations Conference on Environment and Development) (ed) Earth Summit '92. The United Nations conference on environment and development: Rio de Janeiro. The Regency Press, London, pp 9–10
UN (United Nations) (2002) Johannesburg summit 2002: global challenge global opportunity, trends in sustainable development. www.un.org. 15 Aug 2006
UN (United Nations) (2003) United Nations millennium development goals. www.un.org. 04 Jun 2006
UNCED (United Nations Conference on Environment and Development) (1992) Earth Summit'92, The United Nations conference on environment and development, Rio de Janeiro. The Regency Press, London
UNDP (United Nations Development Program) (2004a) The state of human development. http://hrd.undp.org. 11 Oct 2004
UNDP (United Nations Development Program) (2004b) About the human development reports. http://hdr.undp.org. 15 Aug 2006
Williams G (2004) Evaluating participatory development: tyranny, power and (re)politicisation. Third World Q 25(3):557–578
Williams S, Seed J, Mwau A (1995) The Oxfam gender training manual. Oxfam, Oxford
World Bank (2013) Participation and civic engagement. http://www.worldbank.org/projects/search?lang=en&searchTerm=&themecode_exact=57. Accessed 11 Dec 2013
World Resources Institute (2002) Guide to world resources 2002–2004 – decisions for the earth – balance, voice and power. World Resources Institute, Washington, DC
WWF (Worldwide Fund for Nature) (2002) WSSD: World Summit of Shameful Deals. www.panda.org. 15 July 2006
Young E (1995) Third world in the first: development and indigenous peoples. Routledge, London

Chapter 3
An Applied Peoples' Geography as the Basis of the Framework for Cultural Hybridity

Abstract The aim of this chapter is to introduce the four themes that are central to the applied peoples' geography advocated in this book. This applied peoples' geography, coupled with an edge politics (see Chaps. 4 and 5), is the basis of the new conceptual framework for cultural hybridity. This geography enables an investigation into the role of local, Indigenous and scientific knowledge in environmental governance and management. Definitions of the themes of power, knowledge, governance scale and nature are presented in this chapter as the basis for the research epistemology. This epistemology forms the conceptual toolkit for the applied peoples' geography (after Harvey, Prof Geogr 36(1):161, 1984) practised by this research. This applied peoples' geography provides tools to describe, analyse and understand the social world that are empowering and create the basis for social action (Harvey, Prof Geogr 36(1):1–11, 1984). This applied peoples' geography works to open up the local spaces of environmental governance and management and provides the tools necessary for the new conceptual framework for cultural hybridity.

3.1 Power Is an Entangled and Complex Force

> Power is employed and exercised through a net-like organisation. And not only do individuals circulate between its threads; they are always in a position of simultaneously undergoing and exercising this power… individuals are the vehicles of power, not its points of application. (Foucault 1980: 98)

As Foucault (1980) articulates in the above quote, power is a complex phenomenon that pervades all aspects of social interaction and existence. This argument can start with the feminist tenet of the personal is political and can travel simultaneously outwards and inwards with Castree's (2001a: 1) statement that 'society-nature relations extend "all the way down"'. This book constructs power relations through a selected trajectory of theoretical perspectives, empirical accounts and case study analysis. The power of narratives and discourse, the power of governance and the power of participation were referred to in the previous chapter, but little was said about the concept of power itself. This section considers the ways in which power has been conceptualised in the environment and development literatures and in

K. Maclean, *Cultural Hybridity and the Environment*,
DOI 10.1007/978-981-287-323-1_3

related postcolonial and political ecology literatures to produce a working definition for this research.

The work of Dahl (1957) is often quoted as still influential today in conceptions about power. Put crudely, Dahl asserted that power is when A has power over B to the extent that he or she can get B to do something that B would not otherwise do. This suggests a simple one-dimensional relationship between the two actors. The inference is that power is about domination and coercion such as the control of the state over the populous. This view of power is encapsulated in early development discourse relating to the role of the developed world to aid the undeveloped worlds with technology and knowledge transfer (e.g. Rostow 1960). This view ties in with colonial discourse where colonial rule was justified as a means to bring civilisation to the uncivilised. Work by political geographers (e.g. Hinchliffe 2000; Massey 2000; Radcliffe 2000; Thrift 2000) highlights how societies are much more complex and certainly less neat than more orthodox accounts have asserted. The state and more institutionalised forms of power certainly prevail throughout daily life; however, relationships and spaces of power are diverse and pervasive. Hence 'relationships in the power webs of everyday mundane political and social practices are much more entangled – with many more spaces for resistance' (Sharp et al. 2000: 7). This is how power is understood in this book.

Research on the development and workings of social and resistance movements, mainly those groups organised around opposition to the domination of the state or multinational companies, has shed light on a range of forms of resistance. Contemporary examples include the anti-globalisation protests in Seattle: the Battle in Seattle during the World Trade Organization discussions in 1999 (see Reynolds 1999b) and anti-climate change protests in the Hague during the Climate Change Summit in 2000 (see Shah 2000). Academic debates about local everyday forms of resistance developed out of Scott's (1985) work on peasant forms of resistance to dominant rule, such as foot-dragging and sabotage. Equally important was the advent of Subaltern Studies by postcolonial researchers such as Guha and Spivak (1988) and later Bhabha (1994). These researchers called for a new historiography for India. They claimed that Indian history to that point had been written from a colonial point of view, ignoring the important resistant role of the subaltern classes in structuring modern India. Spivak's (1988) work about the subaltern voice, representation and post-colonial literature moves beyond the power of discourse in imperial history and literature to question the role of discourse in rewriting such histories. She asks whether those subjugated under colonial rule can actually move beyond their imposed self-learnt role as other to the colonial self.

Although there is no consensual voice for postcolonial studies (see McClintock 1992; Mohanty 1995; Parry 1995; Slemon 1995; Tiffin 1995; Slater 1998; Sylvester 1999), Rattansi (1997: 481) introduces its central theme well as

> the investigation of the mutually constitutive role played by colonizer and colonized, centre and periphery, the metropolitan and the 'native', in forming in part the identities of both the dominant power and the subalterns involved in imperial and colonial projects of the 'West'.

Willems-Braun (1997) states that there cannot be a global theory of colonial culture, only localised theories and historically specific accounts that provide insight into varied articulations of colonialist and counter colonial representations and practices. Said's (1979) critique of orientalism shows the power of language and discourse in creating and perpetuating exotic notions of place and culture. Said calls this the production of imaginative geographies that construct and calibrate a distance between the colonising and colonised societies (Gregory 2001). In Chap. 5 I practise an edge politics (after Howitt 2001) to investigate the many different ways of knowing the environment in any nation. This investigation uses two case studies located in Australia and works to further unsettle the dichotomies inherent in the colonial project.

A postcolonial conception of power is useful to this research as it highlights the complex, multiple and hybrid nature of colonial and postcolonial spaces. The themes of nationhood, identity and connection to nature are central to environmental governance in a nation such as Australia. Therefore, it is important to critique the influence of colonial rule and the resulting and entangled discourses that influence environmental governance in Australia. This is highlighted by Willems-Braun's (1997) work about the politics of nature in (post)colonial British Columbia. He (1997: 3) states that

> amid the current popularity of notions like sustainable development, biodiversity management…- which risk abstracting natural 'systems' apart from their cultural surrounds - it is essential to recognize the colonial histories and neo-colonial rhetorics that continue to infuse 'commonsense' categories and identities like 'nature' and 'resources'.

In Chap. 4 I use the case study of Australia to engage with these notions of power to provide a way to unpack the way nature is constructed in environmental governance policy in any nation. These critiques highlight the importance of asking 'whose environment' is privileged in environmental governance policies and relating programs.

A coherent, appropriate and relevant critique of power is also provided in political ecology (see Blaikie and Brookfield 1987; Bryant 1992, 1997, 2001; Peet and Watts 1996; Forsyth 2003; Biersack and Greenberg 2006). This critique is useful in the analysis of community involvement in environment and development initiatives practised in subsequent chapters. Political ecology

> combines the concerns of ecology and a broadly defined political economy [to] encompass the constantly shifting dialectic between society and land-based resources, and also within classes and groups within society itself. (Blaikie and Brookfield 1987: 17)

Political ecology draws attention to the ultimate, as opposed to the proximate, causes and forces of environmental degradation and management. In particular, it talks about a politicised environment whereby relationships between actors and links between actors and the physical environment are conditioned by power relations (Bryant 1992, 1997, 2001; Peet and Watts 1996). These relationships are characterised by control: control over access to and use of resources, control over the social prioritisation of environmental projects and regulatory regimes and essentially the control one party has over the environment of another (Adams 1975).

Accordingly, unequal power relations may be inscribed in the environment. I engage with political ecology to assist in unpacking the power relations embedded in projects that focus on engaging the local community in working towards ecologically sustainable development (ESD) at the local scale.

In summary, spaces of power are integral to geographical studies when thinking about the role of the individual and the local in environment and development initiatives and projects. Sharp et al. (2000) provide a useful way of conceptualising power when they speak of entanglements of power, which suggests that there are countless processes of domination and resistance that are always implicated in and mutually constitutive of each other. They use the metaphor of entanglements to suggest the many places, spaces and networks that sustain these power relations. Other postcolonial researchers (see Guha and Spivak 1988; Spivak 1988; Bhabha 1994) also advocate a multi-spaced and hybrid engagement with spaces of power. They question how the subaltern can move beyond a produced history, representation and discourse to create new spaces of self-representation. The postcolonial critique questions the power dynamics inherent in environment and development initiatives in a nation such as Australia. Subsequent chapters in this book engage with these critiques to consider whose knowledge is privileged and whose knowledge is silenced in environmental governance and management. My objective is to show that by listening to the subaltern voice, it is possible to gain insight into the many voices of colonial, neocolonial and postcolonial times. This investigation seeks to demonstrate whether working to recognise these hybrid knowledge spaces enables the third cultural space that exists beyond the dichotomy of self/other. This is the ultimate aim of the new conceptual framework for cultural hybridity that is advocated in this book. The very process of working to support, enable and foster cultural hybridity can give '... rise to something different, something new and unrecognizable, a new area of negotiation of meaning and representation' (Bhabha 1990: 211).

3.2 A Critique of Knowledge Generation

In the previous chapter, I spoke about past development practice as often being about technology and knowledge transfer. I agreed with the conclusion that these perpetuate imperialistic, colonial ideas. I also noted the work of researchers who have criticised the tendency to position local knowledge as the panacea for all environmental and development problems caused by past development practice. Such a stance homogenises local knowledges, ignores the value of so-called universal knowledges and perpetuates the unhelpful dichotomies posited above.

By suggesting that science is a socially negotiated practice, I juxtapose other local knowledge bases, not in opposition to the scientific tradition, nor as the negative to the scientific tradition's positive, but as precisely that: as other local knowledge bases of which science is one. I do not wish to homogenise science by providing a critique that suggests its very philosophy undermines any other form of knowledge generation – there are emerging scientific practices that value other knowledge bases (e.g. ethno-ecology) – nor do I wish to further dichotomise scientific knowledge with other knowledge systems. The critique raised here provides a basis for a conceptualisation of knowledge generation as essentially locally situated and socially derived as a means to engage with the potential for greater interfacing between different kinds of knowledge. My purpose is to investigate whether recognising science as just one knowledge base among many allows an examination of what lies between spaces of knowing the world. I engage with this notion of knowledge to consider what it means to move beyond the dichotomies and binaries discussed in the previous section, towards processes that celebrate diversity as the basis of cultural hybridity. Moving beyond these dichotomies of exploitation creates the potential for processes to support cultural hybridity for knowledge synergies between apparently incommensurable knowledge cultures (discussed in detail in subsequent chapters).

I begin the following section by providing a discussion of the work of the influential social thinkers Kuhn, Foucault and Latour. These researchers are interested in the 'making of natural knowledge' (Golinski 1998). In this discussion, I question the political and social implications of this knowledge. I then examine the ideology that knowledge is locally determined and locally situated. Finally, I consider the idea that knowledge moves through networks between and across time and space rather than through hierarchical structures that work to reinforce the expertness, authority and legitimacy of science. By taking a social constructionist stance, I am in no way suggesting that a physical and material world does not exist; clearly it does. This research study acknowledges that knowledge generation as a social practice is value laden.

3.2.1 A Foray into the History and Philosophy of Science

The scientific tradition claims an objective engagement with the natural world as its basis of knowledge generation. This quest for the understanding of natural processes was the principal focus of the early natural philosophers, the pioneers of modern western science. Until 1960, the philosophy of science saw scientific knowledge as pivotal to human knowledge (Kendall and Wickham 1999). These ideas followed traditions in sociology which accepted scientific fact as universally and objectively true (e.g. see Durkheim 1915) and as progressing in a straight line (see Mannheim 1952; Popper 1963). There were questions relating to how science worked, but not to the content of science itself. Even Marx did not question the practice of science. He saw the growth of capitalism as the direct cause of the development of the natural sciences to their highest point (Kendall and Wickham 1999); he saw science as possibly benefiting the bourgeoisie but believed the scientists' 'knowledge claims within their precise research areas [were] non-ideological' (Mulkay 1979: 10). This claim is not shared by neo-Marxist researchers such as Harvey (1996). For Harvey science is a powerful discourse. He states that

> discourses are manifestations of power… the power of certain kinds of political discourse may derive from the uncanny capacity of those seeking political-economic power to mobilize and promote certain deeply held beliefs, fears and so on, against others and utilize that mobilization to sustain, promote a certain configuration of power relations. (Harvey 1996: 78–79)

Kuhn's (1962) *The Structure of Scientific Revolutions* forced a fundamental re-examination of the nature of science in scholarly circles including the history of science, sociology and later geography. As a historian of science, Kuhn looked at the way science as a discipline had been structured. He stated that, contrary to popular belief, it was not a cumulative or evolving knowledge base but had involved paradigms and revolutions. These revolutions occur when new scientific information goes beyond the confines of the accepted paradigms making the two incommensurable. Kuhn (1962) suggested that a paradigm forms the foundation for the practices of a scientific community. It provides the community with rules and standards to which to adhere, and any subsequent work perpetuates that very research tradition. Unique to this work is the coherence and clarity of the scientific imagination, where certain perceptions and rules emphasised only a portion of the 'too sizable and inchoate pool of information' (Kuhn 1962: 17). This was in contrast to the period of time predating the emergence of the first paradigm (pre-Newton). During this time no standard set of methods was adhered to. This resulted in many and varied descriptions and interpretations of the same phenomena. In addition, without the selected vision that a paradigm provides, early fact gathering of these phenomena was random but also limited to the data at hand. This fact gathering, essential to the establishment of current day science, appears unscientific when confronted with current day standards.

Foucault (1972) published *The Archaeology of Knowledge* a decade after Kuhn's seminal work. Foucault sets out a history of knowledge depicting the way in which the corpus of knowledge has changed with each passing episteme. An episteme encapsulates a period of time where knowledge of the natural world does not exceed the limitations placed upon it by the order of society. An episteme is framed by the 'totality of relations that can be discovered, for a given period, between the sciences when one analyses them at the level of discursive regularities' (Foucault 1972: 191). The episteme itself is not a type of knowledge, but rather is the social formation that leads to knowledge. Unlike Kuhn, Foucault's investigation goes beyond science to the 'total set of relations that unite, at a given period, the discursive practices that give rise to epistemological figures, sciences and possibly formalised systems' (Foucault 1972: 191). Foucault sees the discourse of representation as extremely powerful, considering that everything we know we do so through representation (Kendall and Wickham 1999).

During the classical episteme, classification and order were the driving force for natural philosophy. It was during this time that Carl Linnaeus (1707–1778), the most famous naturalist of the enlightenment, developed his binomial nomenclature whereby the names of all life forms were generated according to taxonomic codes denoting the genus and species. This classifying of nature, the ordering of nature into boxes and tables, resulted in the creation of a hierarchy of nature, a hierarchy of species and a hierarchy in the natural world, where humans inhabited the apex of the pyramid.[1] During this time 'the naturalist is the man concerned with the structure of the visible world and its denomination according to characters, not with life' (Foucault 1970: 161). In Foucault's modern episteme, there is a breakaway from a science that is based on the representation and classification of nature to a more thorough investigation into nature itself. Anatomy and botany become focal points in the need to make visible that which is invisible, to be able to understand the internal workings and secrets of the natural sciences.

Latour's (1987) *Science in Action* study modernises Kuhn's arguments by engaging with the contemporary world of the scientists and taking anthropology into the laboratory. Latour opens an investigation into the practicalities of scientific knowledge, the exhaustive process of refuting an accepted scientific fact. He (1987: 6) states that

> the equipment necessary to travel through science and technology is at once light and multiple. Multiple because it means mixing hydrogen bonds with deadlines, the probing of one another's authority with money, debugging and bureaucratic style; but the equipment is also light because it means simply leaving aside all the prejudices about what distinguishes the context in which knowledge is embedded, and this is knowledge itself.

Latour (1987) situates this procedure and secure culture as the practical process through which objective scientific knowledge is generated. He states that science is a local knowledge, local to the laboratory, but produces immutable mobiles that enable this local knowledge to travel long distances.

I engage with these debates to demonstrate that the generation of scientific knowledge is not purely an objective but also a social practice. Indeed, science practice occurs in myriad places involving many individuals with different skills, voices, practices, technical devices, theories, social strategies and collective work practices. The practice itself cannot exist outside of the agency of human actors as embedded in social process.

3.2.2 Knowledge Is Connected to Place

The work of these researchers questions the foundation of the scientific tradition's claim to objectivity. I engage with these critiques to consider ways of moving beyond dichotomies that locate the scientific knowledge tradition as universal and independent of place, as opposed to other knowledges, such as Indigenous knowledge, as local, inherently place dependent, subjective and thus value laden.

---

[1] Seddon (1997) points out that the hierarchical character of the Linnaean classification system is a reflection of assumptions of the natural and social order at the time. Schiebinger (1996) holds that the basis for the scientific study of nature were sexualised and gendered. At the same time, nature was used as a social reference point dictating the way in which women and men should behave.

This is an important first step on the pathway towards practices and strategies to foster and enable cultural hybridity. The work of researchers of the history and philosophy of science and of social constructivism posits that science is a socially directed practice of knowledge generation and is place dependent. These researchers question nature and its production. They argue that constructions of nature work to reinforce the position of the knowledge makers (Latour 1987; Haraway 1991; Demerritt 1998; Castree 2001b; Castree and Braun 2001). Central to this literature is the role of local knowledges, of which science is one, in generating ideas about nature.

Science, by separating its method of knowledge generation from the subjective and the social, separates itself from the world it is studying and reinforces a binary of objective/subjective or scientific knowledge/local or Indigenous knowledge. This discourse reinforces existing societal power relations, thus enabling the dissemination of scientific knowledge through a normative political hierarchy. In Chaps. 5, 6, 7, 8, 9, 10 and 11, I investigate whether recognising science and, it follows, each disciplinary specialism, as just one knowledge base among many, is the first step in moving beyond dichotomies and binaries that separate the world and social experience into different and opposing categories and creates new spaces from which to consider ESD.

A further critique of scientific knowledge generation points to the use of discourse and narrative as a means of reinforcing the position of the owners of production. It is the owners of the means of production of scientific knowledge who benefit from a system that is supposedly neutral and universal but in fact is grounded in social relations of race, gender and class (Haraway 1989). Haraway (1991: 187) points to the apparent universal concept of nature that is constructed by science, a practice that has been about 'a search for translation, convertibility, mobility of meanings, and universality'. Haraway calls this universality reductionism when the language of science is enforced as the standard for all these translations and conversions. She (1991: 191) refers to the rhetorics of science as 'god-tricks' that promise vision from 'everywhere and nowhere equally and fully'. This practice and discourse does not accept a passive vision of the world but is constantly and actively creating and recreating a way of organising that same world.

Studies into the localness of science, an act conducted by individual scientists in a specific location, subsume many of the previously supposed limitations of other knowledge systems as compared with western science (Watson-Verran and Turnbull 1995). Many arguments have been put forward for the scientific value of local knowledges as a means of moving beyond viewing the local as purely cultural. Perhaps such a stance works to perpetuate the dichotomy it is trying to override. But it cannot be denied in the current socio-political climate that the success of proponents of non-science-based knowledges to acquire government funding, in particular in relation to environment, is often grounded upon their ability to convey meaning within the dominant framework of science. This practice indicates that there is still far to go in actualising equitable knowledge exchange at the environment and development interface. I engage with these debates to consider a new conceptual framework that celebrates and creates the potential for equitable knowledge sharing at the environment and development interface. I contend that conceiving of knowledge as locally situated in place, associated across time and space, is a core foundation of such a new conceptual framework for cultural hybridity.

3.2.3 Situated Knowledges Move Through Networks

In this section I discuss Haraway's (1991) notion of situated knowledges. This ideology considers knowledges as negotiated, situated and partial and thus unique to each locale. This stance calls for a move beyond the realities of universal knowledge-from-above to a more complex and even contradictory view of knowledge as inherently situated in place and in the body. Haraway (1991) challenges what she sees as the rhetorics of science: relativism, totalisation and objectivity with the feminist objectivity that embraces situated knowledges. She argues that the feminist practice of objectivity is about

> limited location and situated knowledge, not about transcendence and splitting of subject and object [...where the] practice of objectivity privileges contestation, deconstruction, passionate construction, webbed connections and hope for transformation of systems of knowledge and ways of seeing. (Haraway 1991: 191–92)

She calls for politics and epistemologies of location, a positioned, situated and partial reality. From this perspective,

> all these pictures of the world should not be allegories of infinite mobility and interchange ability, but of elaborate specificity and difference and the loving care people might take to learn how to see faithfully from another's point of view even when the other is our own machine. (Haraway 1991: 190)

In the previous section, I introduced the social constructivist stance of this research endeavour as a forum for moving beyond the dualisms, dichotomies and binaries that work to perpetuate inequitable power relations in environment and development praxis. This problematic as Murdoch (1997a: 321) eloquently articulates puts human geographers in a position where we constantly have to consider

> unsavoury options... is it the state or the market that should receive our blessings? Should we ally ourselves to nature or society? Do we celebrate global forces of change or local strategies of resistance? Should we be objective analysts or subjective participants? ... it is natural that we should search for a 'third way', a route which permits a careful negotiation of the extremes and the development of a more sophisticated 'in betweenness', a more nuanced 'not quite here or there' kind of approach.

Massey (1991a, 1993) speaks of the power of geometry where place is the location of intersecting knowledge networks. Murdoch (1997b) uses actor-network-theory to speak of a world made up of heterogeneous associations. Watson-Verran and Turnbull (1995) speak of knowledge systems as assemblages of local knowledge. I use the work of these researchers to examine whether the way beyond conceiving of knowledge as hierarchical and dualistic is to conceive of it as the product of the local, but also the extra-local, networked or associated across time and space.

According to Haraway, knowledge is situated and embodied in place. Other researchers conceive of knowledge in similar ways. For example, Escobar (2001: 143) believes that 'we are, in short, placelings… place, body and environment integrate with each other'. Casey (1996: 18) states that 'to live is to live locally, and to know is first of all to know the places one is in'. Basso (1996: 70) points out that many Indigenous cultures focus upon the importance of local understandings of place. He quotes an Apache man saying 'wisdom sits in places'.

In these literatures, there is also the recognition (argued further in Sect. 3.3) that people are not only local but 'indissolubly linked to both local and extra-local places through what might be called networks' (Escobar 2001: 143), and the local is 'certainly not inhabited by rooted or natural identities but very much produced by complex relations of culture and power that go well beyond local bounds' (Escobar 2001: 146). So at once we are all local but also we are all extra-local. Massey's (1993) notion of 'power geometry' shows how space is bounded into particular local and global networks and how these configure particular places. Places are points of intersection where networks of relations meet. Massey (1991a: 28) argues that these networks of relations are 'constructed on a far wider scale than what we happen to define for that moment as the place itself, whether that be a street, or region or even a continent'. In Chap. 8 I engage with these debates to examine whether environment and development projects represent the intersection of environmental governance and management networks and are thus one location where cultural hybridity can be fostered and can form the basis for ESD in any nation.

Murdoch (1997a) says that although Massey's idea of relational networks is similar to the work of actor-network-theory, it ignores the role of non-human entities in these networks. To move beyond the dualisms depicted above, it is necessary to acknowledge the role and agency of the non-human in these networks. Where Massey speaks of the role of human forces in the relations and constellations of networks, Murdoch (1997a: 321) speaks of the need to move towards a 'geography of heterogenous associations' where the material world has agency in the previously mentioned networks; it is not just invested with properties of society and thus becomes the other to society. Actor-network-theory holds there to be exchanges that flow in both directions between the social and the material. This middle passage overcomes all dualisms, binaries and dichotomies argued here as causing the continued separation and universalisation of subject and object. These arguments are helpful in moving beyond the dichotomies of exploitation, discussed above, to an appreciation of the role of the self within a world of heterogeneous associations.

Watson-Verran and Turnbull (1995) state that although knowledge systems are different, a characteristic that they share is their localness. What is interesting is looking at the workings of knowledge systems as a way of understanding power relations both within and between knowledge systems. Watson-Verran and Turnbull (1995) use the term 'assemblages' as a way of considering these power relations. They state that assemblages are also material in much the same way that actor-network-theory speaks of non-human agents, or conceptual such as maps, theories and books, but their 'common function is to enable otherwise incommensurable and isolated knowledges to move in space and time from the local site and moment of their production to other places and times' (Watson-Verran and Turnbull 1995: 118). They exemplify scientific theory building as heterogenous assemblages:

> different viewpoints are constantly being adduced and reconciled...each actor, site or node of a scientific community has a viewpoint, a partial truth consisting of local beliefs, local practices, local constraints, and resources, none of which are fully verifiable across all sites. The aggregation of all viewpoints is the source of the robustness of science. (Star 1988 as cited in Watson-Verran and Turnbull 1995: 127)

In summary, to start from a critique of science as local may seem uneven in a discussion of local knowledges. It may appear to perpetuate the dichotomies and hierarchies central to the continued location of the scientific tradition as universal. I have used it above as a way of reinforcing local knowledge. I develop a critique of knowledge as inherently situated, place dependent and socially directed as a means of investigating whether this assists in moving beyond knowledge dichotomies. It follows that knowledge is simultaneously local and extra-local, where each locale is tied to extra-local knowledges and experiences (Burawoy 1998; Tedlock 2000). I engage with this argument to examine the fact that local knowledge cannot hold all the answers to localised socio-environmental problems because they are essentially extra-local, as are the individuals living them. I examine whether critiquing knowledge as both local and extra-local, situated and networked assists to understand where the individual and place are located across the many scales of environmental management and governance at the environment and development interface in Australia. I practise this critique throughout the research as a means of opening up local spaces of knowing and acting in the world. This is an important part of working towards cultural hybridity. The following section leads an investigation into the conception of scale as a relational social construct when thinking about the important role of the local as a space and place to foster and enable cultural hybridity for ESD in any nation.

3.3 Governance Scale Is a Relational Social Construct

> once scale is constructed or produced, where in the world is it? Scale is not as easily objectified as two-dimensional territorial space, such as state borders. We cannot touch it or take a picture of it. (Delaney and Leitner 1997: 96–97)

As Delaney and Leitner (1997) suggest in the above quote, scale is the product of social relations through time and space, where space itself is defined as a social construct (Lefebvre 1991), and scale is 'a way of framing conceptions of reality' (Delaney and Leitner 1997: 95) where 'the differentiation of geographical scales establishes and is established through the geographical structure of social interactions' (Smith 1992: 73). Developing an understanding of what scale means is essential to the investigation of this research. It provides another way to understand the social world in which this study falls: conceptualising scale as a social construction acknowledges the spatial form and political organisation of social relations. These relations often operate in ways that facilitate the power of dominant actors (Silvern 1999). Such a conceptualisation can enhance social theorising to understand geopolitics (Howitt 1998) and improve attempts to effect real social change (Marston 2000).

Challenging dominant metaphors and narratives about scale and exploring new ways of understanding provides new ways of engaging with the critical geopolitics of environment, difference, place and power (Howitt 2003). Further, Swyngedouw (1997: 147) states that 'scale reconfiguration challenges existing power relations, questions the existing power geometry and, thus, expresses the effects of sociospatial struggles'. A working understanding and definition of scale is pertinent to later analyses in this research project for three reasons. Firstly, it facilitates an understanding of the role of the local scale in environmental governance and management in Australia. Secondly, it encapsulates an acknowledgement of the power and the limitations of the local in environmental governance and management. Thirdly, it enables a consideration of ways to move beyond dichotomies of exploitation that are inherent in a hierarchical notion of scale and thus provides an important step towards fostering and enabling cultural hybridity. The following section gives a brief summary of current debates about scale, locates these debates in empirical cases within the literature and opens a platform from which to consider the relevance of these arguments to the investigation of this research.

What is geographical scale? Howitt (1998) posits that despite being one of geography's foundational concepts, scale has been under-theorised as compared with other core concepts such as environment, space and place. Debates about scale emerged in the 1990s as a way of challenging dominant conceptions of political and social processes (Howitt 2003), and ideas about space and scale continue to be contested in the social sciences. It has been premised as neutral geographical space that is assumed fixed (Kelly 1997). This 'absolute space' is characterised by the separate geographical domains of the global, the international, the regional, the national, the local and the body. Physical geographers use several connotations to describe geographic data issues (Marston 2000). Cartographic scale denotes the relationship between the distance on a map and the corresponding distance on the ground; geographic scale is the spatial extent of a phenomena or a study; and operational scale refers to the level at which relevant processes operate (Lam and Quattrochi 1992). Scale also refers to the measurement or the level of resolution of a study, that is, large scale as opposed to small scale (Marston 2000). Alternatively scale is argued by social theorists to be a social construct reflecting economic and geopolitical interests where the key process is the production of scale. Debates abound about whether scale is an ontological given or an epistemological construct. The debates are central to the investigation of this research.

Scale has conventionally been thought of as hierarchy. Delaney and Leitner (1997: 3) define it as 'the nested hierarchy of bounded spaces of different size, such as the local, regional, national and global'. The idea of scale as hierarchy presupposes that political (also economic and cultural) power and the territorial extent of that power is greater as you move up the hierarchy (Silvern 1999). Such a notion is critiqued by many researchers. For example, Gibson-Graham (2002) speaks about the discourse of globalisation. They see the global as positioned as an abstract space allowing the movement of capital and commodities against the local, characterised and confined by its tradition, powerlessness and locale. This production of scale can work to create a dichotomy that works to undervalue local knowledge and action. In addition the local is positioned as reactive to more global processes. This downplays the importance of the local or regional contexts as formative constituents in the social production of the global scale (McGuirk 1997).

Geographers began to question the representation of scale, its production and the relationship between scale and process in the early 1990s (see in particular Smith 1992; Howitt 1993; Jonas 1994). Since then, many researchers call for a more relational understanding of scale (Howitt 1998, 2002; McGuirk 1997; Swyngedouw 1997). Howitt (1998) states that scale is better understood dialectically rather than hierarchically. He states that scale should be considered as relational. He believes that understanding scale as a factor in the construction and dynamics of geographical totalities rather than simply as a product of geographical relations or a matter of size, as area, or level, as hierarchy, will provide more powerful insights into the nature and dynamic of complex geographical totalities. Swyngedouw (1997: 140) speaks of scale as 'the arena and moment, both discursively and materially [...as] both the result and the outcome of social struggle for power and control... empowerment and disempowerment'. In this way scale can be considered as a network where it is perpetually defined, contested and redefined, where the local and global are mutually constituted. Scales are not discrete entities but are fluid, multidirectional and mutually constitutive (McGuirk 1997).

Cox's (1998) seminal paper mentions scale as a central concept in political discourse. He argues that the relationships that are developed when the struggles at the local move to other scales can be conceptualised as a political strategy of moving between spaces of engagement. Cox (1998) describes spaces of dependence as the fixed localised arenas where individuals are embedded, and spaces of engagement are the sets of relations that extend into and beyond the spaces of dependence. The relationship between these spaces works to 'construct networks of association, exchange and politics' (Jones 1998: 25). At any one physical locale, there are multiple spaces of dependence and multiple associations that extend to spaces of engagement. These spaces of engagement are not necessarily at different 'levels', but rather all scales are mutually constituted and implicated in any conflict or struggle. Scale should not be considered as a place or an arena but, as Jones (1998: 26) states, a network

> or a strategy linking local struggles to regional, national or global events [... in] building these networks, local groups practice politics by actively reshaping the discourses within which their struggles are constituted

So are all politics local? Cox (1998) makes the interesting assertion that as a result of these spaces of engagement, local politics 'appears as metropolitan, regional, national or even international as different organizations try to secure those networks of associations through which respective projects can be realized' (p. 19). In his commentary to Cox's thesis, Smith (1998: 40) suggests that what takes place at the local 'may not be local politics at all but the localization of wider political games involving regional, national or global actors who have found local venues to mine and local actors to express their interests'.

So are the politics of scale inherently local or is the local merely an arena for extra-local politics? This question is central to an examination of the role of the local in environmental governance in any nation. This is because it questions whether the power of local knowledge is confined by the conceptualisation of governance scale as hierarchical. In his work about environmental injustice and racism in North America, Williams (1999) discusses how the production of scale can empower one group while often simultaneously disempowering other groups. Williams (1999: 68) recognises that 'empowerment lies across scales; disempowerment results from being defined by one scale of action'. Taking this further, Jones (1998) points out that the way in which actors link their local struggles to regional, national, global events and struggles is a means of creating scale networks and politically reshaping the discourses within which their struggles are played out: by representing their struggle as a global struggle, they are able to create new spaces of engagement. McGuirk (1997) applies a nonhierarchical way of thinking of scale to an urban development program in an Australian city. She shows that critiquing regulatory planning mechanisms as mutually constituted rather than top-down opens new ways of explaining the active role of the local. She calls for a nonhierarchical approach to scale and a focus on the relationships between scales.

In summary, conceiving of scale as a relational social construct assists the investigation of this research in two ways. Firstly, it assists in a critique into the role of the local in environmental governance in any nation, and secondly, it provides the opportunity for the transformation of existing power relations by seeking to 'mobilize social networks, political institutions, economic resources and territorial rights to the task of creating new geographies, new landscapes of power and recognition and opportunity' (Howitt 2002: 11). Subsequent chapters engage with this critique to consider how the role of the local is constructed in national and regional environmental governance policies and related programs (the two Australian case studies provide a focus for this critique). I investigate whether conceptualising of scale as a relational social construct assists in creating new spaces of engagement that support, foster and enable cultural hybridity. I question whether hybrid and situated knowledge spaces can provide a platform from which social change can be actualised.

3.4 Colonial Discourses of Nature

In the Judeo-Christian tradition, and in mainstream western (scientific) thought, nature is often defined as a singular entity, separate from human culture and society. It has been described as the garden, the temple of God, cultivated by the human hand, and at the same time as wilderness, the wasteland of Satan, beyond civilisation. It has been created as the other and used as a vehicle through which the western self has been justified. Nature has been personified and gendered. It has been acted upon, acted within and made into a muse. It has been romanticised and ostracised. Nature has undergone many transformations, most strikingly from a wilderness to be dominated and cultivated to a wilderness to be protected and left in its natural state. It has been described as a singular 'it'; however, as these myriad descriptions suggest, it is multidimensional, pluralistic and understood in many ways. In this section I briefly touch upon the changing and myriad definitions of nature within the western tradition. A sophisticated understanding of the way in which the natural world has been and continues to be constructed provides yet another way to interpret the social world in which this study falls. This critique is central to an investigation into the role of the local in environmental governance and management in any nation because it highlights the power of entrenched discourses of nature.

'In the beginning…..', Eve took an apple from the tree of knowledge of good and evil and offered it to Adam. This well-known biblical story could be argued as providing the foundation for the way in which nature has been defined in the Old and New Worlds. The Edenic narrative dictates, reinforces and justifies the relations between society and nature in the Judeo-Christian tradition. Man was thrown out of the Garden of Eden tempted by woman and has spent his time ever since trying to get back in. Alternatively he has spent his time trying to recreate such a garden through his labour and skill. This narrative is based upon the dichotomy of the garden as an enclosed sacred place where one can meditate and speak with God versus the wilderness, a place away from God (Merchant 1996).

In Europe during the time of the Renaissance and the enlightenment, wilderness was more a metaphor than a reality because many lands were agricultural. With the advent of scientific endeavour and colonisation, the European imagination came into contact with what it conceived to be wild lands. Accounts by individuals toiling against the ferocity of the wilderness in the New World formed the basis for the national identity of countries like Australia, Canada, USA and New Zealand with notions of the pioneer heroically struggling to tame the supposedly unpeopled and uncivilised wildness of nature.

In contemporary times the unique lands of a nation such as Australia remain as central and pertinent to the national identity. Indeed, the rich and evolving attitudes to country highlight the complexity of what Ward (1965) calls 'The Australian Legend'. The ongoing relationship with country is evidenced in the arts from May Gibbs' fictitious 'Bush Babies' to Dorothea Mackellar's poetic 'I love a sunburnt country'; the political sphere including the Franklin River campaign and the Mabo High Court ruling; and the search for identity with land that still separates Aboriginal and other Australian connections with country encapsulated by the following quote: 'white man got no dreaming' (Muta a Murinbata, cited in Stanner 1979: iii). The majority of migrant Australians choose to live on the east coast for myriad reasons but often for ways that complement A.D. Hope's (1972: 8) metaphor of migrant Australians looking back to Europe. In his aptly named poem 'Australia', he describes the experience of the migrant population by the following words:

> Where second hand Europeans pullulate
> Timidly on the edges of alien shores.

European expansion was driven by several impetuses including the pursuit of gold and profits, the settlement of territories, biological endeavour and dreams of the exotica of India and China (Grove 1995). Expansion for commercial and utilitarian purposes and resultant emerging frameworks of trade and travel also promoted rapid dispersal of scientific and environmental ideas. It also provided contact with other cultures and perhaps broader notions of what nature meant to different peoples and the opportunity for knowledge exchange. Many researchers, particularly those concerned with development (e.g. Sachs 1992; Shiva 1993a; Escobar 1995), argue that the voyages of colonial nations to new and exotic territories in search of new lands, resources and other riches robbed the so-called exotic nations and peoples of their culture, autonomy and territory.[2] Langton (1998: 9) suggests that Aboriginal Australians and their land management traditions have been rendered invisible in Australian landscapes by '…'science fictions' that arise from the assumption of superiority of western knowledge over Indigenous knowledge systems'.

The discourse of orientalism (Said 1979) is relevant to the way in which nature has been classified. Often peoples of distant and different nations were classified not only as the other but as being more closely linked to nature and a natural way of life; terms such as the noble savage (see Cronon 1996; Slater 1996) were coined depicting a people living in harmony with their natural environment. These people could be acted upon and civilised in much the same way as their environment because they were perceived as living so close to nature they could perhaps be identified as primitive wilderness in themselves. This narrative of the noble savage was used as a tool of colonialism; coupled with notions of social Darwinism, it became a tool of the dispossessor. The classification of the land of Australia as *terra nullius* in 1770 as unoccupied and open for claim by the Englishman Captain James Cook reflects this logic. This mindset persisted in Australian Law until the historic Mabo Decision in 1992 when the Australian High Court overturned the notion of *terra nullius*. The ongoing land rights struggle is encapsulated by the words of the chairman of the Central Land Council, a statutory authority set up to represent and promote Aboriginal land rights in the Northern Territory, at the Inaugural Indigenous Land and Sea Management Conference. Ross (2005: 1) states that 'the land needs its people as much as the people need their land'.[3]

[2] Grove (1995) refutes the work of many historians who write about the colonial experience as environmentally destructive and having its roots in ideologically imperialistic attitudes towards the environment. He suggests that much of the ideological and scientific content of the early French and British colonial conservationism was based on a heterogeneous mix of Indigenous, romantic, oriental and other knowledge.

[3] Reynolds (1982, 1992, 1999a, b) speaks of Indigenous resistance to the European invasion of Australia. Indeed the Mabo Decision resulted from the ongoing struggle of Indigenous Australians against colonial laws. Challenges to colonial rule are evidenced by, for example, the historic walk-off staged by Gurindji people working as stockmen at Wattie Creek station (locally called Darguargu) in 1966. This act of protest represented their attempt to reclaim their country from the white pastoralists.

The dual notions of noble savage and social Darwinism as a means of making the continent of Australia wild highlight the problematic term of wilderness. On the one hand, the land of Australia was considered wilderness: a land to which no one had made a prior claim (evidenced by the lack of English forms of property ownership represented by, e.g. agriculture), the uncivilised narrative of wilderness. At the same time, the Indigenous peoples of Australia were seen as part of the wilderness itself. This idea is inherently contradictory and is touted by many researchers (Cronon 1996; Proctor 1996, 1998; Willems-Braun 1997; Castree 2001b; Castree and Braun 2001) as one of the underlying inconsistencies in the definition of '"nature" ("wilderness")… constructed as a realm separate from "culture"' (Willems-Braun 1997: 3). The first claim of the inexistence of the Indigenous peoples is counter to historical fact and contested not only in Australia but in North America and other parts of the world (Haila 1997). The second claim that the subsistence systems of aboriginal cultures had no influence on the natural environment is a complex one but equally false. Langton (1996: 24), an Indigenous Australian, articulates that

> just as *terra nullius* was a lie, so was this European fantasy of wilderness. There is no wilderness, but there are cultural landscapes, those of the environmentalists who depict a theological version of nature in posters, and those of Aboriginal people, present and past, whose relationships with the environment shaped even the reproductive mechanisms of forests.

Undeniably the process of colonialism transformed nature, in particular creating new relations between human and non-human nature; in the process it created new ideologies of those relationships (Shiva 1989). Ideas about nature as either economic resource or reservoir of pristine wilderness were an important element of the colonial ideology (Adams and Mulligan 2003). European colonial power was based upon the separation and exclusion of colonised peoples and nature from civilised society, thereby homogenising their diversity into one single stereotype (Plumwood 2003). There is little doubt this legacy continues, for example, the fortress conservation of colonial Africa. In postcolonial times and nations, what does this legacy of conservation mean? Colonialism was in no way a monolithic practice. It was composed of a range of discourses, knowledges and practices (scientific, religious, aesthetic) in different ways in specific locations. Decolonisation has meant different things according to location. What this means and how it is played out in (post)colonial nations, such as Australia, is of central concern to this research.

In summary, I argue that it is important to trace the way in which the natural environment has been described in western thought to gain an understanding of how it continues to be socially constructed. This claim does not suggest that a biophysical world does not exist but draws attention to the social meanings embedded in this world. It is essential to be aware of the history and present-day conceptions of the biophysical world when considering environmental management and governance in any nation and in particular (post)colonial nations such as Australia.

3.5 Conclusion

This chapter had led a trajectory through relevant theoretical works and debates about power, knowledge, governance scale and nature. These themes are identified as central to an investigation into the role of local, Indigenous and scientific knowledge in environmental governance and management in any nation. The epistemological tools explored in this chapter, which form the basis of the applied peoples' geography, are a conception of power as entangled; knowledge as locally situated, networked and associated across time and space; governance scale as relational and networked; and nature as a social construct. The applied peoples' geography is used throughout this book. It provides the foundation of the new conceptual framework that advocates strategies for cultural hybridity to overcome knowledge dichotomies that impede equitable knowledge sharing for ESD.

References

Adams RN (1975) Energy and structure: a theory of social power. University of Texas Press, Austin

Adams WM, Mulligan M (2003) Introduction. In: Adams WM, Mulligan M (eds) Decolonizing nature: strategies for conservation in a post-colonial era. Earthscan Publications Ltd, London, pp 1–15

Basso KH (1996) Wisdom sits in places: notes on a western Apache landscape. In: Feld S, Basso KH (eds) Senses of place. School of American Research Press, Santa Fe, pp 53–90

Bhabha HK (1990) The third space: interview with Homi Bhabha. In: Rutherford J (ed) Identity: community, culture, difference. Lawrence & Wishart, London, pp 207–221

Bhabha HK (1994) The location of culture. Routledge, London

Biersack A, Greenberg JB (2006) Reimagining political ecology. Duke University Press, Durham

Blaikie P, Brookfield H (1987) Land degradation and society. Methuen, London

Bryant RL (1992) Political ecology: an emerging research agenda in third-world studies. Polit Geogr 11:12–36

Bryant RL (1997) Beyond the impasse: the power of political ecology in third world environmental research. Area 29(1):5–19

Bryant RL (2001) Political ecology: a critical agenda for change? In: Castree N, Braun B (eds) Social nature: theory, practice and politics. Blackwell, Oxford, pp 151–169

Burawoy M (1998) The extended case method. Sociol Theory 16(1):4–33

Casey E (1996) How to get from space to place in a fairly short stretch of time. In: Feld S, Baso K (eds) Senses of place. School of American Research, Santa Fe, pp 14–51

Castree N (2001a) Socializing nature: theory, practice, and politics. In: Castree N, Braun B (eds) Social nature: theory, practice, and politics. Blackwell Publishers Ltd, Oxford, pp 1–21

Castree N (2001b) Marxism, capitalism, and the production of nature. In: Castree N, Braun B (eds) Social nature: theory, practice and politics. Blackwell Publishers, Oxford, pp 189–207

Castree N, Braun B (eds) (2001) Social nature: theory, practice and politics. Blackwell, Oxford

Cox KR (1998) Representation and power in the politics of scale. Polit Geogr 17(1):41–44

Cronon W (1996) The trouble with wilderness, or getting back to the wrong nature. In: Cronon W (ed) Uncommon ground: rethinking the human place in nature. W.W. Norton & Company, London

Dahl RA (1957) The concept of power. Behav Sci 2:201–215
Delaney D, Leitner H (1997) The political construction of scale. Polit Geogr 16(2):93–97
Demerritt D (1998) Science, social constructivism and nature. In: Braun B, Castree N (eds) Remaking reality: nature at the millennium. Routledge, London, pp 173–193
Durkheim E (1915) The elementary forms of the religious life. Allen and Unwin, London
Escobar A (1995) Encountering development: the making and unmaking of the third world. Princeton University Press, Princeton
Escobar A (2001) Culture sits in places: reflections on globalism and subaltern strategies of localization. Polit Geogr 20:139–174
Forsyth T (2003) Critical political ecology. The politics of environmental science. Routledge, Abingdon
Foucault M (1970) The order of things: an archaeology of the human sciences (a translation of Les Mots et les Choses). Pantheon Books, New York
Foucault M (1972) The archaeology of knowledge. Tavistock Publications Ltd, London
Foucault M (1980) Two lectures. In: Gordon C (ed) Michel Foucault: power/knowledge: selected interviews and other writings. Harvester, Brighton, pp 1972–1977
Gibson-Graham JK (2002) Beyond global vs. local: economic politics outside the binary frame. In: Herod A, Wright WM (eds) Geographies of power. Blackwell Publishing, Oxford, pp 25–60
Golinski J (1998) Making natural knowledge: constructivism and the history of science. Cambridge University Press, Cambridge
Gregory D (2001) Post-colonialism and the production of nature. In: Castree N, Braun B (eds) Social nature: theory, practice and politics. Blackwell Publishers, Oxford, pp 84–111
Grove RH (1995) Green imperialism: colonial expansion, tropical island edens and the origins of environmentalism: 1600–1860. Cambridge University Press, Cambridge
Guha R, Spivak G (eds) (1988) Selected subaltern studies. Oxford University Press, Oxford
Haila Y (1997) 'Wilderness' and the multiple layers of environmental thought. Environ Hist 3:129–147
Haraway D (1989) Primate visions: gender, race and nature in the world of modern science. Routledge, New York
Haraway D (1991) Simians, cyborgs and women. Routledge, London
Harvey D (1984) On the history and present condition of geography: an historical materialist manifesto. Prof Geogr 36(1):1–11
Harvey D (1996) Justice, nature and the geography of difference. Blackwell Publishers, Cambridge, MA
Hinchliffe S (2000) Entangled humans: specifying powers and their spatialities. In: Sharp JP, Routledge P, Philo C, Paddison R (eds) Entanglements of power: geographies of domination/resistance. Routledge, London, pp 219–237
Hope AD (1972) Collected poems 1930–1970. Angus and Robertson, Sydney
Howitt R (1993) "A world in a grain of sand": towards a reconceptualisation of geographical scale. Aust Geogr 24(1):33–44
Howitt R (1998) Scale as relations: musical metaphors of geographical scale. Area 30(1):49–58
Howitt R (2001) Frontiers, borders, edges: liminal challenges to the hegemony of exclusion. Aust Geogr Stud 39(2):233–245
Howitt R (2002) Scale and the other: embodiment, emplacement and infinity. Geoforum 33(3):299–313
Howitt R (2003) Scale. In: Agnew J, Mitchell K, Tuathail GO (eds) A companion to political geography. Blackwell, Oxford, pp 138–157
Jonas AEG (1994) The scale politics of spatiality. Environ Plan D: Soc Space 12(3):257–264
Jones M (1998) Restructuring the local state: economic governance or social regulation? Polit Geogr 17(8):959–988

Kelly PF (1997) Globalization, power and the politics of scale in the Philippines. Geoforum 28(2):151–171
Kendall G, Wickham G (1999) Using Foucault's methods. Sage Publications, London
Kuhn TS (1962) The structure of scientific revolutions. The University of Chicago Press, Chicago
Lam N, Quattrochi DA (1992) On the issues of scale, resolution and fractal analysis in the mapping sciences. Prof Geogr 44:88–98
Langton M (1996) Art, wilderness and terra nullius. Ecopolitics IX conference: perspectives on indigenous peoples management of the environment resources. Darwin
Langton M (1998) Burning questions: emerging environmental issues for indigenous peoples in northern Australia. Centre of Indigenous Natural and Cultural Resource Management, Northern Territory University, Darwin
Latour B (1987) Science in action: how to follow scientists and engineers through society. Harvard University Press, Cambridge/Harvard
Lefebvre H (1991) The production of space (trans: Nicholson-Smith D). Blackwell, Oxford/Cambridge, MA
Mannheim K (1952) Essays on the sociology of knowledge. Routledge and Kegan Paul, London
Marston SA (2000) The social construction of scale. Prog Hum Geogr 24(2):219–242
Massey D (1991) A global sense of place. Marxism Today 38:24–29
Massey D (1993) Power-geometry and a progressive sense of place. In: Bird J, Curtis B, Putnam T, Robertson G, Tickner L (eds) Mapping the futures: local cultures, global change. Routledge, London, pp 59–69
Massey D (2000) Entanglements of power: reflections. In: Sharp JP, Routledge P, Philo C, Paddison R (eds) Entanglements of power: geographies of domination/resistance. Routledge, London, pp 279–286
McClintock A (1992) The angel of progress: pitfalls of the term "post-colonialism". Social Text 31/32:84–98
McGuirk P (1997) Multiscaled interpretations of urban change: the federal, the state, and the local in the western area strategy of Adelaide. Environ Plan D: Soc Space 15:481–498
Merchant C (1996) Reinventing Eden: western culture as recovery narrative. In: Cronon W (ed) Uncommon ground: rethinking the human place in nature. W.W. Norton & Company, London, pp 132–170
Mohanty CT (1995) Under western eyes: feminist scholarship and colonial discourses. In: Ashcroft B, Griffiths G, Tiffin H (eds) A post-colonial studies reader. Routledge, London, pp 259–263
Mulkay M (1979) Science and the sociology of knowledge. Allen and Unwin, London
Murdoch J (1997a) Towards a geography of heterogeneous associations. Prog Hum Geogr 21(3):321–337
Murdoch J (1997b) Inhuman/nonhuman/human: actor-network theory and the prospects for a nondualistic and symmetrical perspective on nature and society. Environ Plan D 15:731–756
Parry B (1995) Problems in current theories of colonial discourse. In: Ashcroft B, Griffiths G, Tiffin H (eds) The post-colonial studies reader. Routledge, London, pp 36–44
Peet R, Watts M (1996) Liberation ecology, development, sustainability, and environment in an age of market triumphalism. In: Peet R, Watts M (eds) Liberation ecologies, environment, development, social movement. Routledge, London, pp 1–45
Plumwood V (2003) Decolonizing relationships with nature. In: Adams WM, Mulligan M (eds) Decolonizing nature: strategies for conservation in a post-colonial era. Earthscan, London, pp 51–78
Popper K (1963) Conjectures and refutations: the growth of scientific knowledge. Routledge and Kegan Paul, London

Proctor J (1996) Whose nature? The contested moral terrain of ancient forests. In: Cronon W (ed) Uncommon ground: rethinking the human place in nature. W.W. Norton & Company, London, pp 269–297

Proctor J (1998) The social construction of nature: relativist accusations. Ann Assoc Am Geogr 88(3):352–376

Radcliffe SA (2000) Entangling resistance, ethnicity, gender and nation in Ecuador. In: Sharp JP, Routledge P, Philo C, Padison R (eds) Entanglements of power: geographies of domination/resistance. Routledge, London, pp 164–181

Rattansi A (1997) Postcolonialism and its discontents. Econ Soc 26(4):480–500

Reynolds H (1982) The other side of the frontier. Penguin Books, Ringwood

Reynolds H (1992) The law of the land. Penguin Books Australia, Ringwood

Reynolds H (1999a) Why weren't we told? A personal search for the truth about our history. Viking, Ringwood

Reynolds P (1999b) Eyewitness: the battle of Seattle, BBC News, www.news.bbc.co.uk. Accessed 8 June 2006

Ross D (2005) The country needs its people: the people need their country, Central Land Council. www.clc.org.au. Accessed 9 June 2006

Rostow W (1960) The stages of economic growth: a non-communist manifesto. Cambridge University Press, Cambridge

Said E (1979) Orientalism. Routledge, London

Schiebinger L (1996) Gender and natural history. In: Jardin, Second & Spray (ed) Cultures of natural history. Cambridge University Press, Cambridge, pp 163–177

Scott J (1985) Weapons of the weak: everyday forms of peasant resistance. Yale University Press, New Haven

Seddon G (1997) Landprints: reflections on place and landscape. Cambridge University Press, Cambridge

Shah A (2000) United Nations Framework Convention on climate change conference of the parties (COP6): the Hague conference, global issues. www.globalissues.org. Accessed 8 June 2006

Sharp J, Routledge P, Philo C, Paddison R (2000) Entanglements of power: geographies of domination/resistance. In: Sharp J, Routledge P, Philo C, Paddison R (eds) Entanglements of power: geographies of domination/resistance. Routledge, London, pp 1–42

Shiva V (1989) Staying alive: women, ecology and development. Zed Books Ltd, London

Shiva V (1993) Monocultures of the mind: perspectives on biodiversity and biotechnology. Zed Books Ltd, London

Silvern SE (1999) Scales of justice: law, American Indian treaty rights and the political construction of scale. Polit Geogr 18:639–668

Slater C (1996) Amazonia as edenic narrative. In: Cronon W (ed) Uncommon ground: rethinking the human place in nature. W.W. Norton & Company, London, pp 114–131

Slater D (1998) Post-colonial questions for global times. Rev Int Polit Econ 5(4):647–678

Slemon S (1995) The scramble for post-colonialism. In: Ashcroft B, Griffiths G, Tiffin H (eds) The post-colonial studies reader. Routledge, London, pp 45–54

Smith MP (1998) Looking for the global spaces in local politics. Polit Geogr 17(1):35–40

Smith N (1992) Geography, difference and the politics of scale. In: Doherty J, Graham E, Mallek M (eds) Postmodernism and the social sciences. Macmillan, London, pp 57–79

Spivak GC (1988) In other worlds: essays in cultural politics. Routledge, London

Stanner WEH (1979) White man got no dreaming, essays 1938–1973. Australian National University Press, Canberra

Swyngedouw E (1997) Neither global nor local: 'glocalization' and the politics of scale. In: Cox KR (ed) Spaces of globalization: reasserting the power of the local. The Guilford Press, New York, pp 137–166

Sylvester C (1999) Development studies and postcolonial studies: disparate tales of the 'Third World'. Third World Q 20(4):703–721
Tedlock B (2000) Ethnography and ethnographic representation. In: Denzin NK, Lincoln YS (eds) Handbook of qualitative research. Sage Publications Inc, California, pp 455–486
Thrift N (2000) Entanglements of power: shadows? In: Sharp JP, Routledge P, Philo C, Paddison R (eds) Entanglements of power: geographies of domination/resistance. Routledge, London, pp 269–278
Tiffin H (1995) Post-colonial literatures and counter-discourse. In: Ashcroft B, Griffiths G, Tiffin H (eds) The post-colonial studies reader. Routledge, London, pp 95–98
Ward R (1965) The Australian legend. Oxford University Press, Melbourne
Watson-Verran H, Turnbull D (1995) Science and other indigenous knowledge systems. In: Jasanoff S, Markle GE, Petersen JC, Pinch T (eds) Handbook of science and technology studies. Sage Publications, California, pp 115–139
Willems-Braun B (1997) Buried epistemologies: the politics of nature in (post) colonial British Colombia. Ann Assoc Am Geogr 87(1):3–31
Williams RW (1999) Environmental injustice in America and its politics of scale. Polit Geogr 18:49–73

Part II
Edge Politics in Action

Chapter 4
Political Landscapes

Abstract This chapter practises the edge politics (after Howitt, Aust Geogr Stud 39:233–245, 2001a) advocated by this book to investigate whose notion of environment and whose notion of development are privileged in any given formalised political landscapes. This critique is important to working towards cultural hybridity as it opens up the spaces of exploitation, highlights the dichotomies inherent to the way in which 'top-down' environmental governance is practised in any nation and thus provides a point of departure to move beyond the entrenched and inequitable narratives of ESD inherent to the nexus of environmental governance and environmental management.

Howitt (Rethinking resource management: sustainability, justice and indigenous peoples. Routledge, London, p 234, 2001b) argues that practising an edge politics 'grapples with ambivalence, uncertainty, change, overlap and interaction in ways that dislodge the old-style colonial metaphors of empty spaces and frontier heroics' (In this quote, Howitt (2001b) is referring specifically to historical and contemporary interpretations of the Northern Territory landscape. I engage with his notion of an edge politics as a means to explore the diversity of approaches of land management in any landscape, in particular across Australia and specifically in Victoria and the Northern Territory.). The edge politics practised in this chapter follows the critique provided in Chap. 3 and shows by example the unique and complex politics that are embedded in formal governance structures (policies, programs and related on-ground projects). These formal governance structures are described here as comprising 'political landscapes'.

Two case studies, both located in Australia, are used to explore what this edge politics means. They provide a way to focus the critique, and by example, they illustrate how such a critique can be conducted for the political context of any nation. The political landscapes in which the two case study projects are embedded are critiqued in two ways. Firstly, I detail the policy approach to what is articulated by the Australian Government as regional natural resource management or NRM. I then depict the broader policy landscapes that influenced the two case studies at the time of the research. In the second part of this chapter I use the edge politics to critique the Australian Government notion of 'regionalism' to demonstrate whether it privileges any particular discourse of 'development' and 'nature'. I then engage with

K. Maclean, *Cultural Hybridity and the Environment*,
DOI 10.1007/978-981-287-323-1_4

the applied peoples' geography presented in Chap. 3 to unpack the complexities encapsulated in the Australian Government's regional approach to natural resource management.

4.1 Regional Natural Resource Management in Australia

In Australia, as in other nations, specific government departments administer international conventions, treaties and national strategies. At the time of the research, the Australian Government Department of Environment and Heritage was the national agency responsible for fulfilling Australia's commitment to international environment and development conventions such as the *Convention on Biological Diversity (1992)*.[1] In partial fulfilment of this convention, the Department of Environment and Heritage administered the *National Strategy for Ecologically Sustainable Development (1992)* and the *National Strategy for the Conservation of Australia's Biological Diversity (1992)*.[2] Both strategies[3] emphasise the valuable involvement of all Australians in working towards ecologically sustainable development (ESD). For example, Chap. 22 of the *National Strategy for Ecologically Sustainable Development (1992)* speaks of ensuring 'full participation by Aboriginal and Torres Strait Islander peoples in community progress towards ESD' (ESDSC 1992: 94), and Chap. 32 acknowledges 'that progress towards ecologically sustainable development is supported by community understanding and action' (ESDSC 1992: 10,109). Also Objective 1.8 of the *National Strategy for the Conservation of Australia's Biological Diversity (1992)* works to 'recognise and ensure the continuity of the contribution of the ethnobiological knowledge of Australia's Indigenous peoples to the conservation of Australia's biological diversity' (DEST 1996: 14), and Objective 5 states 'the involvement of all Australians is vital to the conservation of biological diversity' (DEST 1996: 36).

The *National Strategy for the Conservation of Australia's Biological Diversity (1992)* also speaks of managing 'biological diversity on a regional basis, using natural boundaries to facilitate the integration of conservation and production-oriented management' (Objective 1.2, DEST 1996). This is reflected by the commitment of the Australian Federal Government to implement 'regional natural resource management'. At the time of the research, the resulting regional natural resource management program was articulated under the slogan of 'together let's give our land a hand' (see NHT and NAPSWQ 2000: 1). This program integrated the Australian Government's sustainable land management programs of, when

[1]In 2013, this convention is administered by the Australian Government's Department of Environment.

[2]This strategy was revised in 2009. The Australian Government invited public comments on the draft Australia's Biodiversity Conservation Strategy, 2010–2020 (see Environment 2013a).

[3]In 2013, these strategies are administered by the Australian Government's Department of Environment.

relevant, the National Action Plan for Salinity and Water Quality, the Natural Heritage Trust and the National Landcare Program.[4] These programs were the result of the Australian Federal Government's commitment to decentralisation and devolution (discussed in Chap. 2 Sect. 2.7). The push for decentralisation developed from events in both the international and local arenas: Australia's international commitment to ESD and the on-ground development of the Australian landcare movement among farmers in regional Victoria and Western Australia (see Baker 1997).

The Australian National Landcare Program developed from a joint submission of the Australian Conservation Foundation (a national nongovernment organisation dedicated to ecological sustainability; see ACF 2013) and the National Farmers' Federation (the peak national body that represents farmers and agriculture across Australia; see NFF 2013) was entitled *A National Land Management Programme*. The notion of 'landcare' was and still is a community-based approach that has raised awareness, influenced farming and land management practices and delivered environmental outcomes across Australian landscapes (see Baker 1997). Landcare activities include soil conservation, sustainable farming practices, management of erosion and salinity, revegetation, control of weeds and pests, restoration of native habitats and the development of local natural resource management skills and knowledge. It is a voluntary network of more than 6,000 groups across Australia (see DAFF 2009). The evolution of the landcare movement into an Australian Government program is explored in more detail below.

The National Land Management Program was put to the Australian Federal Government in 1989 (see Toyne and Farley 1989). In accordance with this submission, the then Australian Federal Government (Hawke Labour government) declared 1990 the Year of Landcare and the 1990s as the Decade of Landcare. The then Australian Federal Government committed funding packages totalling $A320 million to be rolled out over 10 years (Sobels and Curtis 2001). At the time of the research, the National Landcare Program[5] was administered by the Australian Federal Government Department of Agriculture, Fisheries and Forestry and complemented the delivery of the National Action Plan for Salinity and the Natural Heritage Trust.

[4]The NHT2 evolved into the programs of 'Caring for our Country' and the Indigenous focussed 'Working on Country' in 2008. The Caring for our Country program funds projects across Australia to achieve the national targets to improve biodiversity and sustainable farm practices. The goal of this program, 'an environment that is healthy, better protected, well managed, resilient and provides essential ecosystem services in a changing climate' (CfoC 2013a: 1), reflects seven national priorities. These priorities include the National Reserve System; biodiversity and natural icons; coastal environments and critical aquatic habitats; sustainable farm practices; northern and remote Australia; and community skills, knowledge and engagement. These programs and priorities reflect the same ones that were supported under NHT2. Although the program name has changed and includes contemporary language (e.g. resiliency, ecosystem services, a changing climate), the 'Caring for our Country' and 'Working on Country' programs can be described as the evolution of NHT2.

[5]The National Landcare Program ceased on 30 June 2008. The Australian Federal Government's 'Caring for our Country' initiative (see CfoC 2013a) includes funding for landcare-related activities (DAFF 2013).

The new Australian Government (Howard Liberal government) set up the Natural Heritage Trust in 1997. This was financed with money from the partial sale of the national telecommunications company Telstra. The purpose of the Natural Heritage Trust was to help restore and conserve Australia's environment and natural resources. At the time, it claimed to represent the biggest financial commitment to environmental action by any Federal Government in Australia's history. In 2001, the same Australian Government (Howard Liberal government) extended the Natural Heritage Trust for a second phase of 5 years 2002/2003–2006/2007, a total commitment of $3 billion. The second phase of the Natural Heritage Trust, known as NHT2, signified a move towards strategic planning and investment. This included bilateral agreements between Australian, State and Territory Governments as well as the development of infrastructure for regional delivery of Natural Heritage Trust monies. As a bioregional manager from Victoria describes at the time of the research:

> [the regional authorities] have become the banker for the landcare groups... the Commonwealth and State funding is going through the regions and [...the regional authorities] try to ensure that the funding is hitting the ground.

In addition to the development of these regional authorities (discussed in more detail later), a network of over 800 facilitators[6] was developed to further encourage community involvement in sustainable land management practices (Lane and Corbett 2005). This facilitation network recognised that 'direct human support is a key driver to achieve social behaviour change and therefore on-ground NRM outcomes' (NHT 2005: 10).

Among other things, the role of these facilitators was to assist in the development of integrated natural resource management plans and investment strategies across Australia for the 57 identified regions (see Fig. 4.1). Most regions are based on catchments or bioregions (these bioregions come from the Interim Biographic Regionalisation for Australia; see Fig. 4.2)[7] and where possible they match the National Action Plan for Salinity regions.[8] Integrated natural resource management

[6]This network was comprised of facilitators from the Australian Government, regional facilitators, local government facilitators and local level facilitators and coordinators. The purpose of the network was to increase the engagement of Australians in landcare projects. There was also a 13-person strong Indigenous Land Management Facilitator network. The purpose of this network was to increase the engagement of Indigenous Australians in landcare projects. The need for this additional network highlights the ways in which the institutionalised approaches to landcare have and continue to exclude Indigenous people (see Baker 1997; Lane and Corbett 2005).

[7]The Interim Biogeographic Regionalisation for Australia (IBRA) breaks Australia into 89 bioregions and 419 subregions based upon major geomorphic features in each bioregion. This is used as the reporting unit for assessment of the status of native ecosystems, their protection in the National Reserve System and for use in the monitoring and evaluation framework in the Australian Government's current Natural Resource Management initiatives (Environment 2013b).

[8]In October 2000, the Australian Federal Government (Howard Liberal government) committed $700 million to the first comprehensive national strategy to address salinity and water quality problems in Australia (NAPSWQ 2006). The National Action Plan for Salinity and Water Quality was endorsed by National, State and Territory Governments in November 2000. Twenty-one regions across Australia were identified (see Fig. 4.1).

Fig. 4.1 Map of Australia showing the federal government's natural resource management and national action plan for salinity and water quality regions (Source: See CfoC 2013b)

plans were developed locally in partnership with the local government, industry groups, nongovernment organisations and members of the local communities. Once accredited by State, Territory and Australian National bodies, the plans work as the blueprint for natural resource management planning, investment and on-ground works into the future. They are managed and implemented via regional agencies such as the Catchment Management Authorities in Victoria and the Landcare Council in the Northern Territory.[9] The investment plans and strategies[10] are facilitated via the

[9] At the time of research, the regional body for the Northern Territory was called 'the Landcare Council'. The 'Territory Natural Resource Management' was formed in December 2006 and now manages NRM in the Northern Territory (see TNRM 2013a, b).

[10] These come under various guises across Australia. For example, in Victoria, they are called Regional Catchment Investment Plans, and in the Northern Territory, there is the single Regional Investment Strategy.

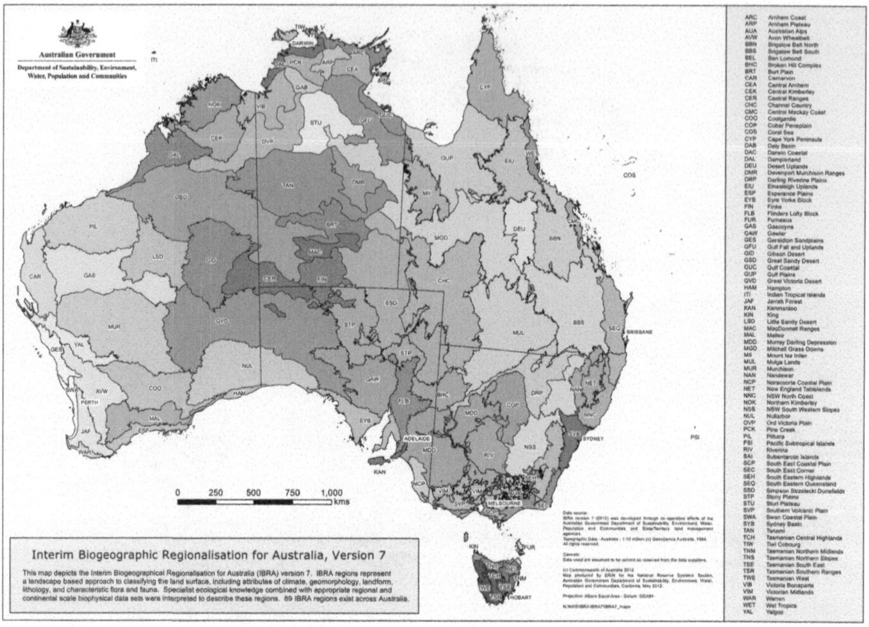

Fig. 4.2 Map of Australia showing the interim biographic regionalisation for Australia (Source: Environment 2013b)

regions with monies from the Natural Heritage Trust and the National Action Plan for Salinity, where regions overlap, and a range of State and Territory funds. Under the Bilateral agreements, State and Territory Governments matched Australian Federal funding from the Natural Heritage Trust. At the time of the research, almost all 56 regions had accredited plans.

4.2 Regionalism in Victoria and the Northern Territory

Predating the second phase of the National Heritage Trust (NHT2), the State of Victoria had been divided into ten regions or catchments to facilitate sustainable land management across the State (see Fig. 4.3). These catchment regions complement the natural resource management notion of regionalism (discussed in more detail later). Collective natural resource management monies are administered in these regions by the Catchment Management Authorities. The Catchment Management Authorities, originally established under the Victorian *Catchment and Land Protection Act (1994)* as Catchment and Land Protection Boards, came into effect in 1997 as statutory authorities. These authorities develop and implement the *Regional Catchment Strategies*. At the time of the research, the Victorian Government

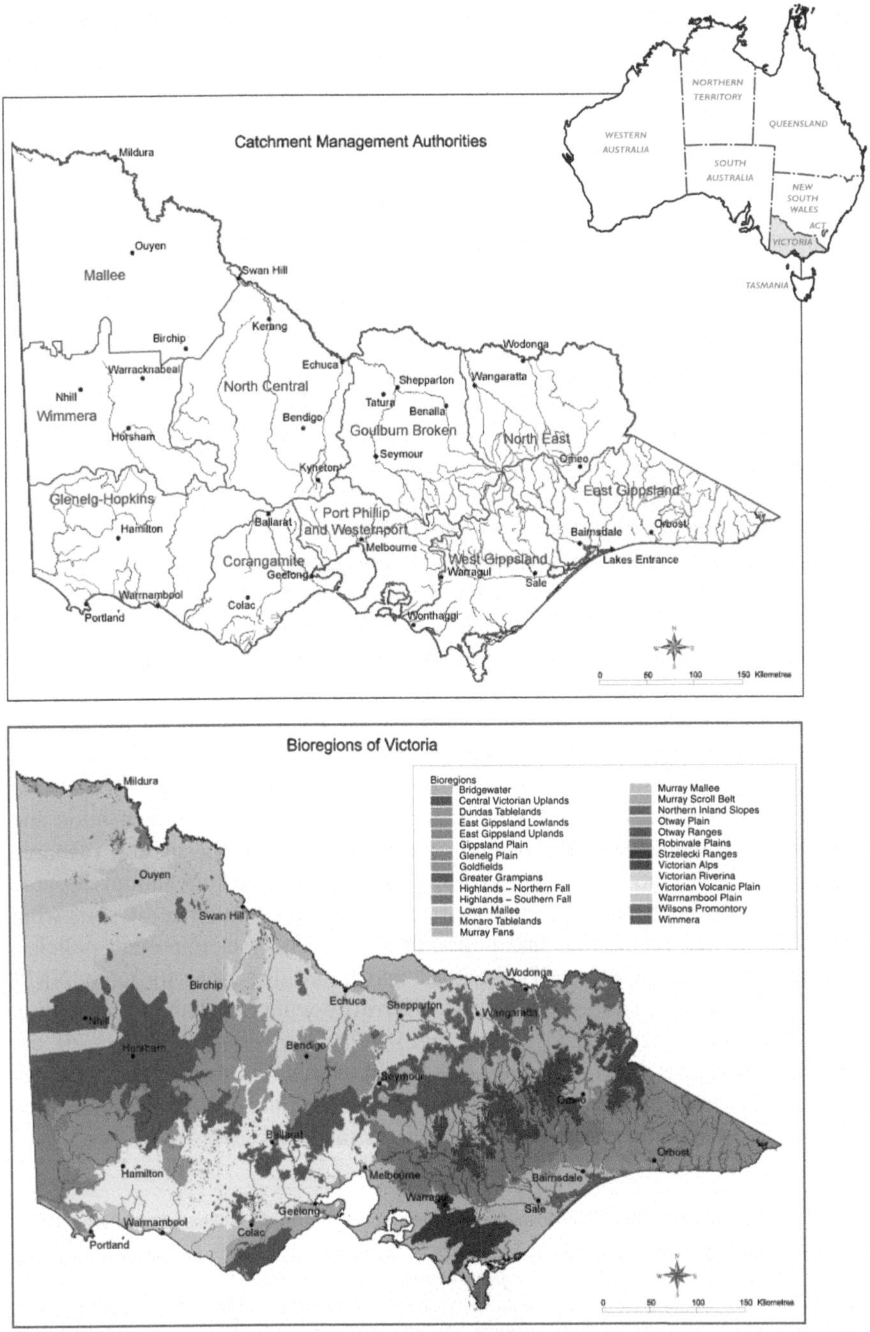

Fig. 4.3 Two maps of the State of Victoria showing the ten Catchment Management Authority regions and the 27 bioregions designated by the *Victorian Biodiversity Strategy, 1997* (Source: DPI 2013b)

Department of Sustainability and Environment[11] was responsible for the administration of the Natural Heritage Trust and the National Action Plan for Salinity across the ten regions. At the time of the research, the Victorian Department of Sustainability and Environment was also responsible for the delivery of the *Victorian Biodiversity Strategy (1997)*. This strategy acknowledges the overarching goals and objectives of the *National Strategy for the Conservation of Australia's Biological Diversity (1992)* and the *National Strategy for Ecologically Sustainable Development (1992)*. It also fulfils the Victorian Government's *Flora and Fauna Guarantee Act (1988)* requirements for a strategy guaranteeing the survival, abundance and development in the wild of all taxa and communities of flora and fauna. This strategy divides Victoria into 27 bioregions for the purpose of biodiversity planning and implementation (see Fig. 4.3). Under this strategy, bioregions are further divided into zones or 'landscapes' to facilitate 'Biodiversity Action Planning', 'Landscape Plans' and the smaller scale 'Local Area Plans'. These plans are developed as partnership projects with the Catchment Management Authorities, local government and nongovernment organisations across Victoria (DSE 2013a). They complement the Regional Catchment Strategies across Victoria.

In comparison to the many regions and subregions of Victoria, the Northern Territory comprises a single region for the regional delivery of natural resource management monies. In 2003, the Northern Territory Landcare Council[12] was designated as the regional body under the Bilateral agreement between the Northern Territory and Commonwealth Governments, for the planning and implementation of integrated natural resource management through the Natural Heritage Trust. The resulting integrated natural resource management plan reflected important principles of the Australian Federal Government's *Environment Protection and Biodiversity Conservation Act (1999)* as well as relevant Territory legislation and policies. At the time of research, and in comparison with the natural resource management policy environment in Victoria, the Northern Territory natural resource management legislation was comprised of a substantial number of somewhat unrelated acts and regulations and pulled upon a diversity of important policies, plans and strategies which clarify the goals and future directions for many NRM issues. Such policies included the Northern Territory-wide Parks and Conservation Master Plan, the related *Territory Parks and Wildlife Conservation Act (1976)*, the Northern Territory *Pastoral Land Act (1992)*, the Northern Territory *Bushfires Act (1980)* and several other Territory Acts. The 2005–2010 integrated natural resource management plan complemented these acts and strategies.[13]

---

[11] This is now called the Victorian Department of Environment and Primary Industries (see DPI 2013a).

[12] The Landcare Council of the Northern Territory was established in 1990 by the Northern Territory Cabinet. At the time of research, the Northern Territory Landcare Council was comprised of two representatives from the government community and 14 representatives from the nongovernment community. The 'Territory Natural Resource Management' was formed in December 2006 and now manages NRM in the Northern Territory (see TNRM 2013a).

[13] The 2010–2015 Integrated Natural Resource Management Plan is the continuation of the 2005–2010 plan. It is arranged under four themes: addressing threats, supporting ESD, managing environmental assets and 'making it happen' (see TNRM 2013b).

4.3 Case Study 1: Threatened Species in the Landscape

As introduced in Chap. 1 (Sect. 1.4), the Victorian case study was a project of the Threatened Species Network of the World Wide Fund for Nature-Australia (see WWF 2006). The Threatened Species Network was described as a partnership project between the World Wide Fund for Nature-Australia and the Federal Government Natural Heritage Trust. The Threatened Species Network provided $500,000 annually to more than 35 community projects conserving threatened species. The Victorian case study project was developed between individuals in the Catchment Management Authority, the then Department of Sustainability and Environment and later, members of the community. The application was submitted to the Threatened Species Network in 2001 with the title of 'Protection and Enhancement of Threatened Species Habitat in the Goldfields Bioregion – Castlemaine zone' (Project Application round 4 2001: 1). This project explicitly linked with *Victoria's Biodiversity Strategy (1997)* and other Victorian policies, as well as the Federal Government's *Environmental Protection and Biodiversity Conservation Act (1999)*. Figure 4.4 provides an illustrative, rather than comprehensive, depiction of the wider international, national and state policy landscape in

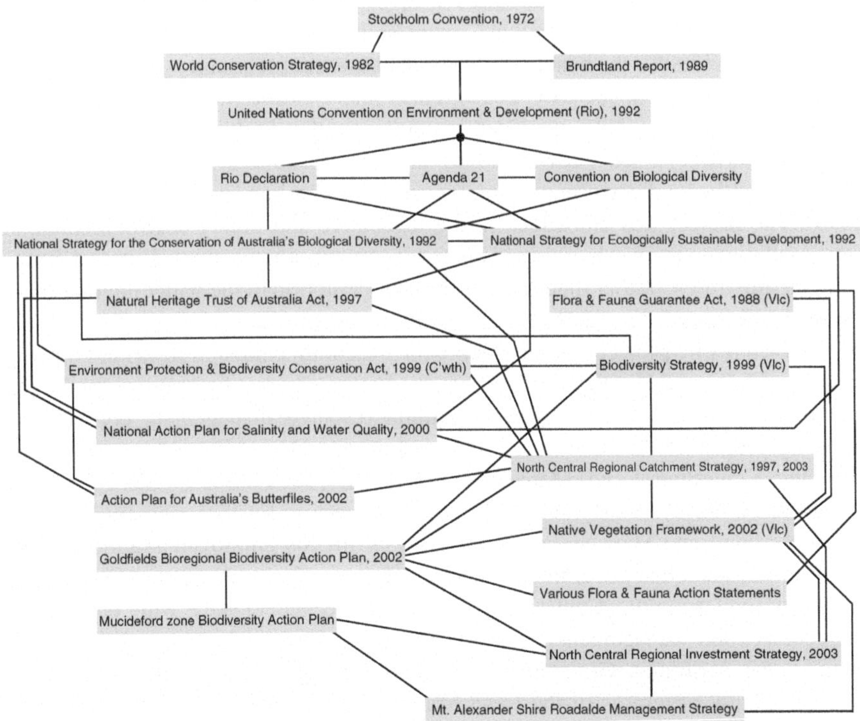

Fig. 4.4 Network diagram depicting the wider policy landscape in which the Threatened Species project was embedded

which the project fits. An intention of the project was to build partnerships between community groups, local government, regional State Government and the regional administrative body of the Catchment Management Authority for ongoing species recovery into the future. Later Threatened Species Network projects that pull upon the original network focussed more specifically on the protection and enhancement of Eltham Copper Butterfly habitat in the Muckleford zone, the locating and protecting of threatened flora species on local roadsides and the threatened species bushland link-up project.

4.4 Case Study 2: Fire in the Landscape

The Northern Territory case study was based upon a project of the Desert Knowledge Co-operative Research Centre (DKCRC). The DKCRC was described as a virtual organisation. This description is indicative of the network of partner organisations and interest groups of which the DKCRC was composed. The case study project was developed in partnership with representatives and interested individuals from various Northern Territory Government agencies including the Bushfires Council (part of the Department of Land Resource Management, they implement the *Bushfires Act* and support landholders with fire mitigation, see LRM 2013), the Central Land Council (an Australian Government statutory authority that provides a number of services for the benefit of 'traditional owners [of country]' and Aboriginal residents in the region; see CLC 2013), Parks and Wildlife (now called 'Parks and Wildlife Commission NT', provides management for Parks and Wildlife in the Northern Territory; see P&WC 2013) and the Centralian Land Management Association (the landcare organisation for central Australian pastoralists; see CLMA 2013). The project was embedded in the legislative and policy environments that direct and dictate the work of these land management organisations. Figure 4.5 provides an illustrative, rather than comprehensive, depiction of the wider international, national and State policy landscape in which the project fits.

The Desert Fire project did not function in a vacuum. Although it was not directly linked to the Natural Heritage Trust as was the Victoria project by virtue of funding, it was indirectly influenced by regional natural resource management policies and resulting programs. At the time of the research, one Desert Fire partner organisation, the Centralian Land Management Authority, was directly funded by the Australian Government's National Landcare Program. Further, one employee of the Centralian Land Management Authority was directly employed as a local facilitator for the Australian government's Natural Heritage Trust. The Desert Fire project representative from the Central Land Council worked closely with one of the Indigenous Land Management Facilitators that formed part of the Indigenous engagement of the Australian Government's Natural Heritage Trust. At the time of the research, many programs of the Land Management Division of the Central Land Council depended upon funding from the then Australian Federal Government Department of Environment and Heritage funding as well as other external funding

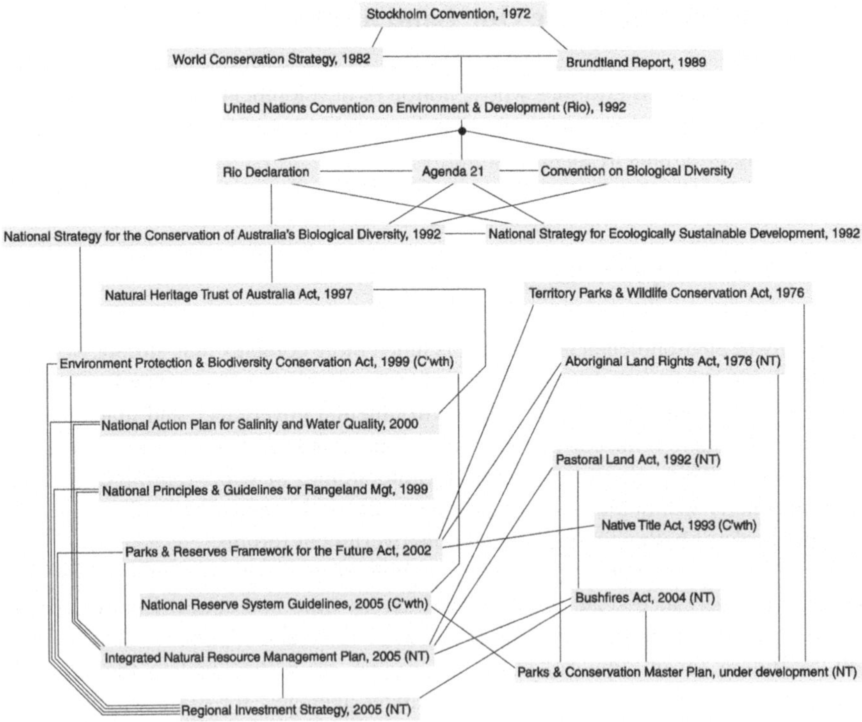

Fig. 4.5 Network diagram depicting the wider policy landscape in which the desert fire project was embedded

sources. Such programs included the Indigenous Ranger Programs and the Indigenous Protected Area Program. In addition, the purchase of the pastoral lease Newhaven was greatly assisted with funds from the National Reserve Program of the Australian Government's Department of Environment and Heritage (see Australian Government 2001). At the time of the research, Newhaven (which formed part of the Desert Fire project area), originally a pastoral lease, had been purchased by Birds Australia (a nongovernment organisation set-up for conservation of bird-related habitat across Australia) and jointly funded by the Australian Government's National Reserve System Program (that was part of the Natural Heritage Trust at the time) to protect the habitat of over 175 bird species (see Australian Government 2001).

The Northern Territory integrated natural resource management plan was developed in conjunction with stakeholders across the many interest groups in the Northern Territory. Many of the individuals connected to the Desert Fire project invested their knowledge in this plan. The core driving principles of this plan, fire, ferals and weeds remain as central importance to land management in the southern Tanami. At the time of research, any projects funded through the Northern Territory Landcare Council to engage in land management in the southern Tanami connected with the principles of Desert Fire.

4.5 Together, Let's Give Our Land a Hand

The following analysis critiques whose notion of development and whose notion of environment are privileged in the regional natural resource management policies and resulting programs in Australia.

4.5.1 The Complexities of 'Togetherness'

The reality of environmental governance is much more complex than simply working together as is implied in the slogan 'together, let's give our land a hand'. The discourse of top-down versus bottom-up environmental governance and management ultimately works to reinforce the destructive 'them and us' dichotomies of the ESD metanarrative. This is because it reinforces hierarchies of scale, reinforces notions of homogeneity within the government sphere and at the same time undervalues the important role of both government and nongovernment forums.

Some pertinent examples of the complexities of togetherness confirm that environmental governance scale is networked across time and space. Environmental governance and management occur along what Lane and McDonald (2005: 712) call 'a sliding (even slippery) scale that ranges from the local to the central'. Individuals working for Australian Government agencies, for example, engage at both the national and the local scale; members of local communities make decisions at the local scale that ultimately inform individuals working at the national scale (as explored in Chap. 6). The evolution of the landcare movement is one case in point which development from the on-ground experiences of farmers in Victoria and Western Australia responding to locally based environmental problems. A key factor driving the development of landcare in these States was the advent of increasing salinity levels across the landscape. As Campbell (1994: 29) expresses 'when you have a rising tide of salty groundwater beneath your farm, it is obvious that (a) you need to act and (b) you cannot solve the problem unless other people also act'. Individuals from the local community arena worked together to develop management plans to address the issue of raising salinity. The development of these plans facilitated local knowledge sharing between farmers, landcare groups and the government. A bioregional manager from the Victorian case study explains the landcare groups *were fundamentally based on communities owning the problem and they were responsible for advising government in how best deal with the problem.*

The same bioregional manager from the Victoria case study elucidates that *when landcare began in the early 1980s there was not much Australian Government investment in NRM at a state level at all [...but] all a sudden landcare groups started popping up [across Victoria] and then the Australian Government got on the band wagon.* The Australian Government's National Landcare Program developed originally from farmers who had little faith in the institutional governance policies and programs and, therefore, took full responsibility for the future of their lands. The bioregional manager testifies that when the

> water tables came to the surface, people who had been farming in that landscape for years suddenly realised that they were basically being beaten by salt and there were two options they could take. One was that they could go or the other was that they could try and deal with it.

What later became known as the Australian Government's National Landcare Program and now receives international acclaim grew from evolving local knowledge about salinity and ways to address it. It could be argued that the National Landcare Program grew out of local resistance to governance structures that neither provided the means nor the process to deal with salinity issues across the Victorian and Western Australian landscapes.

Similar complexities arise in relation to the regional delivery of natural resource management monies. The second phase of the Australian Government's Natural Heritage Trust, NHT2, began in 2002 and signified a shift towards regional strategic planning and investment in Australia. The model for regional governance bodies originated from the successful Catchment Management Authority model that had been active in Victoria since 1997. The bioregional manager from the Victorian case study comments *what the Australian Government has done, it's not immodest to say that Victoria leads the nation in terms of rehabilitation community approaches to NRM*. However, just because this model was successful in local arenas in Victoria, one of the two States where the landcare movement began for good reason did not mean it would be successful across the diverse nation of Australia. The use of similar institutions that appear successful in the more populated, temperate southeast of Australia to govern natural resource management in arid Australia reinforces a narrative of nature that values productive farm lands over lands of desert Australia. Such a narrative perpetuates edenic and colonial discourses of nature as either tamed wilderness or wasteland.

4.5.2 Varieties of Regionalism

The word geography often invokes images of maps, of voyages of discovery, of adventure and of confrontation with the exotic other. The theory and practice of regionalism could be argued as also perpetuating this colonial legacy. This is because, as is discussed in Chap. 5 (Sect. 5.2), the act of understanding a landscape by creating divisions on a map is saturated with discursive practices that enact notions of power as limited and static. The following analysis does not suggest that regional delivery of the Australian Government's Natural Heritage Trust monies was an unproductive practice. Rather, the aim of the discussion is to consider the inherent power inequalities in practices that perpetuate colonial notions of land, landscape and management.

From the narrative shared in the opening section of this chapter, it is clear that regionalism has various connotations across Australia. For example, in Victoria, a jurisdiction covering 227,416 km^2 of land mass (GA 2010) and nine IBRA bioregions, there are ten Catchment Management Authorities further divided into the zones, landscapes and local areas of the *Victorian Biodiversity Strategy (1997)* (see DNRE 1997). In comparison in the Northern Territory, an area encompassing 1,349,129 km^2 of land mass (GA 2010) and 23 IBRA bioregions is recognised as a single region under the natural resource management policies and programs. What do these enactments of regionalism mean for environmental governance and management?

An easy conclusion to draw is that regions are perhaps equated with resident population rather than comparative number of bioregions. In more densely populated parts of Australia, the eastern and southwestern sea boards, the statistics reflect 2.6 people per square kilometre. In the Northern Territory, this figure decreases to 0.1 people per square kilometre. This low ratio is reflected in the Australian Government's funding commitment to land managers in the Northern Territory. Between 1996 and 2002, a total of $44 million was granted through the Australian Government's Natural Heritage Trust for natural resource management in the Northern Territory. This equates to 33.3 cents per hectare during a 6-year period or 5.5 cents per year (DIPE 2004). If the Northern Territory were to be funded the equivalent per area rate of Victoria, this would equate to an approximate total of $1,395 million for that same 6-year period. See Table 4.1 for a comparison of State and Territory Natural Heritage Trust funding over the period 1996–2002.

A genuine devolution of power to the regions to govern regional landscapes must be coupled with sufficient finances to do so. Taking the Northern Territory and Victorian comparison further, this argument becomes more complex when considering studies conducted on landscape health across bioregions (see Morgan 2000). Referring to the IBRA priority bioregions for the National Reserve System (version 5.1) (see Fig. 4.6), it is clear that there are large tracts of country considered as very high priority for conservation in the Northern Territory, as compared with a

Table 4.1 A comparison of State and Territory Natural Heritage Trust funding during the period 1996–2002

Jurisdiction	Total Natural Heritage Trust funding ($Amillion)	Area (million km^2)	Natural Heritage Trust funding/km^2
Australian capital territory	9	0.0024	3,810
Northern territory	44	1.35	33
Tasmania	151	0.068	2221
South Australia	148	0.98	150
Western Australia	185	2.53	73
Queensland	243	1.73	141
Victoria	235	0.23	1,033
New South Wales	308	0.80	384

Source: DIPE (2004: 3)

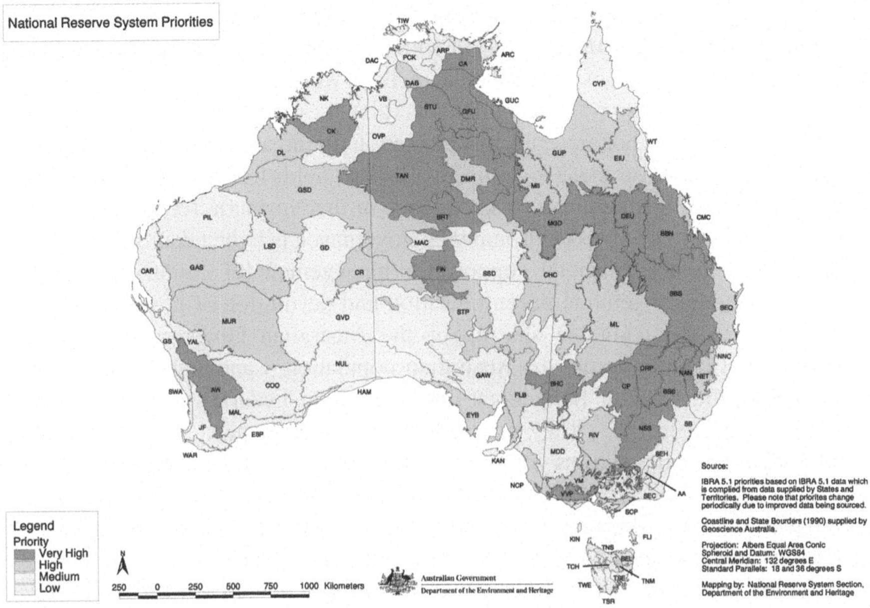

Fig. 4.6 Map of Australia showing the IBRA priority bioregions for the development of the National Reserve System (Source: DEH 2005a)

smaller area in Victoria. There is a clear correlation between landscape health and percentage of remaining native vegetation of these regions. Much of the land area in the Northern Territory is classed as relatively intact, compared with areas in Victoria where the State Government is using a technology called Ecological Vegetation Classes (DSE 2013b) to determine the native vegetation that previously grew in Victoria (discussed in Chap. 5 Sect. 5.4).

At the time of research, conservation land in the Northern Territory totaled approximately seven million hectares or 5.4 % of the total land area. This was held as part of the National Reserve System.[14] This is in comparison to the 4 million hectares that totals 14 % of the land area in Victoria (DSE 2013c). Given the land tenure system of the Northern Territory, new parks and reserves can only be allocated through the acquisitions or resumption of pastoral leases and the development of Indigenous Protected Areas[15] on Aboriginal land. Environmental management

[14] This includes land classified as conservation reserve, coastal reserve, historical reserve, hunting reserve, management agreement area, national park, national park (Aboriginal), nature park, nature park (Aboriginal), other conservation area, protected area, Indigenous Protected Area and National Park (Commonwealth) (DEH 2005b). At the time of research, the Northern Territory also had three protected Marine areas (DEH 2005c).

[15] An Indigenous Protected Area is an area of Indigenous-owned land or sea where the traditional owners of the land and/or sea have entered into an agreement with the Australian Government to promote biodiversity and cultural resource conservation. Indigenous Protected Areas make up over a third of the Australian National Reserve System (see Environment 2013c).

off-park is equally important as is reflected by the developing *Northern Territory Parks and Conservation Masterplan*. In addition, it is more sustainable to protect remnant vegetation and ecosystems than to recreate what previously existed. The aim of this discussion is in no way meant to undervalue the unique environments located in the State of Victoria nor argue against protection for threatened species; rather, it is to point out that the Australian Government allocated funds from the Natural Heritage Trust should have been comparatively higher in the Northern Territory if decentralisation and devolution of environmental governance is to be taken seriously.

In addition to the financial support for management of country across the Australian landmass, genuine decentralisation and devolution of governance must be reflected in the equitable sharing of the Australian Government's Natural Heritage Trust monies across the Australian population. Lane and Corbett (2005: 151) explore the level of Indigenous involvement in Federally funded landcare activities across Australia. They conclude that in the financial year 1999–2000, 'total Indigenous expenditures comprised a mere 1.8 % of total expenditure under the NHT (approximately $A300 million)', and of these funds 'less than 2 % of the national total, were allocated to the management of the Indigenous estate which comprises approximately 15 % of the total land mass' of Australia.

A further interesting comparison between Victoria and Northern Territory relates to the value and relevance of regionalism to each jurisdiction. In Victoria, regional boundaries closely shadow those of the Catchment Management Authorities that have been in place since 1997. In the Northern Territory, genuine commitment to decentralisation and devolution should be indicated by more than one region. Regions could reflect land tenure in the Northern Territory. For example, they could be designated according to Indigenous language groups on Aboriginal land and in relation to arid, tropical or semi-tropical on pastoral lands. This practice would signify genuine devolution by acknowledging the strong connection to place of both Indigenous and pastoral knowledges. This is of particular importance for Indigenous cultures as specific country coincides with traditional ownership and often language.[16]

4.5.3 A Diversity of Hands for Natural Resource Management in Australia

The discussion so far highlights the complexities of the natural resource management policy landscape in relation to the on-ground work conducted by local environmental management and community development projects. Lane and McDonald (2005: 710) comment that community-based environmental planning (and management) embodies inherent conceptual contradictions because it 'seeks to secure the benefits

[16] Since the completion of the research and with the advent of the new NRM body, Territory NRM, the Northern Territory has been divided into four *sub*regions (Top End, Gulf Savanna, Table Lands, Arid Lands) (see TNRM 2013a).

of "bottom-up" knowledge and action yet the opportunities and possibilities of community engagement are framed by State policy and action'. As explored in Chap. 7 (Sect. 7.2), this is particularly pertinent considering there is no single type of community involvement in natural resource management in Australia. As will be demonstrated in Chap. 7 (Sects. 7.2 and 7.3), there are many varieties of environmentalism and varieties of participation in Australia. Do natural resource management policies and programs value the local? Do the governments of Australia fund projects for specific on-ground tangible outcomes, do they fund projects for the purpose of developing intangible processes or do they appreciate both aspects? The following analysis begins with the consultation process of the Australian Government Natural Heritage Trust's integrated natural resource management plans and ends with reflections upon natural resource management project application format.

The integrated natural resource management plans were developed in partnership between Federal, State and Local governments, industry, non-government organisations and local communities. However, the consultation for the plans was done with varying degrees of satisfaction across the regions. A landcare representative from the Victorian case study explains that

> community consultation was the community dragging [the Catchment Management Authority] to the table, so it still wasn't great. Community workshops… didn't have assets for things like the community.

In the Northern Territory, the approach was based upon targeting key organisations such as relevant government agencies, landcare groups, the Aboriginal land councils and so on. As an Australian Government National Heritage Trust facilitator explains, individuals who did not fit within those groups could *access the process through the Internet, if they haven't got Internet they can get information through that post-paid thing to do it*. These statements both raise questions about the extent to which the consultation process was as all-inclusive and equitable as that required for the development of local partnerships and local ownership of planning approaches and documents. The knowledge exchange that could result from such processes appears to be lacking in relation to the monitoring and evaluation of environmental management and community development projects that are funded by the Australian Government's Natural Heritage Trust monies.

The then Australian Government Department of the Environment and Heritage listed the processes of monitoring and evaluation as one of seven core foci of the extension of the Natural Heritage Trust. Indeed, 'the NRM Ministerial Council is overseeing the development and implementation of a national monitoring and evaluation framework' (NHT 2005: 14). Also 'it will be necessary to determine the level of Trust funds required to support monitoring and evaluation at all levels of investment' (NHT 2005: 14). These words suggest that the monitoring and evaluation framework remains to be developed. This appears to support the reality of the project case studies of this research. Individuals involved with the Victorian case study speak of government statistics that include the number of trees planted in a particular year, but neglect to monitor how many actually survived and continue to survive as time passes. Individuals also discredit government reports that speak about the length (in kilometres) of fences built with the Australian Government's Natural Heritage Trust monies but neglect to consider whether funds were adequate for sustainable fencing that will last into the future.[17] These comments reflect the then Australian Government's commitment to local environmental management and community development projects. This attitude suggests that local-scale natural resource management projects are valued as points of contact that fulfil funding mechanisms. If no mechanisms exist to indicate the success of tangible project outcomes, it is hard to imagine that indicators for more intangible, process-oriented outcomes are in place.

Considering how actual project application formats allow for diversity is also a good indicator of how the natural resource management policies and programs value local environmental management and community development project work. Lane and Corbett (2005) report several barriers for Indigenous involvement in devolved government funding projects such as the Australian Government's National Landcare Program and NHT2 projects. Firstly, they State lack of funding for the Indigenous Land Management Facilitator network as well as only 13 facilitators nationwide as compared with 800 non-Indigenous Natural Heritage Trust facilitators. Accordingly, access to these individuals and culturally appropriate advice was limited. The culturally inappropriate language of the natural resource management project funding applications and the length of these documents was a large barrier to involvement in these programs. Other factors include the mainstream western timeframes of projects. These timeframes are difficult enough for non-Indigenous participants to keep to let alone Indigenous individuals living with more complex local realities than mainstream Australia. These realities include working with the right people. For example, there are traditional owners who are the only ones who can speak for certain tracts of country and there are Indigenous residents of communities who may have interests in such projects (Lane and Corbett 2005).

Another barrier for some people is the required project reporting, accounting and administration. This can be overcome with the assistance of local project officers and landcare workers assuming these positions exist. A further factor outside the control of individuals applying for grants is the powerful role of those making decisions about project funding. Often the interests of marginal groups are unrepresented in these fora. The experience of an Indigenous project funded by the Australian Government's Natural Heritage Trust in remote Australia exemplifies how certain views of environment are easily privileged over others. The continued funding of this project relied upon acceptance by the regional Natural Heritage Trust decision-making panel. Individuals on this panel did not believe that fire management work carried out by a group of Indigenous rangers equated with the conservation goals of the Natural Heritage Trust. These experiences echo those shared by Langton (2003) in Chap. 2 (Sect. 2.3) relating to the Northern Territory Government's cut to the very productive ethnobiology program.

---

[17] The practice works to disempower communities because they feel their knowledge and needs are not respected by Australian Governments and results in an increasing lack of confidence in and resistance to government approaches.

4.5.4 The View from the Local

From the narrative and experiences shared above, it would appear the relevant natural resource management policies and programs were not specifically conditioned to celebrate local diversity. Neither were they structured as learning institutions. The lack of direct monitoring and evaluation programs, as well as the ongoing cultural inappropriateness of funding applications for marginal groups, is evidence for this. It would seem these structures are more about tangible project outcomes than intangible project processes of sharing knowledge, realising local capacities and engendering relationship building across governance scales. Given the entrenched power inequalities in these practices, it is understandable why some researchers call for the adaptive management framework to be applied in governance institutions (see Dovers 2003).

In Chap. 6, I engage with the two case studies to consider the following questions. Firstly, how do environmental governance policies and relating programs appear from the local perspective? Are these polices considered as important and do individuals working in environmental management and community development projects engage with these policies?

I have made reference above to the varieties of environmentalism and participation that are experienced by individuals engaged with local-scale environmental management and community development projects in Australia. Despite the limited adaptability of the natural resource management policies and programs of the Australian Government, there appears to be potential for unlimited adaptive management via local environmental management and community development projects. It is at this interface that learning, networking and location-specific innovation occurs. As is explored in following chapters, it would appear that project members and/or gatekeepers pull on the previously mentioned natural resource management policies and programs as best suits the outcomes they are working for.

Project funding from the Australian Government's Natural Heritage Trust was certainly useful for on-ground works. In the two project case studies, innovation and capacity realisation occurred when project members and/or gatekeepers regarded the Australian Government's Natural Heritage Trust money as just one means of sourcing funding for prospective projects. Interest groups are accountable to the stipulations of any government funding, but having or developing a good knowledge of Australian, State and/or Territory and local funding structures as well as maintaining good relationships with individuals working for government agencies means there is potentially a larger pool of funds to access. As mentioned above, often marginalised groups and individuals do not have access to such knowledge or funds. Gatekeepers have a powerful role to play for the potential work of these groups particularly in overcoming the entrenched power inequalities that work to disempower and maintain their marginality.

4.6 Conclusion

This chapter used the conceptual tool of an edge politics as the means to investigate whose notion of environment and whose notion of development are privileged in regional natural resource management policies and resulting programs in Australia. This critique highlighted the complexities of the top-down/bottom-up dichotomy, the notion of regionalism and what it means for these structures to really value the local. In considering whose notion of environment and whose notion of development are embedded in these structures, it is important to consider the reality of ecological uncertainty that complicates decision-making for environmental governance and management across Australia and the world. Lane et al. (2004: 113) argue there is no 'single right scale for management'. Across Australia, there seems to be no single practice of environmental governance. Equally there is no single conception of environment or development across Australia. Social learning that is committed to challenging the status quo has a difficult task precisely because there is no such thing. Systems that assume homogenous local realities and experiences reinforce power inequalities, continue to limit access of marginal groups to resources, perpetuate colonial notions of 'nature' and thereby stifle the potential and resilience of this young nation of Australia to work towards effective and appropriate ESD.

A critique of the formalised environmental governance landscape in any nation is an important part of working towards processes and strategies for cultural hybridity: it is essential to understand how any given environmental governance landscape values different kinds of knowledge (e.g. local and Indigenous knowledge). A focus on 'edge politics' highlights the tensions between working within a formal governance system that does not value diversity and the reality of the diversity of local experience. The new conceptual framework for cultural hybridity provides a way to highlight these tensions. Strategies to foster, support and enable cultural hybridity could include the development of a new system that celebrates the diversity of local realities, engaging with the principles of adaptive management, that value process, conflict and diversity, and thereby developing a system that embraces institutional learning as a way to foster and enable cultural hybridity.

References

ACF (Australian Conservation Foundation) (2013) Who we are. http://www.acfonline.org.au/about-us. Accessed 5 Nov 2013

Australian Government (2001) Launch of birds Australia Newhaven reserve. http://www.environment.gov.au/minister/archive/env/2001/mr10oct01.html. Accessed 05 Nov 2013

Baker R (1997) Landcare: policy, practice and partnerships. Aust Geogr Stud 35(1):61–73

Campbell A (1994) Landcare. Communities shaping the land and the future. Allen & Unwin Pty Ltd, St. Leonards

CfoC (Caring for Our Country) (2013a) What is caring for our country? http://www.nrm.gov.au/about/caring/index.html. Accessed 4 Sept 2013

CfoC (Caring for Our Country) (2013b) Natural resource management. http://www.nrm.gov.au/about/nrm/index.html. Accessed 5 Nov 2013

CLC (Central Land Council) (2013) What the central land council does. http://www.clc.org.au/articles/info/what-the-central-land-council-does. Accessed 5 Nov 2013

CLMA (Centralian Land Management Association) (2013) The Centralian Land Management Association. http://www.clma.com.au/. Accessed 5 Nov 2013

DAFF (Australian Government Department of Agriculture, Fisheries and Forestry) (2009) Landcare. http://www.daff.gov.au/natural-resources/landcare. Accessed 5 Nov 2013

DAFF (Australian Government Department of Agriculture, Fisheries and Forestry) (2013) Former programs. http://www.daff.gov.au/natural-resources/former-programs#2. Accessed 5 Nov 2013

DEH (Department of the Environment and Heritage) (2005a) Summary of terrestrial protected areas in the northern territory by type. www.deh.gov.au. Accessed 18 Mar 2005

DEH (Department of the Environment and Heritage) (2005b) Summary of northern territory marine protected areas by type. www.deh.gov.au. Accessed 18 Mar 2005

DEH (Department of the Environment and Heritage) (2005c) Summary of northern territory marine protected areas by type, Commonwealth of Australia. www.deh.gov.au. 18 Mar 2006

DEST (Department of Environment Sport and Territories) (1996) National strategy for the conservation of Australia's biological diversity. Commonwealth of Australia, Canberra

DIPE (Department of Planning and Infrastructure) (2004) Issue paper: options and opportunities: defining what we want. www.ipe.nt.gov. Accessed 27 Apr 2005

DNRE (Department of Natural Resources and Environment) (1997) Victoria's biodiversity: directions in management. Department of Natural Resources and Environment, Melbourne

Dovers S (2003) Processes and institutions for resource and environmental management: why and how to analyse. In: Dovers S, Wild River S (eds) Managing Australia's environment. Federation, Sydney, pp 3–14

DPI (Victorian Government Department of Environment and Primary Industries) (2013a) Department of environment and primary industries. http://www.dpi.vic.gov.au/. Accessed 05 Nov 2013

DPI (Victorian Government Department of Environment and Primary Industries) (2013b) Victorian resources online. http://www.dpi.vic.gov.au/vro. Accessed 05 Nov 2013

DSE (Victorian Department of Environment and Sustainability) (2013a) Biodiversity action planning – an overview. http://www.dse.vic.gov.au/conservation-and-environment/native vegetation-groups-for-victoria/victorias-bioregions/biodiversity-action-planning-an overview. Accessed 5 Nov 2013

DSE (Victorian Government Department of Environment and Sustainability) (2013b) Ecological Vegetation Class (EVC) benchmarks for each bioregion. http://www.dse.vic.gov.au/conservation-and-environment/native-vegetation-groups-for victoria/ecological-vegetation-class-evc-benchmarks-by-bioregion. Accessed 5 Nov 2013

DSE (Victorian Government Department of Environment and Sustainability) (2013c) Parks and reserves. http://www.dse.vic.gov.au/parks-and-reserves/about-parks-and-reserves. Accessed 5 Nov 2013

Environment (Australian Government Department of the Environment) (2013a) Review of the national biodiversity strategy. http://www.environment.gov.au/node/14490. Accessed 5 Nov 2013

Environment (Australian Government Department of the Environment) (2013b) Australia's bioregions. http://www.environment.gov.au/topics/land/national-reserve-system/science maps-and-data/australias-bioregions-ibra%C2%A0/australias-1. Accessed 5 Nov 2013

Environment (Australian Government Department of the Environment) (2013c) Indigenous protected areas. http://www.environment.gov.au/indigenous/ipa/. Accessed 5 Nov 2013

ESDSC (Ecologically Sustainable Development Steering Committee) (1992) National strategy for ecologically sustainable development. Australian Government Publishing Service, Canberra

GA (Geoscience Australia) (2010) Area of Australia – states and territories. http://www.ga.gov.au/education/geoscience-basics/dimensions/area-of-australia-states and-territories.html. Accessed 5 Nov 2013

Howitt R (2001a) Frontiers, borders, edges: liminal challenges to the hegemony of exclusion. Aust Geogr Stud 39(2):233–245

Howitt R (2001b) Rethinking resource management: sustainability, justice and indigenous peoples. Routledge, London

Lane MB, Corbett T (2005) The tyranny of localism: Indigenous participation in community-based environmental management. J Environ Policy Plan 7(2):141–159

Lane MB, McDonald G (2005) Community-based environmental planning: operational dilemmas, planning principles and possible remedies. J Environ Plan Manag 48(5):709–731

Lane MB, McDonald GT, Morrison TH (2004) Decentralisation and environmental management in Australia: a comment on the prescriptions of the Wentworth Group. Aust Geogr Stud 42(1):103–115

Langton M (2003) The 'wild', the market and the native: Indigenous people face new forms of global colonization. In: Adams WM, Mulligan M (eds) Decolonizing nature: strategies for conservation in a post-colonial era. Earthscan Publications, London, pp 79–107

LRM (Northern Territory Department of Land Resource Management) (2013) About bushfires NT. http://www.lrm.nt.gov.au/bushfires/about#.Ungv61Pd5Bk. Accessed 5 Nov 2013

Morgan G (2000) Landscape health in Australia, department of the environment and heritage, National Land and Water Resources Audit, 11 June 2006

NAPSWQ (National Action Plan for Salinity and Water Quality) (2006) A national action plan for salinity and water quality in Australia. http://www.napswq.gov.au. 11 June 2006

NFF (National Farmers' Federation) (2013) National farmers' federation. http://www.nff.org.au/. Accessed 5 Nov 2013

NHT (Natural Heritage Trust) (2005) Natural heritage trust annual report 2003–04. Commonwealth of Australia, Canberra

NHT & NAPSWQ (Natural Heritage Trust (Australia) & National Action Plan for Salinity and Water Quality (Australia) (2000) Fact sheet: together let's give our land a hand. Australian Government, Canberra

Project Application Round 4 (2001) Protection and enhancement of threatened species habitat in the goldfields bioregion. Threatened Species Network, Melbourne

P&WC (Northern Territory government Parks and Wildlife Commission) (2013) Welcome to the parks and wildlife commission of the northern territory. http://www.parksandwildlife.nt.gov.au/. Accessed 5 Nov 2013

Sobels J, Curtis A (2001) The role of Landcare group networks in rural Australia: exploring the contribution of social capital. J Rural Stud 17:265–276

TNRM (Territory Natural Resource Management) (2013a) Territory natural resource management. http://www.territorynrm.org.au/#6. Accessed 4 Sept 2013

TNRM (Territory Natural Resource Management) (2013b) 2010–2015 INRM plan. http://www.territorynrm.org.au/inrm-plan/2010-2015-inrm-plan. Accessed 5 Nov 2013

Toyne P, Farley R (1989) A national land management program. Aust J Soil Water Conserv 2(2):6–9

WWF (Worldwide Fund for Nature – Australia) (2006) Threatened species network. http://www.wwf.org.au/news_resources/archives/threatened_species_network/. Accessed 5 Nov 2013

Chapter 5
Cultural Landscapes

Abstract This chapter first introduces the two case studies that are used as the lens through which to explore the themes of this book, and second, it practises the edge politics (after Howitt, Aust Geogr Stud 39(2):233–245, 2001a) advocated by this book to highlight the diversity of approaches advocated by a variety of land managers to engage with the biophysical landscape. As introduced in Chap. 3, Howitt (Rethinking resource management: sustainability, justice and indigenous peoples. Routledge, London, p 234, 2001b) argues that practising an edge politics 'grapples with ambivalence, uncertainty, change, overlap and interaction in ways that dislodge the old-style colonial metaphors of empty spaces and frontier heroics' (As already explained in Chap. 4, in this quote Howitt (Rethinking resource management: sustainability, justice and indigenous peoples. Routledge, London, p 234, 2001b) refers specifically to historical and contemporary interpretations of the Northern Territory landscape. I engage with his notion of an edge politics as a means to explore the diversity of approaches of land management across Australia and specifically in Victoria and the Northern Territory). The edge politics practised in this chapter follows the critique provided in Chap. 3 and shows by example the unique and complex politics that occur between different cultural groups. This process is useful to understand the diversity of approaches used by a variety of land managers to engage with the biophysical landscape in any nation. This edge politics looks at unpacking and unpicking the multitude of ways in which any landscape is interpreted and managed. Secondly, it juxtaposes these many ways of knowing the same landscape (which may also be influenced by the social livelihood issues faced by any one group of actors). Thirdly, it demonstrates that celebrating these sometimes conflicting interpretations and management approaches is the first step in working towards the process of cultural hybridity necessary for ESD.

This edge politics explores the tension between historical narratives and contemporary approaches to land management. It acknowledges the importance of historical and contemporary interpretations of the landscape upon contemporary interpretations and resulting land management approaches. I end the discussion by highlighting the importance of considering which environmental governance and management discourses are embedded within any environmental management and community development project. This discussion explains why the edge politics called for in this chapter is an essential step in working towards cultural hybridity at the local scale.

K. Maclean, *Cultural Hybridity and the Environment*,
DOI 10.1007/978-981-287-323-1_5

5.1 Case Study Narratives

5.1.1 Case Study 1: Threatened Species Project, Victoria

The Victorian case study project (hereon called 'the Threatened Species project') was primarily funded through the Community Grants Program of the Threatened Species Network (TSN). At the time of the research, the TSN was:

> Australia's leading species conservation program, with more than 15 years' experience, we bring together science with community needs, on-the-ground action with Australia's decision-makers, and national issues with local concerns to help protect threatened species. (WWF 2006: 1)[1]

The TSN was a partnership between World Wide Fund for Nature (WWF) Australia and the Australian Federal Government's Natural Heritage Trust. Funding for the TSN and the related Community Grants Program was provided by the Natural Heritage Trust and administered by WWF Australia. The Community Grants Program funding was administered by a specified government body. This funding was matched by financial or in-kind support from this government body, as well as the local community groups who have applied for the grant. Spending and reporting had to be completed within a 1-year period, although flexibility of this timeframe was sometimes necessary considering the nature of on-ground conservation works, for example, for the purposes of the effects of drought on revegetation projects. The Threatened Species project was funded via three Community Grants Program rounds.

The Threatened Species project is entitled 'Protection & Enhancement of Threatened Species Habitat in the Goldfields Bioregion' (Project Application round 4 2001: 1). It was located in north central Victoria (see Fig. 5.1). This project developed from a collaboration between a bioregional manager at the regional Catchment Management Authority, a senior flora and fauna officer of the then Department of Natural Resources and the Environment (now the Department of Sustainability and Environment) and the then Victorian coordinator of the TSN. These individuals combined the concepts of landscape planning approaches reflected in the then 'bioregional recovery plans' with the reality of localised biodiversity issues to devise an innovative 'whole of landscape' (encompassing parts of the Goldfields Bioregion) approach to threatened species management. The successful grant application was endorsed by the Catchment Management Authority, the then Department of Natural Resources and the Environment and other partner organisations including the local Shire and the various landcare,

[1]The TSN ceased to exist in 2006 (WWF 2006); however, the important work of this network continues in the WWF, via regional natural resource management bodies across Australia and via work conducted by the wider Australian community.

Fig. 5.1 Map showing the location of north central Victoria (Source: NCCMA 2006)

conservation and naturalist community groups who would be responsible for the on-ground works. Over the 3 years of the project, ten community groups were involved in this project – this case study focuses specifically on the work of three of these groups.

The project had various incarnations since its genesis in 2001. The original project summary was:

> community groups in the [specific zone] of the Goldfields Bioregional Plan will implement actions that protect and enhance habitat of a range of threatened species... integrated predator control, weed control, habitat restoration, and enhancing community participation are key aspects of this project. (Project Application round 4 2001: 2)

The project objectives were:

> to implement priority actions identified in the Goldfields Bioregional Plan. The focus is on protection, management and restoration of habitat by a variety of stakeholders. The project aims to: improve community understanding of and participation in biodiversity conservation activities; implement an integrated community based conservation plan that results in better conservation outcomes for a suite of threatened species and ecological communities. (Project Application round 4 2001: 2)

A project officer was employed by the Catchment Management Authority in 2001 to assist the stakeholder groups in the coordination and management of the overall project. A steering committee, created from representatives from each community group, met monthly with the project officer and the bioregional manager. This was the extent of combined community group involvement as each group worked in their own project area as determined by their interest. However, by virtue of the nature of any rural community, there is much overlay and interconnection between members of different groups, such that the resulting social network was, and remains, strong. A second application to the Community Grants Program of the TSN in 2002 that built 'upon the existing TSN project currently being implemented in the Goldfields Zone' (Project Application round 5 2002: 2) was successful. This worked to 'extend initial works and further strengthen the linkages and networks being supported in the first phase', and this project had the additional aim of working 'to encourage and involve new groups in the processes underpinning the Goldfields Bioregional Plan' (Project Application round 5 2002: 2). As such previous project work continued and additional projects were added. See Fig. 5.2 for a graphic diagram of the various actors and agencies involved with the Threatened Species project.

In 2003, two specific community groups were advised by the Catchment Management Authority project officer to apply separately for funding from round 6 of the Community Grants Program, to develop the work they had begun with money from round 4. Both groups were successful. The Victorian case study looks specifically at the work of these two projects and a third project. The first project, entitled 'Protection and Enhancement of Eltham Copper Butterfly habitat in the Muckleford Zone', 'will enhance and restore two Eltham Copper Butterfly, *Paralucia pyrodiscus lucida*, habitats in [the region]' (Project Application round 6 2003a: 2). The second project entitled 'locating and protecting threatened species on local roadsides' aimed to:

> increase the knowledge on the distribution of threatened species within the Shire via strategic surveys of roadside vegetation – these and selected existing sites will be managed to improve the long-term sustainability of the species present (addressing threats) and extend the range of the species. (Project Application round 6 2003b: 2)

The third project developed from the original project (round 4) (also part of the Victorian case study) was entitled 'Threatened Species Bushland Link-up Project'. Funding for this project continued out of Catchment Management Authority money. The aim of this project was 'to promote and enhance native biodiversity by facilitating movement of native fauna and flora between [a specific] Bushland Reserve and the [a specific] State Forest' (Bushland Link-up Project 2002: 1). I differentiate between project members of the Threatened Species project by describing the arena from which they conducted their work (government arena and the community arena). These project members are depicted in Fig. 5.2.

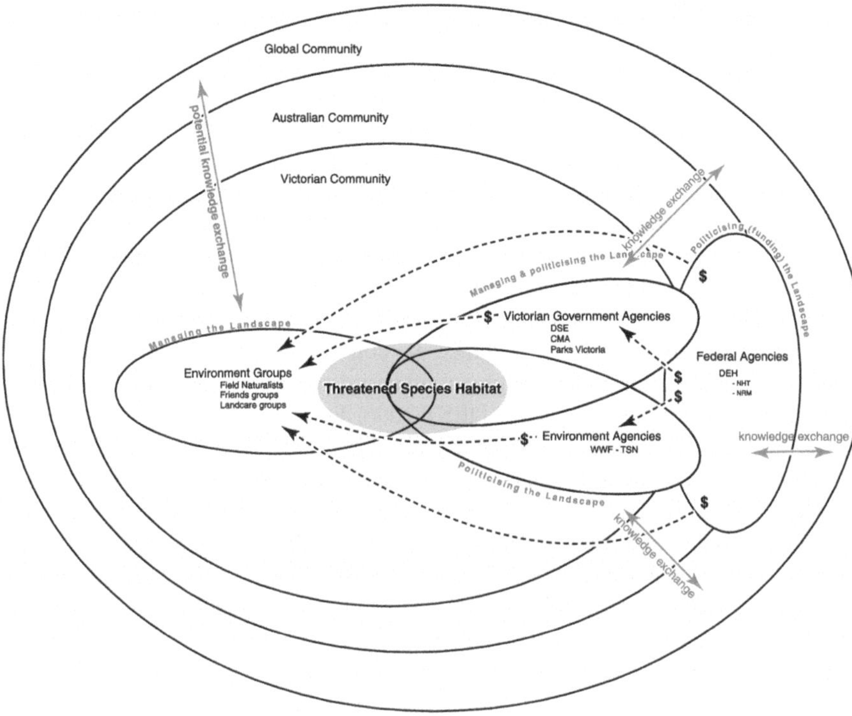

Fig. 5.2 Graphic diagram of the threatened species project

This figure represents the way in which the Threatened Species project is understood and critiqued throughout the book. This diagram locates threatened species habitat as the core focus for the case study. Three groups: environmental groups, Victorian government agencies (the Department of Sustainability and Environment and the Catchment Management Authority) and environment agencies (the World Wide Fund for Nature and the Threatened Species Network), are depicted as active at the project interface. These groups are represented by the three ovals in the centre of the diagram. Knowledge exchange between the groups is represented by the overlapping ovals. Where the three main ovals coincide is the point where the project is created. This point represents the many situated knowledge networks of which the project is composed. Specific Federal Government Agencies are depicted in the diagram (the Department of the Environment and Heritage, the Natural Heritage Trust, the Natural Resource Management program). These agencies were active in financing on-ground environmental management work. The broken arrows represent these financial flows. The grey arrows represent either the actual or potential for knowledge exchange across different environmental governance and management arenas. These arenas include the wider Victorian, Australian and Global communities.

5.1.2 Case Study 2: Desert Fire, Northern Territory

The Northern Territory case study (hereon called the 'Desert Fire project') was a project of the Desert Knowledge Cooperative Research Centre (DKCRC). The DKCRC was one of 72 Cooperative Research Centres 'operating in 6 sectors: environment, agriculture, information and communications technology, mining, medical science, and technology and manufacturing' (DEST 2006: 1). The Cooperative Research Centre (CRC) program was administered by the Australian Federal Government's Department of Education, Science and Training and was established in 1990 to improve the effectiveness of Australia's research and development efforts. The program emphasises the importance of 'collaborative arrangements to maximise the benefits of research through an enhanced process of utilisation, commercialisation and technology transfer' (DEST 2006: 1).

The DKCRC was 'established as an unincorporated joint venture among 15 centre partners, with an additional 14 associate partners and a number of sponsors' (DKCRC 2006a: 1). The DKCRC received $20.7 million from the CRC program, cash and in-kind commitments from its 29 partners. These funds created a total of $90.5 million over 7 years (2003–2010) (DKCRC 2006b).[2] The DKCRC was a 'national research network linking Indigenous and local knowledge with science and education to improve desert livelihoods' (DKCRC 2006a: 1). There were six core projects that complemented the vision and derived key results areas. The case study project was part of core project 1: the development of social livelihoods (based on managing natural and cultural heritage) in desert Australia.

The case study project was part of the DKCRC Desert Fire project. This project encompassed ten subprojects that covered a diversity of fire-related foci across desert Australia. The title of the project upon which the Northern Territory case study was based is 'Desert Fire: Managing Fire in the Southern Tanami'.[3] This project evolved from wide ranging interest in fire as a natural resource management issue in central Australia. This interest developed from widespread fire events between 2000 and 2002 when large areas of country in the southern Tanami region were burnt. These fires were the result of 3 years of above average rainfall across central Australia (a cyclic event that last occurred in 1974–1976) from 1999 to 2001 which contributed to a fuel build-up and 3 years of widespread and extensive fires from July 2000 to December 2002 (see Edwards et al. 2008). The Desert Fire subproject 3a aimed to:

> collate existing knowledge, develop new knowledge and disseminate knowledge for improved management of fire in the southern Tanami desert where frequent, large, uncontrolled wildfires are common [...] the southern Tanami is predominately Aboriginal

---

[2] The DKCRC finished in 2010. The new CRC for remote economic participation evolved from the DKCRC and focuses on delivery solutions to the economic challenges that affect remote Australia; see CRC-REP 2013.

[3] The Desert Fire project includes three subprojects: (1) fire regimes at a continental scale, (2) fire regimes at a regional scale – overview and priority setting, (3) fire regimes at a regional scale: case studies.

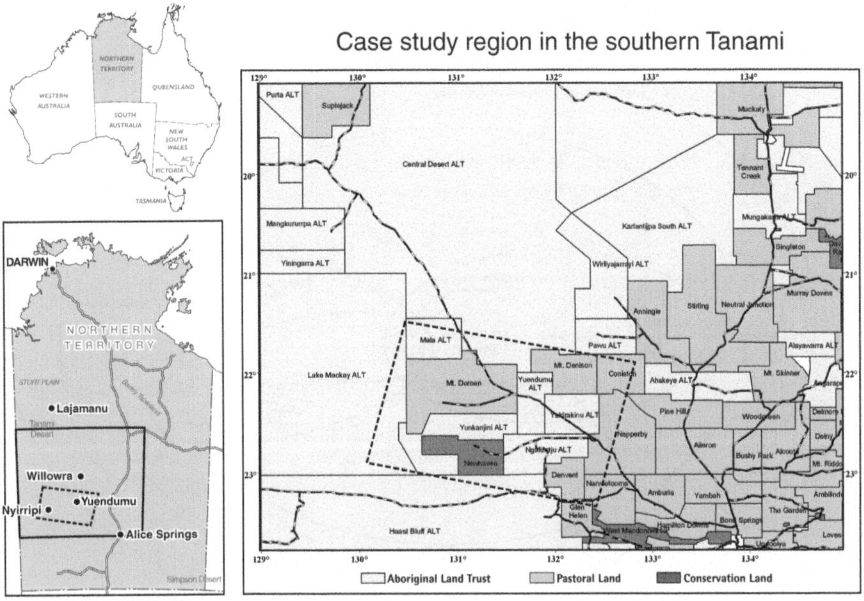

Fig. 5.3 Map showing the case study region in the Northern Territory (Source: Northern Territory land tenure map supplied by G. Allan, Bushfires NT)

> freehold land with fringing pastoral properties in the east and a conservation reserve [Newhaven] in the north. The southern Tanami also contains known biodiversity hotspots which are likely to be threatened by adverse fire regimes. (Desert Fire 2003: 3)

The overall aim of the project was to develop a fire management strategy in a specific area of the southern Tanami, across different land tenures (see Fig. 5.3).

This project was composed of two interest groups. Firstly, the DKCRC partner organisations of which the initial stage of the Desert Fire was composed, which included individuals from the Central Land Council (an Australian Government statutory authority that provides a number of services for the benefit of 'traditional owners [of country]' and Aboriginal residents in the region, see CLC 2013), the Northern Territory Bushfires Council (part of the Department of Land Resource Management, they implement the *Bushfires Act* and support landholders with fire mitigation; see LRM 2013),[4] the Centralian Land Management Association (the landcare organisation for central Australian pastoralists; see CLMA 2013) and individuals from the Northern Territory Parks and Wildlife (now called 'Parks and Wildlife Commission NT', provides management for Parks and Wildlife in the Northern Territory; see P&WC 2013a). I refer to these project members as working

[4]The Bushfires Council, Northern Territory, has since changed names to Bushfires, Northern Territory. Throughout the book, I refer to the council as the Bushfires Council because that was the name at the time of the research.

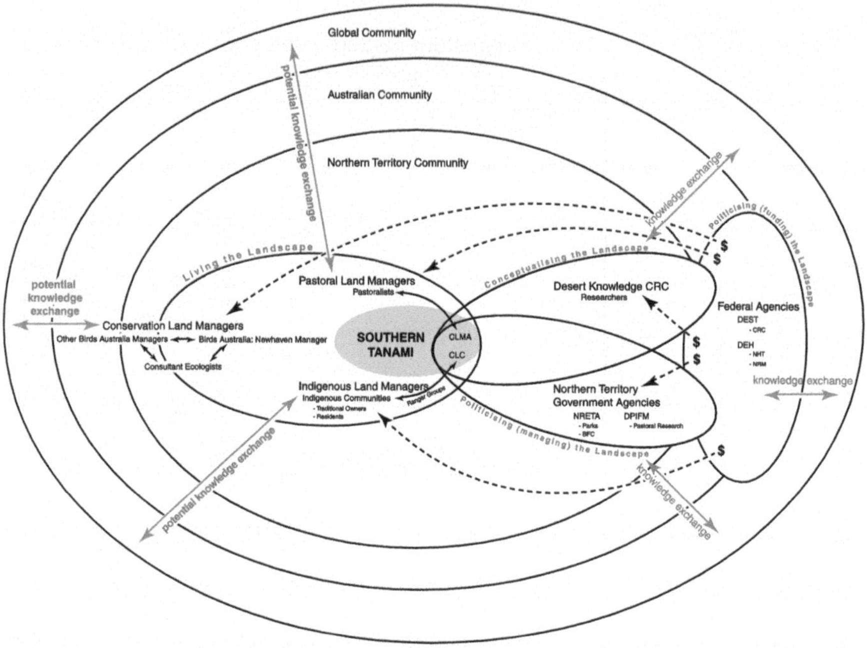

Fig. 5.4 Graphic diagram of the desert fire project

from the government arena. The second interest group includes those individuals and groups who were consulted about fire. These include individuals from the relevant pastoral stations, the conservation land managers of Newhaven, consultant ecologists, traditional owners for country, individuals involved with the Indigenous ranger program and Aboriginal peoples from communities in the region. Throughout the text, I refer to these individuals as from the community arena. The Aboriginal people involved with this project were Warlpiri men and women. These project members are depicted in Fig. 5.4.

Figure 5.4 represents the way in which the Desert Fire project is understood and critiqued throughout the research. This diagram locates the southern Tanami landscape as the core focus for the environmental management community development project in the Northern Territory. Three groups are depicted as active at the project interface: firstly, those who live the landscape which includes pastoral, conservation and Aboriginal land managers; secondly, those who politicise the landscape through specific management approaches including specific Northern Territory Government Agencies; and thirdly, those who conceptualise the landscape including the DKCRC. The Centralian Land Management Association (CLMA) (represent pastoral interests) and the Aboriginal representative body, the Central Land Council (CLC), fit within all three groups. There is overlap between the Northern Territory Government Agencies (the then Nature Resources, Environment and the Arts; the then Primary Industries, Fisheries and Mines) and the DKCRC.

The three groups are represented by the three ovals in the centre of the diagram. Knowledge exchange between the groups is represented by the overlapping ovals. Where the three main ovals coincide is the point where the project is created. This point represents the situated knowledge networks of which the project is composed. Specific Federal Government Agencies are depicted in the diagram (the then Department of Education, Science and Training; the then Department of the Environment and Heritage, including the then Natural Heritage Trust and the Natural Resource Management program). These agencies are active in financing on-ground environmental management work. The broken arrows represent these financial flows. The black arrows represent knowledge exchange across different environmental governance and management arenas. The grey arrows represent the potential for knowledge exchanged across the same arenas. These arenas include wider Northern Territory, Australian and Global environmental governance and management communities.

The remainder of this chapter practises an edge politics (after Howitt 2001a) to highlight the diversity of approaches advocated by a variety of land managers from the Victorian and the Northern Territory case study locations to understand and thus engage with the Australian landscape.

5.2 Historical Narratives

There is much debate about how Australian Indigenous peoples impacted upon the environments in which they lived (e.g. see Jones 1969; Flannery 1994; Bowman 1998; Langton 1998). Although these debates are not the focus of this discussion, I wish to establish that the investigations presented in this chapter are grounded in the fact that 'the land the English settled was not as God made it. It was as the Aborigines made it' (Hallam 1975: vii). The focus of this section is upon the way in which the colonial project interpreted and thus managed the landscape during the establishment of the Australian nation. These interpretations had and continue to have lasting influences upon the Australian landscape and culture. This discussion demonstrates how colonial land management approaches practised in Victoria and the Northern Territory fulfilled the colonial utilitarian narrative of nature as wilderness. The first recorded European visit onto Dja Dja Wurrung lands (overlapping with the area now known as north central Victoria) was by the pastoral lands exploration party of Major Thomas Livingstone Mitchell in June 1836 (Gardiner 1962). The way Mitchell describes the area is indicative of the colonial imagination of the time. Not only do his words reflect notions of *terra nullius*, they also construct the landscape as a resource to be consumed by the colonial project. He writes (from Gardiner 1962: 13):

> a land so inviting, and still without inhabitants! As I stood, the first European intruder on the sublime solitude of those verdant plains as yet untouched by flocks and herds; I felt conscious of being the harbinger of mighty changes; and that our steps would soon be followed by the man and the animals for which it seemed to have been prepared.

The Dja Dja Wurrung people were dispossessed[5] from their lands by this colonial project in two waves (Clark and Cahir 2004). In 1839 they were dispossessed by colonial settlers who were moving inland with their flocks to take up available grazing lands.[6] The second wave resulted from the Victorian gold rush that began in earnest in 1851.[7] The discovery of gold at Ballarat in September 1851 and the alluvial pickings discovered at Forest Creek (in the project case study area) spurned the biggest and richest alluvial gold rush in the world (Serle 1963; Blainey 1969).[8]

The advent and the culture of the gold rush as well as the miners' attitudes towards the landscape reflect the prevalent utilitarian narrative of nature as wilderness. William Howitt (1972: 98) recorded his impressions of the miners during his visit in 1852:

> the diggers seem to have two especial propensities, those of firing guns and felling trees. It is amazing what a number of trees they fell. No sooner have they done their days work, than they commence felling trees.

The resultant clear-felling left a landscape that is described by Slattery (2003a: 11) as:

> heaps of churned over gravels and rocks, creeks of yellow mud running through deeply entrenched gullies, hills denuded of understorey, with feeble coppiced eucalypts struggling to regrow on eroding, soil-less slopes, weeds recolonizing widely, and a dense network of tracks, roads and decaying settlements in many valleys

The vast international immigration to the Victorian goldfields in the 1850s[9] has resulted in the region being proclaimed as the 'cradle of modern Australia, radically reshaping the nation's destiny' (ECC 2001: 147). The importance of this gold mining history is reinforced by the naming of the areas as part of the Goldfields bioregion by the Victorian Biodiversity Strategy (see DNRE 1997). The political uprisings of the Monster Meeting at the nearby Bakery Hill and the Stockade at Eureka[10] in 1854

---

[5] Clark (1995) records 13 murders and massacres in Dja Dja Wurrung lands between 1838 and 1846. These did not all pass without retribution. Clark (1995) records that possibly the first Victorian inquest into an Aboriginal death in custody was held in Dja Dja Wurrung country in 1855.

[6] The Port Phillip Aboriginal Protectorate was created by the Colonial Office in London in 1838 and Assistant Protector Edward Parker set up the Upper Loddon Aboriginal Reserve in 1840 (Culvenor 1992).

[7] Annear (1999) states that people had been finding gold in the Port Phillip District from as early as 1842 and when gold was discovered in May 1851 in NSW, it was 'as bad as a declaration of war against the embryonic Victoria' (p7). A Gold Discovery Committee was formed offering 200 guineas reward for the discovery of a workable goldfield within 200 miles of Melbourne. Three months later the gold rush begun.

[8] Some Dja Dja Wurrung people had a role in the gold rush. A publication documenting this involvement was released in 2004 (see Clark and Cahir 2004).

[9] During this time, the population of Victoria grew from 77,000 in 1851 to 540,000 by the end of 1859 (Powell 1976).

[10] The Eureka Stockade was a rebellion fuelled by the 'diggers' over the system of licensing enforced by government officials and police troopers, some of whom were corrupt. This was based on the fact that gold deposits were and still are the property of the crown. Many miners claimed the license was unfair and a tax upon labour.

are heralded by some to have 'precipitated Australia into nationhood' (Annear 1999: 313). These two statements further illuminate the way the Victorian landscape was interpreted and managed during the early stages of Australian nation-building. They reflect how the historical descriptions of Australia as *terra nullius* also worked to inform the Australian national identity at the time.

Similar interpretations, descriptions and land management approaches perpetuated the colonial narrative of nature as wilderness on the lands of central Australia. Historically, central Australia was described as the wasteland and desert heart of Australia. These metaphors encapsulated the colonial confrontation with alien environments and with, as Howitt (2001b) describes, the incomprehensible Indigenous other. These lands were depicted as the frontier and the edge of the metropolitan centres of colonial outpost of Australia. Furthermore, the heart of the Australian landscape was conceptualised as the primitive and inferior other to the superior lands and culture of the colonial centre. This narrative was further enforced by the then fashionable notion of social Darwinism whereby Australia was depicted as a land of living fossils, primitive nature and primitive peoples.

At this edge of empire, the aim of this colonial project was to empty the landscape of its primitivism and to fill it again with elements of European development. Indicators of this development included pastoral land tenure and related infrastructure as well as education and history. European plant and animal species were brought in to physically colonise these inferior landscapes. Griffiths (1997) argues that the practise of ecology and empire was interchangeable. Changing the local ecology, subverting the natural order and taming the great southern land were all part of a biological imperialism to control the dangerous and ancient landscape of Australia.

In central Australia, the mapping of property by practises of demarking land with fixed boundaries perpetuated the colonial notion of Australia as *terra nullius*. This conceptualising of place as purely spatial property excluded other ways of knowing the landscape. For example, in contemporary times, Indigenous Australians often describe their relationship to land in terms of their movement through it and their special relationships with particular places. Indeed *jurkurrpa* (the Dreaming) is dependent upon people walking, singing and performing in the country.

Early colonial narratives that depicted pioneering men and women living at the edge of empire toiling to subdue the primitive and wild centre of Australia formed the basis of the pastoral myth that is sometimes represented in contemporary times by the not entirely in jest motto of: 'if it moves shoot it, if it doesn't, cut it down'. The myth of the noble savage aligned Indigenous peoples with the land as wild, natural and having no imprint upon the landscape. These myths not only perpetuated the colonial narrative of development versus primitivism and the inherent discourse of settlement versus a nomadic lifestyle, but they depicted two opposing groups of harmonious and homogenous communities. This dichotomy simplified both pastoral and Indigenous cultures and left unsaid the diverse experiences and histories of place that formed the basis of life in the region. These narratives represent the colonial interpretation of the social and physical landscape that silenced all other ways of knowing the land and thus ignored diversity. The following discussion touches upon the tension between these historical narratives and how contemporary practises allow for alternative readings of the diverse historical confrontations with the Australian landscape.

5.3 Contemporary Realities

Contemporary readings of the Australia landscape increasingly reflect the voices and experiences that were silenced by the colonial project. Although the ideology of Australia as *terra nullius* before British settlement remains strong in certain parts of contemporary Australian culture, the challenge to the 'Great Australian Silence'[11] (see Stanner 1968) began a recognition and investigation into Indigenous history. Autobiographical writing by Aboriginal people as well as Aboriginal life histories written and recorded by nonindigenous authors (e.g. Beckett 1958; Stanner 1960; Batty 1963; Rose 1969; Hardy 1976; Shaw 1981, 1983; Morgan 1987; Marshall 1989; Vaarzon-Morel 1995) has confronted the previous orthodoxy of Australian history. These accounts have in turn encouraged some Australian historians to reappraise and rewrite Australia's past (e.g. the work of Reynolds 1982, 1992, 1999). These works also speak about the complicated personal relationships shared between some colonists and white settlers and some Indigenous peoples that did not always reflect the dichotomy of the coloniser and the colonised (e.g. Baker 1999).

Having briefly discussed the cultural shift into the changing Australian narrative of Indigenous history, I now investigate how changing interpretations of the Australian landscape influence contemporary management approaches. I focus upon specific changes in land management in north central Victoria and parts of the Northern Territory. The declaration in November 2002 of the Box-Ironbark Forest and Woodlands national, state parks and reserves across the State of Victoria (DSE 2005a) symbolises contemporary interpretations of the Victorian landscape. The declaration of these parks and reserves was complemented by the introduction of the National Parks (Box-Ironbark and other Parks) Bill into the Victorian Parliament (DSE 2005b). These parks and reserves resulted from 5 years of Victorian State Government and community consultation. The *Box-Ironbark Forests & Woodlands Investigation Final Report* (ECC 2001) was the main outcome of these consultations. As is declared by the Victorian Government Department of Environment and Sustainability (DSE 2005a: 1):

> over 105,000 hectares of public land in north central and north east Victoria is now protected in a series of parks and reserves to halt the serious environmental decline in the Box-Ironbark area…[these] landscapes are unique. Not only do they have enormous environmental values, but also very strong cultural and community ties and traditions. These areas have been used by Aboriginal people for thousands of years, followed by the industry and recreational uses that have evolved since European settlement.

---

[11] The Great Australia Silence refers to the many written historical accounts that excluded the indigenous side of the story of colonisation and rendered the indigenous peoples as passive and inactive (see Attwood and Foster 2003).

The long history of land use includes rich Aboriginal, non-Aboriginal, mining, forestry and more recently conservation heritages.[12] All the heritages are recognised by the declaration of these parks and reserves. Some parks, such as the first ever National Heritage Park declared in Australia, focus more upon certain cultural heritage values than others. The name of this park, 'the Diggings National Heritage Park', reflects the rich mining heritage that is protected by its declaration. Much of the work carried out by the project members of the Victorian case study is conducted in or around this park. The remaining discussion focuses upon the discord between the different cultural heritages represented in this park.

The declaration of the Castlemaine Diggings National Heritage Park represents the tensions between the historical colonial narratives of nature as wilderness represented by the discussion of the Forest Creek Goldfields above and the great diversity of contemporary interpretations of the same landscape that represents rich Aboriginal heritages and the rich and important biodiversity played out upon and embedded within contemporary readings of the landscape. These tensions are articulated by a local community member from the North Central Victorian case study region, who, at the time of the research, also worked as a cultural heritage advisor to the Victorian Government's Heritage Council and Parks Victoria agencies:

> there was no way [the environmental lobby groups] were going to get a national park here because biodiversity just wasn't good enough. We [Heritage Victoria] stepped in and made a case that [the region] had this incredible cultural heritage. We [environmental and heritage conservationists] are in general agreement that we can protect both values, but that's not the issue, it's more an ideological one: whether you have culture first or nature first and whether you celebrate the act that you think was responsible for destroying a wilderness.

Although this comment does not speak directly of the rich Aboriginal heritage in the region, the speaker (who also works closely with Dja Dja Wurrung people in the region and was instrumental in the release of the first publication documenting Aboriginal involvement in the Forest Creek gold rush; see Clark and Cahir 2004) is making a point about the tensions between culture and nature. A local historian encapsulates these tensions by proclaiming 'it's a Goldfield, not a Box-Ironbark forest' (Slattery 2003b: 455). These comments and local realities reflect what researchers of the social construction of nature (see Castree and Braun 1998; Demerritt 2002) advocate: that nature is culture and cultural interpretations of nature construct the way in which land is managed. These tensions are also evident in the contemporary approaches to land management in the Northern Territory.

The advent of the *Aboriginal Land Rights (Northern Territory) Act 1976*, the historical High Court's *Mabo Decision 1992* and the *Native Title Act 1993* challenged previously held attitudes about the role of Indigenous people in Australia at the time of British colonisation. In the Northern Territory, these changes have had very real impacts upon the lives of Indigenous peoples. The Federal Government fostered land settlement and rural development until the 1970s and used lease tenures as policy instruments towards these goals (Holmes 2002). Remaining vacant

---

[12] Other recognised land use practises include apiculture, recreation, tourism, eucalyptus oil production, grazing as well as water production and distribution (ECC 2001).

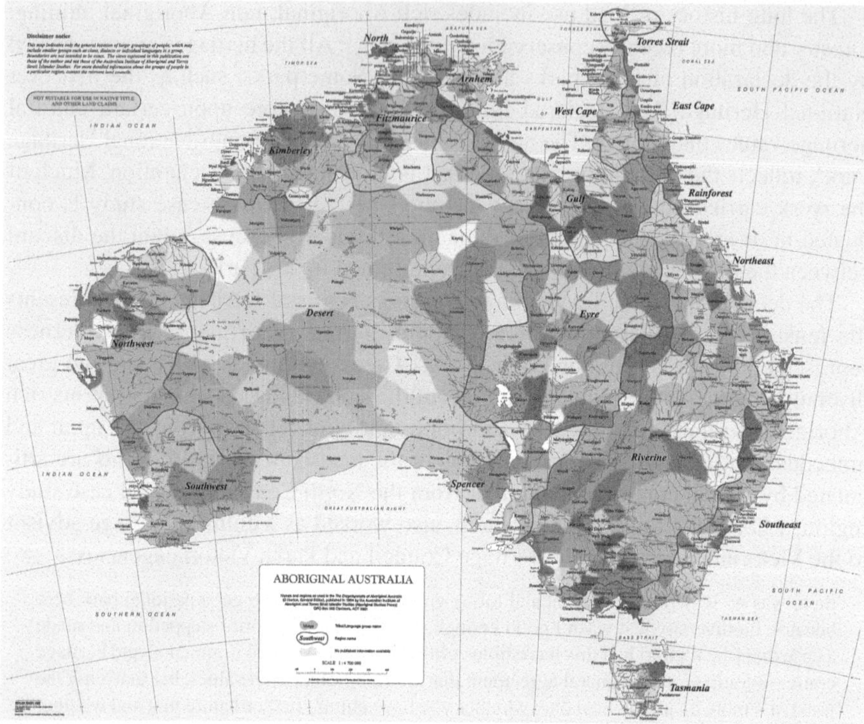

Fig. 5.5 This map is just one representation of many other map sources that are available for Aboriginal Australia. Using published resources available between 1988 and 1994, this map attempts to represent all the language, social or nation groups of the Indigenous people of Australia. It indicates only the general location of larger groupings of people which may include smaller groups such as clans, dialects or individual languages in a group. Boundaries are not intended to be exact. This map is *not suitable for use in native title and other land claims*. David R Horton, creator, © Aboriginal Studies Press, AIATSIS and Auslig/Sinclair, Knight, Merz, 1996. No reproduction allowed without permission (Source: Horton 1996)

crown land, considered unable to support viable pastoral business, was declared inalienable freehold land. Following the *Aboriginal Land Rights* (*Northern Territory*) *Act 1976*, these areas were claimed by Aboriginal people and are now administered by a number of Aboriginal land trusts. These land trusts represent the Aboriginal connection to the Australian landscape that was silenced by the colonial project. The land trusts also celebrate the great diversity of Aboriginal cultures and languages that were homogenised under colonial rule. Figure 5.5 shows the diversity of Aboriginal languages in Australia and, more specifically, in central Australia.

Slogans of the Indigenous statutory organisations, the Northern Land Council and the Central Land Council, that were set up to fulfil the land allocation that resulted from the *Aboriginal Land Rights* (*Northern Territory*) *Act 1976*, further challenge colonial narratives of the centre of Australia as hostile wasteland or timeless desert. These slogans, current at the time of the research, describe this landscape as 'Our Land, Our Life' (CLC and NLC 1995) and 'The Land is Always Alive' (CLC 1995), and stand in testament against it being the edge, frontier or outback of some omnipotent centre.

Autobiographical accounts by some pastoralists are also beginning to contest notions of the pastoral community as homogenous and harmonious (see Bowman 1991; Chisholm 1999; Coppock 1993). Accounts of the land management practises of some pastoralists are challenging long-held perceptions that all pastoralists practise unsustainable land management: a small number of pastoralists advocate land management approaches that value the quality of the land over the quantity of stock it can support (see Purvis 2004). This diversity is also demonstrated by the various attitudes that pastoralists in the southern Tanami have towards fire.

Despite the growing landcare concern among pastoralists, there is no doubt that the environmental aspect of colonial conquest (Griffiths 1997) has brought large numbers of hard-hoofed animals to the centre of Australia and has led to the spread of exotic grass species[13] across parts of central Australia. Equally, there is little doubt that since the Horn Expedition (see Morton and Mulvaney 1996) wove its way through the central Australian landscape in 1894 conducting the first European ecological survey, there has been rapid land degradation, extinction of species and a noticeable change in vegetation communities and animal populations. The introduction of feral animals such as foxes, cats, camels and donkeys has also greatly affected the biota of central Australia.[14] Changing fire regimes that have resulted from a reduction in the number of people who burnt as they walked the country, introduced plant species such as buffel grass, and the increased ability of people to travel much further in a shorter length of time has had a marked impact upon the landscape.

Many Indigenous Australians are concerned with this ongoing land degradation. But with the advent of the *Aboriginal Land Rights (Northern Territory) Act 1976*, they are voicing concern about the role placed upon them as traditional owners to overcome the degradation caused by decades of pastoral occupancy. The ongoing development of the Federal Government's Indigenous Protected Area Program (see Environment Australia 2013c) is the first attempt to finance the important conservation works that can be conducted by traditional owners and Aboriginal people living on these lands. In central Australia, there is the potential for the expansion of the federally funded Indigenous ranger programs. These programs offer training and employment for individuals who are interested in working in the land management sphere.

As is the case across much of Australia, many pastoralists in central Australia also express concern at the impacts of past land management practises upon their

[13] The introduction of buffel grass in the northern territory continues to be a highly contentious issue between pastoralists and conservationists. Pastoralists value buffel as feed for their livestock with some trying to encourage the spread of seeds. Conservationists argue the grass should be listed as a noxious weed. This exotic species that is colonising the central Australian landscape is also highly flammable.

[14] The introduction of higher-order predators has led to the extinction or close to extinction of many endemic animal species (see Paltridge 1998, 2002; Edwards et al. 2001a, b, 2002; Paltridge and Southgate 2001).

pastoral leases. This concern is reflected by the existence of the Centralian Land Management Association. This association is described by its coordinator as the largest landcare group in Australia with a membership of over 40 pastoral properties in the Alice Springs region (Johnson pers com 2004).

The need to understand the multidimensional complexity of the central Australian landscape is reinforced by the reality of what Holmes (2002) calls the post-productivist transition. He argues that in Australia's most marginal lands 'pastoral occupance is being displaced by renewed Indigenous occupance, conservation and tourism, with significant changes to land ownership, property rights, investment sources and power relations' (Holmes 2002: 362, 2011). There is certainly a growing imperative for the arid lands of central Australia to be managed in an ecologically sustainable manner.

Scientific research into land degradation in central Australia highlights the importance of ecologically sustainable land management with an increased focus upon biodiversity conservation (Ledgar and Stafford Smith 1996). The introduction of various government legislation and programs is indicative of the changing land management cultures in the Northern Territory. These include the previously mentioned Federal Government's Indigenous Protected Area program funded through the Natural Reserve System; the negotiations for joint management of parks and reserves in the Northern Territory following the *Parks and Reserves Act 2003* that have provided new opportunities for the conservation of biodiversity and Aboriginal communities across the Northern Territory (see P&WC 2013b); the review of the *Pastoral Lands Act 1992* to address issues relating to access, development, native vegetation clearing controls and Aboriginal community living areas on pastoral lands; the development of the *Integrated Natural Resource Management Plan 2005* (see LCNT 2005) and, at the time, the ongoing development of the *Northern Territory Parks and Conservation Master Plan* (see NRETA 2005). These plans certainly indicate the impetus for changing land management approaches in the Northern Territory; however, it remains to be seen whether Federal and Territory Governments are willing and able to commit the funds necessary.

Herein lies the challenge of the Northern Territory case study project: Desert Fire. How can such a project incorporate the multiple values of pastoral production, biodiversity conservation and Aboriginal contemporary practise in considering the management of fire in the region? The following section of this chapter highlights further complexities of these tensions. It illuminates the diversity of ways that the interest groups from each case study location interpret and experience the same environment.

5.4 Difference and Diversity Across the Landscape

The previous section illuminated the way in which cultural interpretations of the Australian landscape determine specific land management approaches. This section further unpacks the basis of these cultural interpretations. Firstly, it examines how the interest groups of each case study know about the landscape where they work. This discussion draws attention to the diverse ways that the same landscape can be known. It investigates how threatened species are known in north central Victoria and how fire is known in the southern Tanami region of the Northern Territory. Secondly, this section reflects upon the diversity of social livelihood issues confronting the many interest groups. This analysis demonstrates the additional factors that influence why these people choose to be, or not be, involved with the environmental management and community development project that is the focus of each case study.

When analysing the different knowledges of the Australian landscape, it is important to remember the reality of ecological uncertainty. Policy writers depend upon the knowledge of scientists who specialise in landscape mechanisms and interactions, such as ecologists, biologists, zoologists and so on, to determine best practise environmental management. This scientific knowledge is based upon statistical prediction and thus can never be 100 % accurate. This uncertainty is confounded by larger-scale environmental interactions such as global warming and the effects of variables yet to be identified let alone researched. Ecological uncertainty in relation to the management of species habitat in Victoria is reflected by the use of ecological vegetation classes.

In relation to the management of fire in the Northern Territory, ecological uncertainty is reflected by the fact that relatively little is known by western scientists about the effects of fire on biodiversity in central Australia. Indeed, it was not until work such as Jones (1969) that scientists began to consider fire as an essential part of the landscape. This ecological uncertainty is articulated by an ecologist who is part of the Northern Territory case study. In the following quote, he speaks about ecological uncertainty but also the possible irrelevance of current scientific approaches to the ecological study of the central Australian landscape. He explains:

> it took me years and years to realise that most other scientist just weren't seeing how it was happening out there they are just walking around blind. Aborigines say a lot of people walk round the bush like blind people, they can't see anything… I've tried to do experimental stuff… to show what was happening and… I soon realised that there is a lot of noise in the system… it is to do with the fact that Australia is the oldest continent on earth so it is messy… when you have got the mess on top of an incredibly complex system in a mess, science doesn't work… I just think that Australian science is going the wrong way. They are trying to apply the experiments that work in physics where you can control everything nicely to the most complex system in the world.

An interesting contrast that will become apparent in a reading of the following discussion relates to the number of ways that individuals know about threatened species in Victoria as compared with the number of ways that individuals know about fire in the Northern Territory. In Victoria the knowledge of individuals from the local community arena, of individuals from the government arena and of individuals from the science community is based upon the scientific method. In comparison, the knowledge of individuals from the local community arena including pastoralists and Aborigines is not always based upon the scientific method.

The title of the Victorian Threatened Species project reflects the project goal 'Protection and Enhancement of Threatened Species Habitat in the Goldfields Bioregion' (Project Application round 5 2002: 2). These habitats are classified according to what the *Victorian Biodiversity Strategy 1997* calls 'pre-1750 Ecological Vegetation Classes'. They include the ecological communities of 'Grassy Woodland, Creekline Grassy Woodland, Alluvial Terraces Herb-rich Woodland and the Temperate Woodland Bird community' (Project Application round 5 2002: 2). I consider there to be three main ways in which these threatened species and communities are known by individuals involved with the project.

Firstly, threatened species and ecological communities are known by certain individuals involved with the project through the practise of the scientific method. The species and ecological communities that are the focus of the case study project have been listed as threatened under the under the Victorian *Flora and Fauna Guarantee Act 1988* and the Federal Government's *Environment Protection and Biodiversity Conservation Act 1999* according to specific scientific evidence.[15] This scientific evidence is generated by individuals engaged in applying the scientific method to natural systems. This work includes that of a PhD student who uses scientific methods to investigate the ecology and life cycle (preferred egg-laying habitat, egg production rates and mortality rates) of the threatened Eltham Copper Butterfly. She also uses mathematical models to determine population viability of this threatened species, and this data reflects the habitat size necessary to sustain genetically healthy populations of the species. Also a zoologist who wrote the Action Plan for Australian Butterflies (Sands and New 2002) uses scientific methods to investigate the taxonomy of related attendant ant species. These methods include the examination of specimens collected at specific sites to determine anatomy, physiology and invertebrate structures of species.

Scientists working for the government also use taxonomic methods to identify, classify and ultimately manage flora and fauna species. Individuals working for government sometimes rely on local amateur scientists, who they describe as local gurus, to feed information relating to the identification and location of threatened plant species into the State-wide herbarium database located at the Arthur Rylah Institute for Environmental Research, Melbourne. Clearly these local amateur scientists are following rigorous scientific practises respected by professional scientists. As such these individuals also know threatened species according to their practise of science. This ongoing knowledge generation is essential for the management, protection and enhancement of threatened species habitat in Victoria.

The second way that individuals know threatened species in north central Victoria is by using derived scientific information for management purposes. The ecological

---

[15] Under the Flora and Fauna Guarantee Act 1988 a taxon or community is eligible to be listed if it is in a demonstrable state of decline that is likely to result in extinction or significantly prone to future threats that may result in its extinction (DSE 2006a). Under the Environment Protection and Biodiversity Conservation Act 1999, a native species (or ecological community) is in the critically endangered, endangered or vulnerable category if it meets any of the five criteria (or six criteria for ecological communities) as specified under the Act (Office of Legislative Drafting 2000).

communities that are the focus of the Victorian case study projects are units of vegetation that have been derived for specific management approaches. Government representatives use pre-1750 Ecological Vegetation Classes as the benchmark for the conservation status and conditions of lands in Victoria to make decisions about biodiversity policy and management. Ecological Vegetation Classes are defined as consisting of one or a number of floristic communities that exist under a common regime of ecological processes within a particular environment and bioregion or broader scale (see DEPI 2013).[16] Scientists have used remaining remnant vegetation, ecological processes and landscape ecology to determine what vegetation communities would have existed across the Victorian landscape prior to European clearing of the country. The notion of the 'pre-1750 condition' was proposed as the primary measure of naturalness prior to European development of the country (see Hopkins 1999).

Pre-1750 Ecological Vegetation Classes are the basic mapping unit for the conservation status and condition of lands in Victoria. These mapping units are used in conjunction with the methodology of 'habitat hectare' (Parkes et al. 2003) and the principle of 'net gain' (see Oliver et al. 2002) as the basis for *Victoria's Native Vegetation Management: A Framework of Action* 2002. Community conservation projects are funded according to the conservation status of ecological communities. As is explored further in Chaps. 7 and 8, some individuals from the government and local community arenas engage proactively with these management languages to gain funding for locally desired conservation land management.

Finally, threatened species are known by certain individuals according to prescribed on-ground work. These individuals engage with both scientific and management principles to conduct on-ground species recovery works. These include individuals from the local community groups, amateur and professional scientists and government representatives working with the Victorian project case study. These individuals apply 'mechanisms for more efficiently conserving key biodiversity assets and enhancing community participation, further effective integrated predator control, weed control and habitat restoration' (Project Application round 5 2002: 2). They also work to educate the community 'through planting days, weed control and education material is seen as a key element of this project' (Project Application round 6 2003a: 2). Furthermore, they strive to 'increase the knowledge on the distribution of threatened species within the Shire' as well as 'enhance biodiversity values of sites and provide long-term protection of threatened species, identify and mitigate threats to the threatened species on roadsides and put in place roadside conservation management strategies' (Project Application round 6 2003b: 2). As is explored in Chaps. 8 and 9, individuals engaged in on-ground species recovery work in Victoria know these species according to the impacts of potentially threatening anthropocentric activities.

[16] Ecological Vegetation Classes are a feature of Broad Vegetation Types. Broad Vegetation Types categorise a diversity of indigenous vegetation assigned on the basis of existing vegetation and other biophysical parameters such as geology, rainfall, elevation and soil type (see DEPI 2013).

The ways in which fire is known by people working with the Desert Fire project in the Northern Territory is more complex than the ways in which threatened species are known by people involved with the Threatened Species project in Victoria for reasons expressed previously. The impetus for the project is reflected in the project title: 'Desert fire: Managing Fire in the Southern Tanami, Northern Territory'. The project is embedded within the larger Desert Knowledge Cooperative Research Council network that is *aimed at generating new knowledge, new ways of doing things, new ways of thinking about things*. The success of this project is dependent upon understanding the three ways in which fire is known by people working with the project (see also Maclean 2009).[17]

Firstly, some people know fire through the practise of science. These practises include those pertaining to the management of biodiversity for conservation, for example, the research work carried out by individuals working for the Northern Territory Parks and Wildlife Service. These practises also include the mapping of fire across the landscape, for example, the geographical information systems mapping and the related ground-truthing work conducted by a scientist at the Bushfires Council. This valuable work increases knowledge of fire histories and effects of fire upon biodiversity with a view to improve management of fire in the region. However, the application of this knowledge is not without its complexities. This touches upon the points made previously about ecological uncertainty. These complexities highlight the tension between government policy, management practises and the scientific knowledge upon which these practises are founded.

Scientists in central Australia openly admit their evolving knowledge of the region. Although there has been an increase in recent ecological research into the effects of fire on vegetation communities (see Griffin et al. 1983; Saxon 1984; Allan and Southgate 2002; Allan et al. 2003; Nano 2006) and bird communities (see Leavesley 2008), relatively little is known about the effects of fire on biodiversity. For example, there is a lack of detailed information on the responses of most individual species, communities or environments to changed fire regimes (LCNT 2005).

Large areas in the southern Tanami region are managed by pastoral landholders. As such the practise of pastoral knowledge is important to the management of fire in region. As explored in Chaps. 8 and 9, attitudes to fire vary between pastoral landholders. Some individuals wish to keep it out of their leases because they see it as a threat to pastoral grasses and infrastructure. Others use it as often as they can; as such, the incidence of unwanted fires travelling onto their leases is greatly decreased. Others use fire primarily to create firebreaks. Although knowledge of fire on pastoral leases varies, the purpose for the management of these lands remains the same, as one pastoralist from the region explains: the *cattle take precedence*. However, there are also various approaches to the management of the country for cattle. For example, one pastoralist who describes fire as a grazing management tool and uses it as often as he can also speaks about the benefits of managing the land to promote diverse native grass species. In contrast he speaks of *old school pastoralists*,

[17] See Verran (2002) for a postcolonial critique on alternative firing regimes of environmental scientists and Aboriginal landowners in northeast Arnhem Land, Northern Territory.

residing outside the southern Tanami region who come under the watchful eye of the government because, as he explains, they *don't think of the quality of stock, just the number.*

The project case study area is predominately on Aboriginal freehold land. The practise of Aboriginal knowledge of fire in the region is paramount to the management of fire in the region. Although the ecological knowledge of many Indigenous Territorians still remains to be extensively documented and applied to land management issues, there is increasing interest in and recognition of the important role this knowledge can play. For example, work by some researchers gives voice to traditional ecological knowledge (see Latz 1995). The ongoing expansion of the land management division of the Central Land Council is indicative of increasing interest in, and government funding for, Indigenous land management. The ongoing development of Indigenous Protected Areas and Indigenous ranger programs in the Northern Territory is evidence of this two-way interest. As is discussed in Chaps. 8 and 9, Aboriginal knowledge of fire in the region varies between individuals, and its application is closely entwined with traditional ownership. Individuals describe fire in relation to 'caring for country' under traditional law. For example, it is used to clean the country to make way for new growth. Fire is also described as important for living effectively in the region. For example, people speak about using fire for hunting, cooking and heating. Fire is also pivotal for cultural practises such as ceremony. Individuals also speak about the important role of fire as a communication tool in the event of an emergency such as car failure.

What is evident from the discussion above is that the same landscape can be known in many different ways. This confirms a point made earlier that land management approaches depend upon cultural understanding of the landscape. Sometimes these understandings may be in conflict as is the case with the use or the perceived use of fire in the southern Tanami. As the coordinator of the Centralian Land Management Association clearly articulates:

> [fire] is a potential tool but it can get misused or underestimated. People may be [using it] for their right but these reasons might be someone else's wrong reasons [as such it is] a mis-valued tool.

As explored in Chap. 8, the politics of local knowledge, that is, the way that others perceive the knowledge held by different interest groups, are equally important to equitable and sustainable environmental governance and management. Of similar importance to equitable and sustained environmental governance and management are the social livelihoods issues faced by individuals that influence their choices to engage in environmental governance and management.

Individuals become involved with environmental management and community development projects for a variety of reasons. Chapter 7 explores these reasons for the two case study projects, and Chap. 7 discusses the responsibilities of environmental management and community development projects to also provide for the development of sustainable social livelihoods. The remainder of this section presents the social livelihood issues faced by individuals from the local community arena of each case study project. What becomes clear is the diversity of social livelihood issues faced by individuals engaged in environmental governance and management across Australia. This complements the claims made in Chap. 2 (Sect. 2.7) that relate to the varieties of environmentalism that exist in Australia.

All individuals involved with the case study project from the local community arena in Victoria regard themselves as proactively engaged in working to protect and enhance the habitat of threatened species. Some of these individuals classify themselves as part of the community landcare movement, others speak of themselves as environmental conservationists, others speak of being political lobbyists and a final group of active community members define themselves as apolitical field naturalists. Many of these individuals are retired or semiretired and have either chosen to relocate to the region for lifestyle reasons or have been living in the region for an extended period of time.

These individuals are aware of the power of their local knowledge and action. Indeed, many of them could be described as empowered individuals using government policy and funding networks to meet the requirements of their on-ground project work. Some individuals believe their work is limited by parochial small picture thinking among other community members and limited government recognition and funding. However, there is no doubt that these individuals choose to volunteer their time to engage with environmental management projects for the benefit of the whole community.

In contrast, the social livelihood issues faced by individuals from the local community arena, including pastoralists and Aboriginal people, involved with the Northern Territory case study project are more complex. These complexities are reflected by the development of the Desert Knowledge Cooperative Research Centre research network that aimed to link 'Indigenous and local knowledge with science and education to improve desert livelihoods' (DKCRC 2006a: 1). As such a core objective of this network is to 'deliver sustainable livelihoods for desert peoples that are based on environmentally and socially sound natural resource and service enterprise opportunities' (DKCRC 2006d: 1). In relation to engaging with the project case study, individuals living in the southern Tanami are more socially disadvantaged than those in north central Victoria. This is particularly the case for Aboriginal people living in the region. As an individual working for the Central Land Council articulates, *people have got more important things to do with their lives like providing a roof over their head… or getting their kids to school or just finding enough to eat for the day.*

Some Indigenous Australians are considered as third world in the first world (Young 1995) or as fourth world people (Dyck 1985) living in a supposedly developed society but not benefiting equitably with the rest of society. Evidence shows that Indigenous Australians living in remote parts of Australia are one of the most disadvantaged groups in Australia. They have a lower life expectancy[18] and lower

[18] The Australian Bureau of Statistics (ABS) estimates (from data during the period 2005–2007) that life expectancy at birth for nonindigenous males was 78.7 years, females was 82.6 years as compared with indigenous males 67.2 years and females 72.9 years (ABS 2011). Indigenous Australians also continue to be at a greater health disadvantage to other Australians.

attendance at schools. In fact, most remote communities in the Northern Territory do not offer postprimary education.[19] There are currently very few employment opportunities for Aboriginal people living in the southern Tanami region.

Although the situation for pastoralists is not as difficult as it is for Aboriginal people living in the southern Tanami, they face social livelihood issues that are more challenging than those faced by individuals living in north central Victoria. For example, individuals who live in remote regions of Australia[20] have decreased access to many of the services, such as health and education, offered by more populated centres. The livelihoods of pastoralists are also influenced by external factors. As a regional manager from the Northern Territory Government Department of Natural Resource, Environment and the Arts explains, pastoralists are also *trying to make a living [...they] go from high to low [in relation to drought, interest rates and so on].*

As these descriptions suggest, the social livelihood issues faced by individuals living and working in the southern Tanami region are more complex and confronting than those faced by individuals living in north central Victoria. As such there must be tangible livelihood reasons for these individuals to choose to be involved in the case study project. Indeed, in contrast to individuals from the local community in Victoria, none of these land managers can afford to volunteer their time in working to meet project objectives and on-ground works.[21] In summary, the diversity of social livelihood issues faced by the individuals from the local community arena of each project influences their motivations for being involved with the project.

5.5 Embedded Powers Across the Landscape

The two projects that are the focus of the research clearly highlight the varieties of environmentalism that are held and practised by land managers across Australia. For example, the knowledge held by pastoralists and Aboriginal land managers relating to the role of fire in the southern Tanami is quite different to each other as well as to the knowledge held by individuals working for the different arenas of government in Australia. Indeed, these knowledges may sometimes be in conflict. It is imperative to evaluate the environmental governance and management discourses that are embedded in any environmental management and community development project because if the project structure silences any one group, it will perpetuate the challenges that it is attempting to overcome.

[19] Statistics reflects that in 2011 the apparent high school retention rate (year 7–12) for indigenous students was 48.7 % compared to the total retention rate of all students of 79.3 % (2012).

[20] Remoteness is calculated by the Australian Bureau of Statistics using the road distance to different-sized urban centres, where the population size is considered to govern the range and type of services available. The five remoteness areas are major cities of Australia, inner regional Australia, outer regional Australia, remote Australia and very remote Australia (ABS 2004).

[21] All individuals interviewed for this research study did so of their own accord and no payment was made.

Asking whose environment and whose development, if any, is favoured by the project structure is the first step in overcoming any embedded power inequalities. Engaging in strategies to overcome these inequalities is the second step in working towards equitable and sustainable environmental governance and management in Australia. In Chaps. 9 and 10, I critique and demonstrate how the two project case studies exemplify the potential for working to overcome current levels of environmental and social degradation in Australia.

5.6 Conclusion

This chapter has practised an edge politics (after Howitt 2001a) to highlight the diversity of approaches advocated by a variety of land managers to engage with the Australian landscape. Howitt (2001b: 234) argues that practising an edge politics 'grapples with ambivalence, uncertainty, change, overlap and interaction in ways that dislodge the old-style colonial metaphors of empty spaces and frontier heroics'. An edge politics allows for a celebration of difference. Further it provides the practical means to begin the process of cultural hybridity that Bhabha (1990) argues is necessary to reach a third cultural space of cultural representation and understanding. These concepts are explored in detail in Chap. 10.

Practising an edge politics acknowledges the historical antecedents that continue to influence contemporary environmental governance and management practises. It also challenges historical narratives by juxtaposing them with contemporary institutions and counter-narratives. This juxtaposition opens the opportunity to reflect upon these complex and sometimes conflicting narratives. Critiquing these narratives paves the way for a conceptualisation of environmental governance and management as composed of different knowledge cultures and land management approaches and as motivated by diverse social livelihood issues. An edge politics unpacks and unpicks the many knowledges of environmental governance and management and provides strategies (as presented in Chap. 9) to consider ways to overcome the conflict that arises from these different and diverse environmentalisms. It also considers who is silenced within any environmental management and community development project and how they are silenced and thereby affords the first step in overcoming the power inequalities that are embedded in any project.

References

ABS (Australian Bureau of Statistics) (2004) Australian social trends, work: aboriginal and Torres Strait Islander people in the labour force. Australian Bureau of Statistics, Canberra

ABS (Australian Bureau of Statistics) (2011) 4704.0 The health and welfare of Australia's aboriginal and Torres Strait Islander peoples, Oct 2010. Australian Government. Australian Bureau of Statistics, Canberra

ABS (Australian Bureau of Statistics) (2012) 4102.0 Australian social trends 2014 (education and training). Australian Government. Australian Bureau of Statistics, Canberra

Allan GE, Southgate RI (2002) Fire regimes in the spinifex landscapes of Australia. In: Bradstock RA, Williams JE, Gill AM (eds) Flammable Australia:the fire regimes and biodiversity of a continent. Cambridge University Press, Cambridge

Allan GE, Phillips NR, Hookey P (2003) Learning lessons from an exceptional period of fires in central Australia: 1999 to 2002. In: Proceedings of the 3rd international wildland fire conference, Sydney, 3–6 October

Annear R (1999) Nothing but gold: the diggers of 1852. Text Publishing, Melbourne

Attwood B, Foster SG (2003) Introduction. In: Attwood B, Foster SG (eds) Frontier conflict: the Australian experience. National Museum of Australia, Canberra, pp 1–30

Baker R (1999) Land is life. From bush to town: the story of the Yanyuwa people. Allen & Unwin, St. Leonards

Batty JD (1963) Namatjira: wanderer between two worlds. Hodder and Stoughton, Melbourne

Beckett J (1958) Marginal men: a study of two half-caste aborigines. Oceania 29:91–108

Bhabha HK (1990) The third space: interview with Homi Bhabha. In: Rutherford J (ed) Identity: community, culture, difference. Lawrence & Wishart, London, pp 207–221

Blainey G (1969) The rush that never ended. Melbourne University Press, Carlton

Bowman B (1991) A history of central Australia volume II: the Coniston story and tales of the north west sector. Swift Printing Services, Alice Springs

Bowman DMJS (1998) Tansley review no. 101. The impact of aboriginal landscape burning on the Australian biota. New Phytol 140:385–410

Bushland Link-up Project (2002) Draft action plan: threatened species Bushland link-up project. Taradale & District Walking and Landcare Group, Taradale

Castree N, Braun B (1998) The construction of nature and the nature of construction: analytical and political tools for building surviviable futures. In: Braun B, Castree N (eds) Remaking reality: nature at the millennium. Routledge, London

Chisholm J (1999) Destined for the desert: memoirs of 35 years in central Australia. NTU Press, Darwin

Clark ID (1995) Scars in the landscape: a register of massacre sites in western Victoria 1803–1859. Aboriginal Studies Press for the Australian Institute of Aboriginal and Torres Strait Islander Studies, Canberra

Clark ID, Cahir DA (2004) Tanderrum, 'freedom of the bush': the Djadjawurrung presence on the goldfields of central Victoria. Friends of the Mount Alexander Diggings, Castlemaine

CLC (Central Land Council) (1995) The land is always alive: the story of the Central Land Council. Central Land Council, Alice Springs

CLC (Central Land Council) (2013) What the Central Land Council does. http://www.clc.org.au/articles/info/what-the-central-land-council-does. Accessed 5 Nov 2013

CLC (Central Land Council) & NLC (Northern Land Council) (1995) Our land, our life: aboriginal land rights in Australia's northern territory. IAD Press, Alice Springs

CLMA (Centralian Land Management Association) (2013) The Centralian Land Management Association. http://www.clma.com.au/. Accessed 05 Nov 2013

Coppock RR (1993) Central Australian cattle station woman. Rose Rawlins Coppock, Alice Springs

CRC-REP (Cooperative Research Centre for Remote Economic Participation) (2013) About us http://crc-rep.com/about-us. Accessed 04 Sept 2013

Culvenor CC (1992) The boundaries of the Mount Franklin aboriginal reserve. Jim Crow Press, Daylesford

Demerritt D (2002) What is the 'social construction of nature'? A typology and sympathetic critique. Prog Hum Geogr 26(6):767–790

DEPI (Victorian Department of Environment and Primary Industries) (2013) Native vegetation information management. http://www.depi.vic.gov.au/environment-and-wildlife/biodiversity/native-vegetation/native-vegetation-information-management. 14 Jan 2014

DEST (Department of Education Science and Training) (2006) Cooperative research centres, Australian government. www.crc.gov.au. 17 July 2006
DKCRC (Desert Knowledge Cooperative Research Centre) (2006a) Desert Knowledge Cooperative Research Centre, Desert Knowledge Cooperative Research Centre. www.desertknowledge.com.au. 13 June 2006
DKCRC (Desert Knowledge Cooperative Research Centre) (2006d) CRC objectives, Desert Knowledge Cooperative Research Centre. www.desertknowledge.com.au. 21 Jul 2006
DNRE (Department of Natural Resources and Environment) (1997) Victoria's biodiversity: directions in management. Department of Natural Resources and Environment, Melbourne
DSE (Department of Sustainability and Environment) (2005a) Victoria's box-ironbark forests and woodlands, the Victorian State Government. www.dse.vic.gov.au. 26 May 2006
DSE (Department of Sustainability and Environment) (2005b) National parks (box-ironbark and other parks) bill, the Victorian State Government. www.dse.vic.gov.au. 26 May 2006
DSE (Department of Sustainability and Environment) (2006a) Flora and fauna guarantee act. The Victorian State Government, Melbourne
Dyck N (1985) Aboriginal peoples and nation-states: an introduction to the analytical issues. In: Dyck N (ed) Indigenous peoples and the nation-state: 'fourth world' politics in Canada, Australian and Norway. Institute of Social and Economic Research, Memorial University of Newfoundland, Newfoundland and Labrador, pp 1–25
ECC (Environment Conservation Council) (2001) Box-ironbark forests & woodlands investigation final report. Environment Conservation Council, Melbourne
Edwards GP, De Preu N, Shakeshaft BJ, Crealy VI, Paltridge RM (2001a) Home range and movements of male feral cats (Felis catus) in a semiarid woodland environment in central Australia. Austral Ecol 26:93–101
Edwards GP, Eldridge SR, Wurst D, Berman DM, Garbin V (2001b) Movement patterns of female feral camels in central and northern Australia. Wildl Res 28:283–296
Edwards GP, De Preu N, Crealy IV, Shakeshaft BJ (2002) Habitat selection by feral cats and dingoes in a semi-arid woodland environment in central Australia. Austral Ecol 27:26–31
Edwards GP, Allan GE, Brock C, Duguid A, Gabrys K, Vaarzon-Morel P (2008) Fire and its management in central Australia. Rangel J 30(1):109–121
Environment Australia (Australian Government Department of the Environment) (2013c) Indigenous protected areas. http://www.environment.gov.au/indigenous/ipa/. Accessed 14 Jan 2014
Fire D (2003) Desert knowledge CRC project proposal form & guidelines for initial round of projects: desert fire. Desert Knowledge CRC, Alice Springs
Flannery T (1994) The future eaters. Reed Books, Chatswood
Gardiner L (1962) Thomas Mitchell. Oxford University Press, Melbourne
Griffin GF, Price NF, Portlock HF (1983) Wildfires in central Australia 1970–1980. J Environ Manage 17:311–323
Griffiths T (1997) Introduction. In: Griffiths T, Robin L (eds) Ecology and empire: environmental history of settler societies. Melbourne University Press, Melbourne, pp 1–16
Hallam S (1975) Fire and hearth: a study of Aboriginal usage and European usurpation in South-western Australia. Australian Institute of Aboriginal Studies, Canberra
Hardy B (1976) Lament of the Barkindji. Rigby, Adelaide
Holmes J (2002) Diversity and change in Australia's rangelands: a post-productivist transition with a difference? Trans Inst Br Geogr 27:362–234
Holmes J (2011) Land tenures as policy instruments: transitions on Cape York Peninsula. Geogr Res 49(2):217–233
Hopkins A (1999) National land and water resources audit vegetation theme. Condition of vegetation: a discussion paper. Conservation and land management, Wanneroo
Horton DR (creator) (1996) Aboriginal Australia wall map. Aboriginal Studies Press/AIATSIS and Auslig/Sinclair, Knight, Merz, Canberra
Howitt W (1972, 1855) Land, labour and gold or two years in Victoria with visits to Sydney and Van Diemen's land. Lowden Publishing Company, Kilmore

Howitt R (2001a) Frontiers, borders, edges: liminal challenges to the hegemony of exclusion. Aust Geogr Stud 39(2):233–245

Howitt R (2001b) Rethinking resource management: sustainability, justice and indigenous peoples. Routledge, London

Jones R (1969) Fire-stick farming. Aust Nat Hist 16:224–228

Langton M (1998) Burning questions: emerging environmental issues for indigenous peoples in northern Australia. Centre of Indigenous Natural and Cultural Resource Management, Northern Territory University, Darwin

Latz P (1995) Bushfires & Bushtucker: aboriginal plant use in central Australia. IAD Press, Alice Springs

LCNT (Landcare Council of the Northern Territory, now Territory NRM) (2005) Integrated natural resource management plan for the northern territory. http://www.territorynrm.org.au/inrm-plan/2005–2010-plan. Accessed 14 Jan 2014

Leavesley A (2008) The response of birds to the fire regimes of central Australian mulga woodlands. http://www.nintione.com.au/resource/Adam-Leavesley-The-response-of-birds-to-the-fire-regimes-of-mulga-woodlands-in-central-Australia.pdf. Accessed 28 Oct 2013

Ledgar R, Stafford Smith M (1996) Dead centre or living heart? Habitat Aust 24(2):17–26

LRM (Northern Territory Department of Land Resource Management) (2013) About bushfires NT. http://www.lrm.nt.gov.au/bushfires/about#.Ungv61Pd5Bk. Accessed 5 Nov 2013

Maclean K (2009) Reconceptualising desert landscapes: unpacking historical narratives and contemporary realities for sustainable livelihood development in central Australia. GeoJournal 74(5):451–463

Marshall P (ed) (1989) Raparapa Kularr Martuwarra. All right, now we go 'side the river, along that sundown way. Stories from the Fitzroy River Drovers. Magabala Books, Broome

Morgan S (1987) My place. Fremantle Arts Press, Fremantle

Morton SR Mulvaney DJ (eds) (1996) Exploring central Australia: society, the environment and the 1894 horn expedition. Surrey Beatty & Sons PTY Limited, Baulkham Hills, NSW

Nano C (2006) Ecology of mulga-spinifex mosaics in central Australia. University of New England, Armidale. Unpublished Doctor of Philosophy thesis

NCCMA (North Central Catchment Management Authority) (2006) Map of north central Victoria catchment management region. North Central Catchment Management Authority, Huntly

NRETA (Natural Resources Environment and the Arts) (2005) Northern territory parks and conservation masterplan, northern territory Department of Planning and Infrastructure. www.nt.gov.au/. 26 May 2006

Office of Legislative Drafting (2000) Environment protection and biodiversity conservation regulations. Attorney-General's Department, Canberra

Oliver I, Smith PL, Lunt I, Parkes D (2002) Pre-1750 vegetation, naturalness and vegetation condition: what are the implications for biodiversity conservation? Ecol Manage Restor 3(3):176–178

P&WC (Northern Territory government Parks and Wildlife Commission) (2013a) Welcome to the Parks and Wildlife Commission of the northern territory. http://www.parksandwildlife.nt.gov.au/. Accessed 5 Nov 2013

P&WC (Northern Territory government Parks and Wildlife Commission) (2013b) Joint management. http://www.parksandwildlife.nt.gov.au/manage/joint#.UtRsr_vd5Bk. Accessed 14 Jan 2014

Paltridge R (1998) Occurrence of the marsupial mole (*Notoryctes typhlops*) remains in the faecal pellets of cats, foxes and dingoes in the Tanami desert, NT. Aust Mammal 20:427–429

Paltridge R (2002) The diets of cats, foxes and dingoes in relation to prey availability in the Tanami desert, northern territory. Wildl Res 29:389–403

Paltridge R, Southgate R (2001) The effect of habitat type and seasonal conditions on fauna in two areas of the Tanami desert. Wildl Res 28:247–260

Parkes D, Newell G, Cheal D (2003) Assessing the quality of native vegetation: the 'habitat hectares' approach. Ecol Manage Restor 4(Supplement):S29–S38

Powell JM (1976) Environmental management in Australia 1788–1914. Oxford University Press, Melbourne
Project Application Round 4 (2001) Protection and enhancement of threatened species habitat in the Goldfields Bioregion. Threatened Species Network, Melbourne
Project Application Round 5 (2002) Protection and enhancement of threatened species habitat in the Goldfields Bioregion. Threatened Species Network, Melbourne
Project Application Round 6 (2003a) Protection and enhancement of Eltham copper butterfly habitat in the Muckleford zone. Threatened Species Network, Melbourne
Project Application Round 6 (2003b) Locating and protecting threatened species on local roadsides. Threatened Species Network, Melbourne
Purvis B (2004) Practical biodiversity. In: Purvis B (ed) Australian rangeland society 13th biennial conference: living in the Outback Alice Springs
Reynolds H (1982) The other side of the frontier. Penguin Books, Ringwood
Reynolds H (1992) The law of the land. Penguin Books Australia, Ringwood
Reynolds H (1999) Why weren't we told? A personal search for the truth about our history. Viking, Ringwood
Rose L (1969) Lionel Rose: Australian, the life story of a champion. As told to Rod Humphries. Angus and Robertson, Sydney
Sands DPA, New TR (2002) The action plan for Australian butterflies. Environment Australia, Canberra
Saxon EC (ed) (1984) Anticipating the inevitable: a patch-burn strategy for fire management at Uluru (Ayers Rock-Mt Olga) National Park. CSIRO, Melbourne
Serle G (1963) The golden age: a history of the colony of Victoria 1851–1861. Melbourne University Press, Carlton
Shaw B (1981) My country the Pelican dreaming: the life of an Australian Aborigine of the Gadjerong, Grant Ngabidj, c. 1904–1977. Australian Institute of Aboriginal Studies, Canberra
Shaw B (1983) Banggaiyerri: the story of Jack Sullivan as told to Bruce Shaw. Australian Institute of Aboriginal Studies, Canberra
Slattery D (2003a) Cultural perspectives on the box-ironbark country. Change in a threatened landscape. Department of Natural Resources and Environment, Melbourne
Slattery D (2003b) Australians and 'the bush': a changing identity from gold rush to nature conservation? In: Pedersen K, Viken A (eds) Nature and identity: essays on the culture of nature. Norwegian Academic Press, Norway, pp 247–264
Stanner WEH (1960) Durmugam: a Nangiomeri. In: Casagrande J (ed) In the company of men. Harper, New York
Stanner WEH (1968) After the dreaming: black and white Australians, an anthropologist's view. The Australian Broadcasting Commission, Sydney
Vaarzon-Morel P (ed) (1995) Warlpiri karnta karnta-kurlangu yimi. Warlpiri women's voices. Our lives our history. IAD Press, Alice Springs
Verran H (2002) A postcolonial moment in science studies: alternative firing regimes of environmental scientists and aboriginal landowners. Soc Stud Sci 32(5–6):729–762
WWF (Worldwide Fund for Nature – Australia) (2006) Threatened species network http://www.wwf.org.au/news_resources/archives/threatened_species_network/. Accessed 5 Nov 2013
Young E (1995) Third world in the first: development and indigenous peoples. Routledge, London

Part III
Local Voices in the Landscape

Chapter 6
Spaces of Environmental Governance

Abstract The aim of this chapter is to show how the first question of this research enables an exploration of the tensions that exist at the nexus between environmental governance and environmental management. This chapter (and the next) asks, how do knowledges of best practice environmental management move across and between international, national and local scales of environmental governance and community-based environmental management? The literature reviewed for this research, the applied peoples' geography and the edge politics practised in this research suggest that knowledges of best practice environmental management move through local spaces of environmental governance and environmental management. This analysis uses the conceptual framework for cultural hybridity to demonstrate that a sophisticated awareness of how these individuals perceive environmental governance is integral to equitable and sustained environmental governance and management. This is because as the conceptual framework for cultural hybridity illuminates, environmental governance consists of place-based, relational, networked and entangled local spaces of environmental management. Environmental governance is connected to place.

6.1 Environmental Governance Is Connected to Place

As elucidated in Chap. 5, the projects in this study are located in specific geographic places that have multiple political histories of place and nation. The projects have evolved from these geographic places according to the identified issues of threatened species habitat destruction in Victoria and the increased incidence of large-scale fires in the Northern Territory. The projects have been developed by local personalities and are defined by local politics. Project success (as discussed in Chaps. 8 and 9) is contingent on but not confined by local knowledge of these specific geographic places. This local knowledge is tied to place.

The geographic places where the projects are situated are also the point of intersection of knowledge networks. These knowledge networks are composed of people, of environmental governance policy and of environmental management practice including on-ground project work. As such these place-based spaces of environmental governance are the product of knowledge networks (after Massey

K. Maclean, *Cultural Hybridity and the Environment*,
DOI 10.1007/978-981-287-323-1_6

1991a, b, 1993). These networks connect the local to the extra-locale. As Escobar (2001:143) articulates "we are all indissolubly linked to both local and extra-local places." It follows that place-based spaces of environmental governance are "very much produced by complex relations of culture and power that go well beyond local bounds" (Escobar 2001:146). For example, the two case study projects gained Federal and State or Territory Government funding because the management of threatened species habitat and the incidence of fire have national implications. These complex relations are clearly exemplified by the wider networks of the two projects. The Victorian project has its genesis in a program embedded within and created by networks. A woman who was instrumental in the development of the Threatened Species Network articulates that

> [the Threatened Species Network is] designed to take a state based approach... its very make up is looking at a regional approach but within the context of a nation because all of the work that the network does is boiled down from the National Strategy for Biodiversity and the Environmental Protection and Biodiversity Conservation Act... it operates at a local scale... but within the context of a national scale and in many cases with the species [for example migratory birds] on a global scale

The Northern Territory project was embedded within the networks of the Desert Knowledge Cooperative Research Centre (DKCRC). A manager of DKCRC describes it as

> a research network. Primarily its work is aimed at generating new knowledge, new ways of doing things, new ways of thinking about things, through various types of research... it is about rubbing shoulders between research and every day aspects of society. That's where we try to leave a lasting knowledge: in the development of a greater understanding of how to manage the self

The answer to the first question of this research (How do knowledges of best practice environmental management move across and between international, national and local scales of environmental governance and community-based environmental management?) supports the first foundation of the conceptual framework: environmental governance is place-based and, therefore, locally situated and connected to other locales by networks. The two project case studies provide the means to unpack these complexities and investigate what constitutes environmental governance. In particular, following the conceptual framework for cultural hybridity, they provide the means to consider how environmental governance appears from these place-based locations (hereafter referred to as local spaces).

6.2 The Relational Characteristics of Environmental Governance

Project members from the government and local community arenas in Victoria and the Northern Territory speak of their work as having local, regional, national and global environmental governance ramifications. The following discussion elucidates how the findings of this research show that local environmental management decisions and actions cross multiple environmental governance scales. These findings support the arguments made in Chap. 3 (Sect 3.3) for an understanding of environmental governance scale as relational.

The first analysis of this chapter shows that project members from the government arena of the two case study projects perceive their work as crossing multiple environmental governance scales. Individuals choose to work in government and non-government organisations for diverse reasons. They do so to conduct scientific research for the purposes of sustainable land management, to explore notions of community development and social justice and to develop strategic landscape management approaches. This work extends over different environmental governance scales. It may encompass the national scale, for example, the work of the Federal Government's national, regional or local natural resource management facilitators. It may encompass specific jurisdictional scales, for example, the work of the ten Threatened Species Network coordinators based in each state and territory of Australia. It may span specific biogeographic scales determined by the Interim Biogeographic Regionalisation for Australia (IBRA) (discussed in Chap. 4, Sect. 4.1) to facilitate regional environmental governance across Australia such as the work of the many integrated catchment managers of the Victorian Catchment Management Authorities. It may extend over statewide governance scale as, for instance, the work of local project officers of specific Victorian Catchment Management Authorities. Or it may span a specific geographic scale as determined by any environmental management and community development project, for example, the Desert Fire project of the DKCRC.

Project members from the Victorian project speak of their work as having global ramifications. The project officer points out that one aspect of her role concerns raising community awareness of the fact that local actions have global impacts. She explains that *the personal is political… you can have an impact and this is what it is all about.* Scientists and land managers from the regional division of the Victorian Government's Department of Sustainability and Environment speak about their local threatened species work in the global context. One man explains that *the Eltham Copper Butterfly only exists in Victoria [...at] an international level it is the only population in the world [...accordingly] we have a responsibility to ensure that the habitat is protected for the species' ongoing survival.* These words bring attention to the connection between environmental governance decisions and environmental management actions. The local decisions made about best practice management of threatened species habitat in Victoria have regional, national and global ramifications. This is further highlighted by the Desert Fire project in the Northern Territory.

One aspect of the Desert Fire project is its role as a scoping case study to determine what it means to manage fire across different land tenures in the arid region of Australia. This scoping case study will inform national environmental governance because it evolved from national discussions about natural resource management in the arid zone. The project leader explains that

> fire kept on coming up as a key issue [at facilitated natural resource management meetings] so that brought together a group of… people across Australia who were interested in fire in the arid area.

In a similar way, the project will also inform international natural resource management because as the project leader articulates *fire issues are global issues and fire in desert landscapes is a global issue*. These words highlight the fact that regional, national and global environmental governance occurs at the local scale and is about place-based environmental management actions.

The importance of place-based environmental management actions and place-based ecological research actions for national and global environmental governance is further highlighted by the following words of Desert Fire project members. A land manager from the Central Land Council speaks of the local, regional, national and global significance of Aboriginal land management work. He explains that

> the Indigenous Protected Area program, which is like the brand for Aboriginal land management, […has] got national recognition […and] international recognition. [The Aboriginal land managers] are not just regarded as black hippies any more: people are actually doing something.

A researcher from the Northern Territory Parks and Wildlife Service speaks of the importance of place-based ecological research actions to inform environmental governance policy. He explains that

> the [Federal] Government puts up a lot of money for… big strategies… but there is not enough money going into the research and management that could be increasing our knowledge and implementing knowledge to make a difference.

In summary, project members from the government arena in Victoria and the Northern Territory speak of their environmental management work as having local, regional, national and global environmental governance ramifications. This is because decisions made about best practice threatened species habitat management in Victoria and fire management in the Northern Territory inform environmental management actions. These actions influence the longevity of threatened species and the spread of large-scale wildfires for the whole of Australia and the world. As such these decisions constitute environmental governance. In essence, the multiple scales of environmental governance are performed through the enactment of place-based environmental management action as exemplified by the on-ground work of the two project case studies.

The following analysis clarifies how project members from the local community arena in Victoria and the Northern Territory perceive their environmental management work in light of environmental governance scale. Project members from the local community arena involve themselves in project work for various reasons. In Victoria project members engage with the Threatened Species project for the purposes of documenting the locations of threatened species, such as the work of the Field Naturalists Clubs. They engage in this work to develop land management networks across the landscape as individuals involved with landcare groups do. Other people such as those involved with environmental lobby groups are motivated to work with the Threatened Species project as a means of holding the government accountable to environmental legislation. A further group of individuals, such as those involved with Friends Groups, work with the project in order to protect and conserve specific areas of threatened species habitat. The following discussion reflects the views of their government counterparts because individuals from the local community arena in Victoria believe their work has local, regional, national and global ramifications.

Project members perceive the on-ground project work as constituting *something of global significance*. This is because although working with threatened species is a local priority, species extinction has global ramifications. For this reason local environmental management work must not be undervalued. A local farmer states that *if lots of people do tiny little bits, it all happens*. Another project member believes that the local is political. His attitude reflects the words of the project officer who advocates that the personal is political. This project member explains that global outcomes result from place-based actions because

> changes of industrial technology on a national basis to effect greenhouse outcomes actually depend upon making decisions and taking actions to change those. That involves corporate, national arrangements and funding and policy decisions, but it has to come down to practical physical actions.

Another project member maintains that the power of local action can be likened to *a network, if everyone is doing something, it will improve it regionally and eventually it will improve it globally*. The words of an active landcare member reveal that the power of local action is also about informing and inspiring people working in other locales. She elucidates that

> [local successes] can inspire people at different levels: nationally, regionally even globally. Stories do come out, you are always reading wonderful stories of people in India or Bangladesh they take on some sort of local issue [...and] they produce something that is outstanding, so you have that link coming through, it can be a strong link from the local to the global.

In the Northern Territory, project members from the local community arena may choose to engage with the Desert Fire project for diverse reasons. Project members from the conservation community may be involved for the purposes of researching the effects of fire on local ecosystems to improve the management of conservation reserves such as Newhaven. Project members from the pastoral community may be involved because they wish to protect pastoral infrastructure from fire. Project members from the Aboriginal community may be involved as a means of 'caring for country' under traditional law and as a means of developing employment opportunities for their young people.

The words of these project members further expose local perceptions of what constitutes environmental governance. All project members speak of their environmental management work as connected to place. Some speak of this place-based work as having wider environmental governance ramifications. Interesting to note is that the places identified by land managers in the southern Tanami as their local area are likely to be described by land managers in north central Victoria as regional or even state. These perceptions about what constitutes environmental governance scale reinforce the complex notions of environmental governance scale as a social construct. They give life to the arguments put forward in Chap. 3 (Sect. 3.3) explored relating to how notions of environmental governance scale as a fixed hierarchy have worked to undervalue and marginalise local environmental management work.

All project members from the pastoral community speak of being locally situated in their part of the southern Tanami, but they have different views about the ramifications of their place-based environmental management actions. For example, one man speaks of his work as dictated by weather conditions in his part of the southern Tanami. His words highlight the variability of climate across central Australia where each pastoral station may experience different weather conditions. He explains that his station has not suffered from drought like other pastoral lands and this brought home to him the fact that his pastoral station *is the centre of the world as far as we are concerned.* In comparison, other pastoralists perceive their work as crossing multiple scales. Firstly, one pastoralist speaks of his role as an advisor to pastoral boards, committees and lobby groups across central Australia. Secondly, another pastoralist perceives his work as having national ramifications and being part of the *big picture of actually catering not only for yourself but also other families.*

The work of individuals from the conservation community in the southern Tanami is also connected to place. One researcher explains that the mess and noise of the southern Tanami (as discussed in Chap. 5 Sect. 5.4) dictates that the skills of observation necessary to understand plant ecology can only be developed in situ. This locally derived and place-based knowledge informs environmental governance policies for the region and is often financed by national environmental governance programs. For example, the work of a local ecologist[1] is considered important to environmental management of the southern Tanami region. This work is often funded by Federal Government programs. Some of this work also feeds into decisions made about best practice environmental management of the Newhaven reserve. Although at the time of the research Newhaven had a committee of managers located across Australia, it was the locally based manager at Newhaven who ultimately made decisions about on-ground management actions.

As a manager of Birds Australia who is based in Melbourne explains,

> there is a bit of trying to manage Newhaven from Melbourne which is quite a challenge… the committee is spread all over Australia, with teleconferencing and email we seem to have done pretty well but we couldn't possibly do it… without a person on the ground.

For the Aboriginal community, caring for country under traditional law is also determined by place. Traditional ownership determines who can speak for the country and conduct management activities on the country. Ownership is locally situated and culturally defined. One Aboriginal woman reflects upon the connection between place, traditional ownership and the use of fire for land management: *we only burn our own country… we can't burn on other's country.* Knowledge of country is also locally situated. However, this does not limit the reach of this knowledge and expe-

---

[1] Her work considers the responsibility of predators including cats, foxes and dingoes, for the decline of medium-sized mammals in the region (see Paltridge 2002).

rience: locally situated knowledge is shared with others through networks. For example, many Indigenous land managers from all over Australia came together to speak of their local experiences at the Indigenous Land Management Conference held just outside of Alice Springs in 2005. At this conference land managers were able to learn from other people's local experiences and locally situated work. This example reinforces a comment made by a Victorian project member: local work and local stories can inspire people from across Australia. The work and lives of these land managers are tied to place for the reasons previously mentioned. But these local lives can have bearing on other place-based land management approaches. In the same way that place-based ecological research and pastoral experience informs environmental governance approaches, the experiences of place-based Aboriginal land managers should also inform governance approaches by acknowledging that environmental governance is closely connected to environmental management work that is inherently connected to place.

In summary, a significant number of project members interviewed from the government and local community arenas of both projects locate their work across multiple scales of environmental governance. They describe their work as having local, regional, national and global environmental governance and management ramifications. There are three ramifications of this. Firstly, environmental management work that protects species habitat in north central Victoria protects species that are found nowhere else in the world, and managing fire on specific pastoral, Aboriginal or conservation lands amounts to the management of fire over vast tracts of the central Australian landscape. Secondly, decisions that inform best practice environmental management actions in these places amount to environmental governance. Thirdly, these decisions and knowledge generated from resulting management actions can inspire and inform environmental governance and resulting management actions in other locales. This final ramification connects strongly with notions of ecological uncertainty discussed in Chap. 5 (Sect. 5.4).

The findings of this research provide evidence for the first assertion of the framework for cultural hybridity: the conception of environmental governance scale as relational rather than as hierarchical. Firstly, environmental governance scale is relational because successful governance of the biophysical environment is entwined with knowledge of place. Secondly, the notion of governance scale is a social construct that is understood by individuals according to perceptions of their own place within the physical landscape and their own role within environmental governance policy structures. These findings provide the platform from which to consider how knowledges of best practice environmental management move from locale to locale.

6.3 The Networked Characteristics of Environmental Governance

Common to both the Victorian and Northern Territory projects is the importance of knowledge networks for successful environmental governance and management. In Victoria a significant number of project members locate the work of others within wider networks that cross environmental governance scales. In the Northern Territory, where project members perceive themselves as working in networks that cross environmental governance scales, the potential and possibilities for local environmental management expand. Indeed, most individuals who are not working in networks wish to be. The following discussion clarifies how the findings of this research show that local spaces of environmental governance are linked to the extra-locale by knowledge networks.

The Victorian project involves local community working with individuals from different government agencies in the region to protect and conserve threatened species habitat on specific areas of public and private lands. Project members from the government arena speak of the importance of networks for environmental governance. The bioregional manager explains that the Threatened Species project facilitates network connections that link people who operate at different scales of environmental governance. The longevity and success of this project depends upon the role of project structure to *leverage a lot of good connections [...enabling the project to] develop into something more long term or larger*. The local landcare coordinator speaks of his role to facilitate networks between community groups and government based upon two-way knowledge exchange. He highlights that effective and sustained environmental governance is improved by networks and partnerships between people who work in different jurisdictions and who have diverse areas of expertise. He is particularly enthusiastic about the *unpredictable synergies* that can occur as a result of these networks, generating creative solutions to cross-jurisdiction challenges.

Project members from the local community arena in Victoria locate their work within a network of bigger picture environmental governance. As one landcare member articulates *[...the governance approach] has to be total picture stuff for it to be really effective*. She believes that the development of community-government networks is essential for local environmental governance because these *give a focus for all the interest groups and government departments to work together to achieve something in the community*. These networks are based upon two-way knowledge exchange. In essence, project members who work in the government arena are described by those from the local community arena as pathfinders for ongoing community environmental management work. For example, project members from the local community arena describe their government counterparts as facilitators. They facilitate the development of local networks, inform the community of funding opportunities and update them on relevant changes to environmental governance policy. As a project member from the local community arena who is also employed by the Department of Sustainability and Environment explains, this is an important role because *sometimes community groups can be too green and it gets too political for them*. As such, project members from the government arena have an important role to assist local community groups to *keep an eye on the bigger picture*. Project members from the local community arena have the important role to provide information to project members from the government arena. This two-way knowledge exchange is essential because, as this active landcare member explains, *[government representatives] have to be able to work through people at local levels because if you can't have that, it is never going to happen*.

The success of the Desert Fire project in the Northern Territory also depends upon the success of knowledge exchange between project members from the government arena and project members who live and work in the southern Tanami region. The project is fundamentally about cross-agency collaboration between project members from the government arena with project members from the local community arena to foster strategic approaches to fire management in the region. Project members from the government arena recognise that engagement of individuals living and working in the southern Tanami is fundamental to the management of fire in the region. This engagement complements the knowledge brokering role that some individuals perceive they have. For example, a project member from the Northern Territory Parks and Wildlife Service describes his role as linking scientific research work with Federal and Territory environmental governance policy. He explains that *sometimes my role is straddling that academic science and the land management government bureaucracy of looking after park estate*. Another project member who works for the Central Land Council explains his role as about two-way knowledge exchange for environmental governance in the region. He states that individuals such as himself work as

> gatekeepers to help [Aboriginal] people that don't have ready access [to environmental governance structures and related] western and scientific information, but we are also gate keeping when [Aboriginal] people put across their ideas to people who are the government and other agencies.

The coordinator of the Centralian Land Management Association describes her work with pastoralists in similar terms. She explains that a *lot of pastoralists say [to me] 'you are here to de-bofinise this stuff'…we get information and help people to decipher it*. For project members from the local community arena who live and work in the southern Tanami, successful local land management is contingent upon knowledge networks. Some individuals regard the success of their work as partly due to their involvement with government. For example, some pastoralists advise individuals from the government arena on their land management approaches and needs. One pastoralist speaks of how he shares localised information with government agencies. He explains that he has given *so much information to so many different people that we sometimes forget who we gave information to*.

This pastoralist explains that he works closely with government because he has not

> got the resources to do the mapping, to set up paddock areas, to monitor phosphorus soil levels [indeed] most of the things we have done on the place have been done through the government agencies.

Other pastoral managers speak of a lack of such networks. Two individuals speak of their powerless relationship with the government. One man gets exasperated by what he perceives as the top-down approach of government. He feels that the government *are telling us what to do: we are living it and we are breathing it!* Another pastoralist suggests that changes in government approaches have resulted in bad relationships. He explains how he declined a telephone survey with a government representative by saying:

> I haven't seen anyone from [the department] I haven't talked to anyone there so… in the old days when they were stocking us, they used to teach you, like they taught you how to spray and that sort of stuff but they aren't doing that anymore.

This lack of networking is regarded by a researcher from the conservation community as the main issue that confounds the successful management of fire in the region. He explains that the development of networks between the specific interest groups is essential for fire management in the region. This is because

> we know what to do, the problem is getting everyone concerned happy with how we go about doing what we know we need to do […we need to] get everyone together and work out the politics, the social aspects of [fire management].

Other project members from the conservation community believe that these networks are essential for the successful management of biodiversity in the region. A manager from Birds Australia who is based in Melbourne explains how they value the networks they can develop with individuals from the Northern Territory government and in particular with the traditional owners of Newhaven.

Individuals from the Aboriginal community also speak of the importance of networks between individuals working for government and pastoralists to the strategic management of fire in the region. One Aboriginal man explains that *if we can get all together to talk about it, we can get some plan together.* He also points out that although government agencies have wanted to work with traditional owners and Aboriginal communities in the past, it has never come to fruition. He believes the breakdown of these potential networks can be traced back to the additional challenges of finding funding for fire management work on Aboriginal land. He explains that *whenever [the government agency] come near to doing [fire management training, they] have a problem with money.*

In summary, a significant number of individuals interviewed for this research locate the work of individuals from the government and the local community arenas as forming part of their local network. The perceived success of both projects is based upon networks for three reasons. Firstly, networks facilitate two-way knowledge exchange between the government arena and the local community arena. Secondly, networks facilitate the exchange of resources, for example, government funding and expertise to members of the local community arena. Thirdly, networks facilitate the development of relationships between project members that are the basis of successful environmental management.

The findings of this research provide evidence for the first assertion of the framework for cultural hybridity: the conception of environmental governance scale as networked rather than as a hierarchy. The success of the two projects is dependent upon these knowledge networks. These networks exemplify how knowledge of best practice environmental management moves from one locale to another. These relationships highlight the value placed upon local knowledge within these networks, either through choice or necessity. They also exemplify how perceiving environmental governance scale as hierarchical can severely limit the potential of place-based environmental management.

6.4 The Entangled Characteristics of Environmental Governance

Project members from Victoria and the Northern Territory speak with varying authority about the environmental governance policies related to their environmental management work. The following discussion reveals how all project members perceive environmental governance policy as only as relevant as it is locally appropriate and informed. The findings of this research show that the power and capacity of environmental governance policies to inform and direct local-scale environmental management are entangled with the power and capacity of local environmental governance and management practices.

Individuals from the government arena in Victoria locate their work as influenced by national governance policies and strategies more so than international governance conventions and agendas. The bioregional manager acknowledges that international conventions, national strategies and regional policies share common aims, goals and language, but he believes that the regional environmental governance policy interface as exemplified by the Regional Catchment Strategy (discussed in Chap. 4, Sect. 4.2) is of most importance for his work. This is because he feels that it is at this interface that the local community can inform policy. He enthuses that

> to get really good [environmental governance] outcomes you need to involve the community, provide them with information, help them to interpret that information and acknowledge … the diversity of opinions and aspirations that exist.

He explains that this interaction is essential because *enacting [environmental governance] on the ground has to happen at [the local community] scale*. Taking this argument further, a regional employee of the Victorian Government Department of Sustainability and Environment speaks of the importance of local action and ownership of governance policy. He feels the Regional Catchment Strategy is evidence of the importance of local action and ownership. He describes it as *very appropriate for this region, and it's our document so we are very happy with [it]*.[2]

Considering that no project members from the government arena in Victoria identify the international *Convention on Biological Diversity, 1992*, as an influence on their work, it may not come as a surprise that most project members from the local community arena in Victoria have not heard of the Convention, although many have heard of the Rio Earth Summit. Indeed, many of them are not familiar with the corresponding *National Strategy for Ecologically Sustainable Development, 1992*, and the *National Strategy for the Conservation of Australia's Biological Diversity, 1992*. More had heard of the *Environment Protection and Biodiversity Conservation Act*, 1999; the *Flora and Fauna Guarantee Act, 1988*; and the related *Victorian*

---

[2]There are also criticisms of the community consultation process for the Regional Catchment Strategy. For example, the project officer explains that the original draft did not include *the people in the picture*.

Biodiversity Strategy, 1997. The words of this active landcare member reflect the way most project members from the local community arena feel about these environmental governance policies: *[the policy documents would] look fantastic in a library somewhere*. A member of a local 'Friends of Group' explains that: *I would be paralysed [if I tried to keep up with it all] if there was one document to read I would read it*. Project members who have a good knowledge of these policy documents do so because they perceive that an aspect of their environmental management role is to hold the government accountable to these documents because *they are often breached* and *they are not policed enough*.

As a reflection of the bioregional manager's words reported above, most project members from the local community arena have heard of the *Regional Catchment Strategy, 2003*. Some had been involved in its development. One project member regards this document as instrumental to land management in the region. She explains that although *it seems like a lot of paper work at the end of the day it does make a lot of sense*. One local farmer and president of his landcare group believes it is essential to be familiar with this document because *you've got to read these things if you want to argue with [government representatives] about things*. Another project member reflects that this document is valueless if there is *no government commitment to staff their departments and make sure that it is put into play. Do they have the people on the ground to make sure that that stuff works?*

Project members from the local community arena are aware of environmental governance policies; however, they regard individual personalities and localised networks as more important to their work. This is demonstrated by the fact that some people perceive the Threatened Species project as a vehicle through which to further develop local networks to deliver on-ground project outcomes. The secretary of a local landcare group explains that the Threatened Species project work is neither about regional strategies nor Federal Government policies; rather it is about people. She articulates that

> even though we've had this great presentation with the plan that was drawn up by [the Threatened Species project officer] we have to get commitment and if you don't have that kind of commitment and energy that will basically take people along with you, then it won't happen, and that's the same thing on the larger scale.

In the Northern Territory, the DKCRC developed from the need for research into sustainable desert livelihoods. This local vision was supported by the Federal Government. A leader of the Desert Fire project explains that

> over the past few years [the Federal Government] has identified issues of the draining of rural Australia, people moving to the big cities or the coast [...and] so I guess the Federal Government has been actively trying to address that issue.

The DKCRC can be regarded as working to fulfil certain aspects of the Federal Government's responsibility to international conventions and agendas. At the same time it is trying to deliver sustainable livelihoods, benefit sharing and protection of intellectual property, especially in relation to traditional ecological knowledge and biodiversity conservation. A manager of the DKCRC explains that this bottom line will assist in facilitating *the involvement of Indigenous people in land management.*[3]

In essence the Desert Fire project exemplifies the interface where international and national environmental governance policy intersects with local livelihoods. In fact project success depends upon listening to, engaging with and developing networks with individuals living in the southern Tanami. This project must work hard to overcome institutionalised bias that has neglected the Aboriginal point of view. As this individual who works closely with Aboriginal people explains,

> historically Parks and Wildlife and certainly Bushfires Council have written down or have expressed ideas about fire management that has been pretty much exclusively western and from a particularly pastoral point of view, parks and wildlife, certainly the Aboriginal world view has been left out of it or [has been] a token add on.

The various perspectives and attitudes of individuals living in the southern Tanami further exemplify the interface between environmental governance policy and the lived local realities of land managers. Project members from the pastoral community speak of the Northern Territory *Pastoral Land Act, 1992*, as influencing their work and lives. One pastoralist explains how members of the pastoral board police this Act:

> if [they] come out and see that the country is deteriorating year by year then they will step in and advise you or reprimand you… if you don't take notice of their recommendations then they will look seriously at the lease.

Another pastoralist believes that personal relationships with members of the pastoral board are more important to the policing of this Act than the Act itself. He believes that lease renewal depends on *how well, I s'pose you get along with the person… whether he understands the situation or whether he is straight from university and hasn't got a clue.* Other Acts highlighted by pastoralists as impacting upon their livelihoods include the recently reviewed Northern Territory *Bushfires Act, 2004*. Some pastoralists were directly involved with the review. The words of the following pastoralist reflect those of an environmental lobbyist in Victoria previously mentioned who explains that environmental governance policies are only as good as the government's commitment to adequately resource them. This pastoralist explains that the *Bushfires Act, 2004*, is only as good as the local scale policing of it:

> I was one of the people who pushed very hard for the new fire fines in the Territory and all that, but that's only as good as the courts and catching the people doing it and I think that we are extremely weak in that.

---

[3] Ironically because of the innovative focus upon creating networks between disciplines for better and more sustainable desert livelihoods and because the DKCRC is outside the box of the typical Cooperative Research Centre (CRC) industry mould, it may be a one-off experiment, with the Federal Government reverting to more traditional science research structures. As an active Desert Fire project member states, *[in] the next round of CRCs that have just gone through… similar socially oriented CRCs didn't get up.*

The *Aboriginal Land Rights Act, 1976*, and *Native Title Act, 1993*, are also cited by pastoralists as influential to their livelihoods. They speak of excised living areas and land claims as influencing their lives and the management of pastoral property. They also speak about how these Acts, in conjunction with the *Pastoral Land Act, 1992*, allow traditional Aboriginal practices such as the use of fire on pastoral lands.

Individuals from the conservation community are influenced by various Federal and Territory policies. A manager of Birds Australia based in Melbourne speaks in similar terms as the bioregional manager in Victoria about the relevance of environmental governance policies. He explains that they know about the international Convention on Biological Diversity, 1992, but it *is a long way from Newhaven*. He states that the management plan for Newhaven *implicitly integrates those pieces of legislation [Northern Territory's Pastoral Land Act, 1992; and Mining Act, 1980] but not in an obvious way.*

Individuals from the Aboriginal community in the southern Tanami are influenced by various Federal and Territory environmental governance policy, but, as previously mentioned, professionals from the Central Land Council often work as gatekeepers for Indigenous communities to assist them to navigate these environmental governance policies. Some Aboriginal people have been involved in the integrated natural resource management planning process (described in Chap. 4, Sect. 4.1). However, national and international strategies are too far removed from life in the southern Tanami to receive much direct attention by Aboriginal land managers. This is not to say that if they were familiar with them, they would not be interested in them. Attitudes to the *Bushfires Act, 2004*, exemplify the relevance, cultural appropriateness and practicalities of such governance policies. An Aboriginal woman, who was not familiar with the *Bushfires Act, 2004*, before our interview, speaks about the important role of gatekeepers from the Central Land Council. She explains that *some people would have [heard of the Bushfires Act, 2004] some wouldn't have. Depends if land council has been telling people about it or not*. She also points out how this Act is probably inappropriate to the lifestyles and relationship to country of Aboriginal people living in the southern Tanami. She describes how difficult it would be for Aboriginal land managers to get a permit from the Bushfires Council each time they wished to burn their country. If she were to ring the Bushfires Council to get a permit, the conversation would be as follows:

> She would say: *oh yes, send it out to us*
> to which individuals working with the Northern Territory Bushfires Council would respond:
> *ok, where are you now?*

She explains this in the context of a very large expanse of country with few phones, even fewer faxes to facilitate the permit process and high mobility of people travelling through.

In summary, it is clear that many local community arena project members from Victoria and the Northern Territory are not familiar with formal environmental governance policies. Where they are, there is a very strong consensus from individuals in both the government arena and the local community arena that these environmental governance policies are only as important as they are locally appropriate and informed. Project members from the government arena in Victoria speak about the importance of local ownership of policy documents to satisfy local environmental management aspirations and approaches. Project members from the government arena in the Northern Territory recognise that project success depends upon developing successful networks with interest groups living and working in the southern Tanami.

The findings from this research show that local spaces of environmental governance are entangled. As described in Chap. 4, the two project case studies are embedded within specific environmental governance policy landscapes. Both projects are funded by programs of this environmental governance policy landscape, and so without this funding, the projects would not exist in their current form or would cease to exist. However, environmental governance policies and programs are dependent upon the networks of individuals working to manage their local environment. Both the Threatened Species project and the Desert Fire project evolved as a result of individuals from the government arena navigating these policies and programs. For example, project members from the government arena in Victoria worked to create opportunities within this landscape, which resulted in the innovative whole of landscape Threatened Species project approach. Similarly the DKCRC evolved out of a group of individuals who pushed the boundaries of these policy landscapes, to fund locally situated and appropriate environmental management practices.

6.5 Conclusion

This chapter showed how the first question of this research enables an exploration of the tensions that exist at the nexus between environmental governance and environmental management. This chapter asked, how do knowledges of best practice environmental management move across and between international, national and local scales of environmental governance and community-based environmental management? The two empirical case studies provided a way to investigate how individuals working with the Victorian and Northern Territory local environmental management and community development projects perceive environmental governance. The findings of this chapter demonstrate a complex and entangled conception of environmental governance that suggests environmental governance scale is a relational social construct rather than an asocial hierarchy. Firstly, the findings show that environmental governance is place based. Secondly, they demonstrate that environmental governance consists of locally situated environmental management actions that have ramifications for regional, national and global environments. Knowledge generated from these actions has implications for regional, national and global environmental governance and management approaches. Thirdly, the success of locally situated environmental management depends upon two-way knowledge exchange that occurs through networks rather than hierarchical governance scale. These networks link locally situated environmental management places to extra-local environmental management places. These places constitute the intersection of diverse and various knowledge networks, the two case study projects exemplifying such places. Fourthly, these knowledge networks shed light on the entangled intersection between place-based environmental management and big picture environmental governance policy. In essence, the environmental management and community development projects in Victoria and the Northern Territory exemplify the point of intersection between environmental governance policy and the lived local realities of place-based environmental management. The entangled connection between the rhetoric of environmental governance policy with the lived local realities of individuals working in environmental management and community development projects highlights the fact that it is sometimes difficult to conceive where environmental governance ends and environmental management begins.

References

Escobar A (2001) Culture sits in places: reflections on globalism and subaltern strategies of localization. Polit Geogr 20:139–174

Massey D (1991a) A global sense of place. Marxism Today 38(June): 24–29

Massey D (1991b) The political place of locality studies. Environ Plan A 23:267–281

Massey D (1993) Power-geometry and a progressive sense of place. In: Bird J, Curtis B, Putnam T, Robertson G, Tickner L (eds) Mapping the futures: local cultures, global change. Routledge, London, pp 59–69

Paltridge R (2002) The diets of cats, foxes and dingoes in relation to prey availability in the Tanami Desert, Northern Territory. Wildl Res 29:389–403

Chapter 7
Spaces of Environmental Management

Abstract The aim of this chapter is to further address the first question of this research to enable an exploration of the tensions that exist at the nexus between environmental governance and environmental management. This chapter also considers how knowledges of best practice environmental management move across and between international, national and local scales of environmental governance and community-based environmental management. As established in Chap. 6, knowledges of best practice environmental management move through local spaces of environmental governance and community-based environmental *management*. In this chapter, the conceptual framework for cultural hybridity illuminates that these local spaces are comprised of many different arenas of 'participation' which are in turn influenced by the varieties of environmental management practised at each project location.

7.1 Project Success Is Synonymous with Community Involvement

The discourse of participation is central to ecologically sustainable development (ESD) (discussed in Chap. 2), but debates continue about what it actually entails. The multiple definitions and expectations of participation range from passive participation to self-mobilisation (Pretty 1995), participation as a means or as an ends to the goals of ESD. In Australia Ross et al. (2002) speak of participation ranging from community-based management to agency-based management. Other researchers (Guijt 1996; Cooke and Kothari 2001) speak of the tyranny of participation. The first analysis of this chapter demonstrates that the success of environmental management and community development projects is synonymous with community involvement. The following discussion illuminates how project members from the government arena perceive community involvement.

In the Victoria case study, project members from the government arena perceive community involvement as important for project success for various reasons. Firstly, project members from the local community arena carry out valuable work that otherwise would not be done by government agencies because they do not have the time or the resources. As an employee of Parks Victoria explains *there are a few*

K. Maclean, *Cultural Hybridity and the Environment*,
DOI 10.1007/978-981-287-323-1_7

parts to community [involvement]: it's ownership, it's understanding and it's also then turning round to say [their work saves the Government money]. Secondly, as a project member working for the Department of Sustainability and Environment expresses, the role that project members from the local community arena play in locating, recording and protecting threatened species *is integral to a lot of species survival.* Thirdly, as the following words of a bioregional manager from the Catchment Management Authority illustrate, the success of local environmental management projects is often dependent upon local community groups using environmental governance policies and programs to meet their own requirements, rather than being dictated to by these policies and programs. He explains that

> historically the [community groups] that are really successful were the ones that have stuff happening at the local level and understood the planning landscape or the political landscape so they could make the system work for them instead of just being at the mercy of the system.

Project members from the government arena in the Northern Territory articulate that the future of the Desert Fire project is dependent upon the interest expressed by individuals from the community arena who are living in the southern Tanami. The perception that project success is contingent on community involvement is demonstrated by the ethos of the Desert Knowledge Cooperative Research Centre (DKCRC) that dictated projects must be practice driven rather than research driven. As a manager of the DKCRC articulates, the community *have to want it… [because at the end of the day] we don't want to see the money used to do research that isn't used.* Project members also speak of the fact that the management of fire in the region is based upon community involvement. As this project member who is well versed in the scientific method articulates, *there is a growing recognition that there are a lot more social aspects to fire management than we have probably paid a lot of attention to in the past… we can't solve this simply by satellites and mapping fire. That is not what it is about.*

Community involvement is integral to the management of fire in the region for the following three reasons. The first reason is based upon the fact that the land in the region is either freehold land or held under pastoral lease. Therefore, as this project member who works for the Central Land Council clearly articulates, *nothing operational can happen without traditional owners being involved.* The same holds for land managed by pastoral and conservation land managers. The second reason that is closely related to the first is that, as this project member from the government arena explains, *stakeholder consultation [is fundamental …] if you don't have those people on side, irrespective of their backgrounds, you are doomed to fail.* Finally, as the Desert Fire project leader makes clear, the future of the project that includes the development and implementation of a fire management strategy *depends on the stakeholders [in the southern Tanami] and their perceptions [of the strategy].*

The findings of this analysis clearly reveal the valuable, powerful and integral role that individuals from the local community arena play in managing local environments. In the context of the two case study projects, it becomes clear that we need to question who exactly is participating within the environmental management programs that result from Federal, State and Territory environmental governance policy. This question is explored in the following analysis. The second analysis of this chapter demonstrates that there are multiple arenas of participation active at any local environmental management project interface. The implications of these findings are twofold and are elucidated in detail below.

7.2 Varieties of Participation

As discussed in Chap. 6, project members working from within the government arena do so within specific environmental governance policy and programs. Some project members perceive their work as connected to international conventions but most locate their work within regional and local arenas. Some of these project members have been involved in the development of regional plans such as the *Regional Catchment Strategies* and *Regional Investment Strategies* in Victoria and the *Integrated Natural Resource Management Plan* and the *Regional Investment Strategy* in the Northern Territory.

Although the Threatened Species project is located in north central Victoria and administered through the Catchment Management Authority, it is primarily funded through the Natural Heritage Trust (discussed in Chaps. 1 and 4). The words of the project officer illuminate how her work is limited by the agenda of this policy landscape. She speaks of the potential of her role as limited by government funding structures: *I had 11 landcare groups when I first started on 20 hours a week to work with; it was obvious to me; I had to let go*. Another local project officer speaks of the reduced longevity of on-ground works because the money made available from the Natural Heritage Trust is

> to fund a slightly dodgy fence… that reflects back on the project, on the Catchment Management Authority and ultimately on the Federal Government as well because the money has not been provided to do the job as well as it could be.

Although the local environmental management work is determined by the previously mentioned government agendas, it is dictated to by the community. The project officer explains that

> it is not always easy to follow the strategic line when you are working with community groups as you really have to work with where they are at and what their needs are and that can sometimes take you away from the big picture.

The local landcare coordinator exemplifies how project members from the government arena are working for the government but also they are working for the community. He locates his work within the Natural Heritage Trust agenda, as physically housed in the local government office, but his role is guided by a community-elected steering committee. He perceives his role as assisting the community to voice their dissatisfaction with government priority setting. Also he sees himself as a resource broker for the community, assisting them to

> work their way through the maze of agencies and to assist community volunteer groups to increase their capacity to operate [within the bureaucracy... thus empowering] people to take control of the natural resource.

All individuals from the government arena are themselves participating within specific environmental governance policy and program landscapes. At the same time, they believe their work is dictated to according to *where the community is at* and perceive the focus of their work is to empower the local community in the ways presented above. These perceptions raise questions about who is participating with whom.

The words of an individual who has been working with local community groups in the management of threatened species habitat for a number of years clearly articulate how the discourse of community participation within Federal Government environmental management programs does not reflect reality. She argues that

> the whole issue of community involvement needs to be looked at because... it's a vital ingredient but who is it and what does 'the community' mean?...when funding programs talk about it they mean Joe Bloggs on the ground in the country...they are not including the big companies, the statutory authorities, themselves. They are saying here is us and there is the community... [this approach is] inherently flawed.

The voices shared above illuminate the complexities of the discourse of participation. This is because they expose the reality that the local community is not the only interest group who is participating. Project members from the government arena in Victoria and the Northern Territory are themselves participating within Federal, State and Territory environmental governance landscapes. The implications of this investigation show that just as it is difficult to perceive when environmental governance ends and environmental management begins (see Chap. 6), it is also difficult to perceive where the role of project members as environmental governors ends and their role as participants within those same governance landscapes begins. A further complexity of this discourse becomes apparent when we consider the genesis of each of the two case study projects.

In the same way that project success is contingent on community involvement, so too is it contingent on project members from the government arena participating within the environmental governance landscape to create new and innovative approaches to environmental management. This is demonstrated by the fact that project members from the government arena in Victoria and the Northern Territory have been instrumental in tailoring the concepts of the two projects to capture funding opportunities as they arose. For example, the innovative whole-of-community landscape-scale Threatened Species project was engineered by three individuals working in state and regional government arenas in Victoria. Once conceived, the project was introduced to several community groups for their potential involvement. The second example is that of the collaborative Desert Fire project. This project was further developed within the innovative DKCRC by a group of eclectic individuals based in Alice Springs and working as representatives for on-ground interest groups. The project was then taken to the specific interest groups to gauge its ongoing viability.

At each environmental governance and management interface, these individuals were working from within governance structures to create new environmental governance and management approaches. According to the typology of participation distilled by Pretty (1995) (presented in Chap. 2, Table 2.1), these individuals could be classed as self-mobilising. Thus, individuals who are employed by institutions set up to further the principles of ESD are themselves participating. The findings of this analysis demonstrate the many and complex varieties of participation active within the government arena of the two project case studies. Further complexities of the discourse of participation become apparent from an analysis of what it means to participate from the local community perspective. The following analysis reveals that there are also varieties of participation active within the local community arena of the two project case studies.

Within the narrative of ESD, individuals from the community arena are encouraged to participate within given governance policies and programs in working towards localised ESD. This discourse undervalues the knowledge and work of individuals from the local community. Equally, it perpetuates a knowledge hierarchy that places the project leaders and administrators at the top. Evidence from both case studies clearly contradicts this discourse. In Victoria, project members from the local community arena use environmental governance policies and programs to assist them to conduct on-ground works that they have identified as important. This attitude is demonstrated in three ways. Firstly, one project member points out the importance of developing capacity and experience to engage with the environmental governance landscape. He explains that *you can have all these wonderful ideas but until you actually are able to use the system, the bureaucracy and the funds that are available, they will always stay nice ideas.* Secondly, another project member from the local community arena reveals how the involvement of his group in the Threatened Species project is more about leveraging funding for the whole of park conservation. He points out that *the Eltham Copper Butterfly project is simply a specific focus… a lever for us to get* (a) *interest,* (b) *participation and* (c) *resources to look after the park generally.* Finally, another project member builds upon this point by highlighting how the Threatened Species project is a means to an already determined end. He explains that, for his community group, the Threatened Species project is

> one project of about four or five we have this year, apart from the other activities that are not grant driven projects so we are very busy… as long as we can see good things happening, coming out of the projects, that's all we want to achieve.

Project members from the local community arena articulate that they are engaging with the Threatened Species project on their own terms. For example, one project member recalls how the project officer approached her landcare group for support. She recollects that *the types of things that [the project officer] was wanting some support with [fitted in with] the types of things we were doing*. Another project member speaks of the interdependent relationship between environmental governance and environmental management. He explains that in order for the Catchment Management Authority to gain funding for the project, they *needed [the community group] to apply.*

The comments of another project member further articulate the complex notion of community participation. She speaks of the proactive role that she perceives her landcare group has in relation to the wider community. By working to convince others to participate in the Threatened Species project, they are taking responsibility for project success. This is because it is in this role that *the responsibility comes back to the landcare group: to be able to encourage and convince people it is worthwhile saving or protecting these things*. The findings of this analysis clearly articulate the many varieties of participation active within the local community arena of the Threatened Species project interface.

Within the local community arena of the Desert Fire project in the Northern Territory, the local community responses to the project were still developing. This was because the project was still at a scoping stage. As such individuals were not able to reflect on project approaches to date; however, analysing the value they place on the aims of the Desert Fire project, and their potential role in this, illuminates similar perceptions about what it means to them to be involved in such a project.

Although individuals from the pastoral and Aboriginal communities in the southern Tanami have various attitudes about fire, it is interesting that their attitudes about what it would mean to be involved with the project are fairly similar. Comments from a variety of people suggest that involvement with the project will be on their terms. The following words of a pastoralist from the region clearly articulate this attitude. He explains that you can't *get people together who don't want to come together*. At the time of the research, consultations with the Aboriginal communities that fall within the Desert Fire case study area were still progressing. Aboriginal land managers are a vital part of the process and the potential project outcomes. Whether or not individuals are interested or willing to speak about fire on country is embedded within the wider context of living in remote Australia. In any project meetings and country visits with local traditional owners and members of the community, there is no sense that any traditional owners and community residents are participating. If anyone is participating, it is the project members from the government arena. This is because at any time they are dependent upon the wilful involvement of traditional owners and Aboriginal people living in the southern Tanami. Consultations depend on how much people are willing to, or wanting to, share their time to work with fire on country. Indeed, as a cultural advisor who is related to families in the communities by virtue of marriage states, *some people like to sit around and impress white fellas with what they know. But others get sick and tired of it*. In relation to his own consultation work related to education, he might *ask 'are you interested in talking about this' and they reply 'no' so that's that.*

Potential project members from the pastoral, the conservation and the Aboriginal communities speak about the importance of working together to manage fire in the region. None of these groups speak about participating within government-led projects. The findings of this research demonstrate that working together has a different meaning according to each interest group. Individuals from the pastoral community have differing views about how the project will facilitate working relationships. The words of this pastoralist indicate that he is fairly sceptical about the approach of the project so far. He believes that

> anything is possible, if you chuck enough resources at it, people will learn more about fire, raise awareness, management outcomes… there is only one certainty, and that is the scientific community is quite excited about it, they will get papers out of it, but a lot of good practical outcomes? I don't know.

Another pastoralist speaks of the fundamental importance of working together for the successful management of fire in the region. He articulates that the project must get *as many stakeholders as possible involved, working together with fire. As it is now everybody is on their own, they go out on their own, there is no real communication between people.*

Individuals from the conservation community speak of good relationships with traditional owners and neighbouring pastoral managers as essential to their work. Although a manager from Birds Australia who is based in Melbourne had not heard of the project, he notes that *the Aboriginal aspect to fire management in that region is just so important… we've really got to communicate and it's not easy, if that project facilitated that it would be brilliant.* The then manager of Newhaven states that *if [land managers] can't get on with the Aboriginals, they will hit a brick wall.* An ecologist speaks of the importance for equitable involvement of all interest groups in the Desert Fire project *[…we need] to get everyone together and work out the politics, the social aspects of it.*

When asked what it would mean to manage fire on country across different interest groups in the southern Tanami, two Aboriginal land managers explain that *[we] can all work together and look after the country and work better to look after country* and

> there is only one thing missing: understanding, we need to get together… got to make people understand. That would be the first time that that has happened [meeting to speak about fire]. That would be good.

The findings of this analysis demonstrate that project members from the community arena in Victoria are self-mobilising within given environmental governance landscapes to achieve self-determined outcomes (see Pretty 1995). The findings also demonstrate that in the Northern Territory it is the project members from the government arena who must participate with pastoral and Aboriginal interest groups. Indeed, they rely upon the wilful involvement of the on-ground interest groups for project success. To them, this success includes the development and implementation of a fire management strategy in the region. For pastoral, conservation and Aboriginal interest groups, success depends upon working with each other to better manage country, to understand other ways of managing fire and to overcome any past misunderstandings. However, as is explored in Sect. 7.3, being able to work together to manage fire in remote Australia requires more than choosing to do so and using the environmental governance landscape to self-mobilise as is the case in Victoria.

The implications of these findings are twofold. Firstly, they challenge the notion that environmental management is about community participation in predetermined environmental governance initiatives. This is because there is no clear delineation about who is participating with whom. The entangled social landscape of what it means to participate in environmental management and community development projects shows that there are multiple arenas of participation. Project members from the government arena operate within a given environmental governance landscape, but they also are directed by and dependent upon the wilful involvement of project members from the local community arena. Individuals and project members from the local community arena in Victoria self-mobilise within the environmental governance landscape to achieve desired on-ground project outcomes. While individuals from the local community arena in the Northern Territory only engage in project work if it is going to benefit their desired outcomes, many of them highlight the fact that they are dependent upon building and developing relationships with other interest groups to better manage fire in the region. The wider implication of this finding is that individuals and project members from the local community arena in Victoria and the Northern Territory are engaged in and making decisions about best practice environmental management rather than merely participating in environmental management projects where project leaders, scientists and administrators are making the decisions on their behalf.

The second implication further illuminates the complexity of environmental management and community development projects. The experiences of individuals and project members from the local community arena in the Northern Territory as compared with those in Victoria suggest that just as there are multiple arenas of participation, there are also varieties of participation. This is because the entangled and complex social livelihood issues faced by pastoralists, conservation land managers and Aboriginal communities living in the southern Tanami region of the Northern Territory (discussed in Chap. 5) dictate that these individuals are not able to self-mobilise. Indeed, although project members from the government arena are dependent upon their wilful involvement with the project, individuals from the local community arena are themselves dependent upon gatekeepers, such as land managers working for the Central Land Council or the Centralian Land Management Association, to navigate given environmental governance landscapes on their behalf. The genesis and evolution of the Desert Fire project is an example of this navigation.

The varieties of participation that are demonstrated by the findings of this research further exemplify how environmental management and community development projects revolve around varieties of environmental management. This is because, as demonstrated above, environmental management and community participation are complexly entwined. Furthermore, individuals from the local community arena are involved or choose to be involved in environmental management and community development projects for diverse reasons. The implications of these varieties of environmental management are investigated in the following discussion.

7.3 Varieties of Environmental Management

Chapter 2 touches on the complex issues surrounding the varieties of environmentalism across the developing and developed worlds. This is a pertinent issue in the 'post'-colonial nation of Australia where, as discussed in Chap. 5, certain groups of citizens experience conditions not dissimilar to those in developing nations. For example, many Indigenous Australians are confronted with livelihood issues relating to poverty, social and environmental injustice and inequality. It is certainly pertinent and interesting to consider these issues when contrasting the two case studies of this research and considering a concluding remark made above that working with the Desert Fire project requires more for some interest groups than choosing to self-mobilise. The final analysis of this chapter demonstrates the varieties of environmentalism or the varieties of environmental management at the local environmental management and community development project interface. The findings illuminate why individuals from the local community arena in Victoria and the Northern Territory choose to be involved in environmental management and community development projects. These findings further the discussion begun in Chap. 5 relating to the diversity of social livelihood issues faced by these different interest groups. The implications are discussed below.

As highlighted in Chap. 6, project members from the local community arena in Victoria engage with the environmental management and community development project for diverse reasons. All choose to engage in volunteer work. Some project members are project drivers; others are satisfied with simply doing the hard physical on-ground works. Some regard their work as community advocacy; others choose to remain apolitical naturalists. Political or apolitical, all are making a political choice to negotiate environmental governance landscapes to meet self-defined outcomes. Project success equates with the protection and enhancement of threatened species habitat. To many project members, this success is about tangible project outcomes.

One project member from the local community arena explains that overall project success is about longevity of species. He believes he would know if the project had been successful if they *come back in 100 years and see that [the threatened species on roadsides] are still there*! Species longevity depends upon several tangible factors including knowledge. As this project member explains: *we must learn from [the scientists] how to better recognise areas that are suitable habitat*; *there would be a better awareness of the park itself and the existence and rarity of the butterfly* and planning for the future. This project member elucidates further:

> it's going to have to be ongoing, it can't just keep being a 12 month thing and not knowing what kind of on-ground work will be going for one year to the next, and a more broad action plan on what needs to be done in the park, just to give it a long term goal.

Intangible indicators of success include the strengthening of community networks: *it's getting a few extra people wanting to participate and do the tree planting and whatever they have to do, getting more and more landholders involved.* Also, as one project member explains, the existence of the project itself is an indicator of success because *it gives a focus for all the interest groups and government departments to work together to achieve something in the community, it's that networking [that is important].*

In Victoria, individuals from the local community are already empowered; they consider themselves as working in networks with individuals from government agencies. It is not important who administers the project monies. What is important is achieving on-ground outcomes such as linking up areas of bushland for habitat of the threatened brush-tailed phascogale, learning how to survey and locate habitat of the Eltham Copper Butterfly for future protection and locating and recording threatened plant species to develop better management outcomes into the future.

As highlighted in Chap. 6, project members from the local community arena in the Northern Territory may engage with the environmental management and community development project for diverse reasons. They all do so as a means of improving their chosen approaches to localised land management. Additionally, their choice to be involved with the Desert Fire project is closely connected to social, cultural and economic survival. This is highlighted by the fact that these individuals do not volunteer their time to work with the project rather they are confronted with these livelihood issues daily. Although one pastoralist highlights the fact that the development of a fire management strategy in the southern Tanami means stopping fires to protect property because if *you stop people lighting fires, you save pastoral property*. A significant number of individuals from the pastoral, conservation and Aboriginal communities identify social relationships and communication as central to improved management of fire in the region. For example, a pastoralist who uses fire as a management tool on this land explains that he would choose to be involved with the Desert Fire project because it would create working relationships between different interest groups to work *together with fire… Aboriginal, pastoralists, because of the majority of the land up there is owned by Aboriginal people they have got to be fair stakeholders in it.*

Land managers from Birds Australia explain that the Desert Fire project would facilitate stronger relationships with the traditional owners of Newhaven. These relationships would be grounded in knowledge sharing about best practice fire management. Knowledge sharing would potentially evolve from conservation land managers working with traditional owners to manage Newhaven. Ultimately, as a previous manager of Birds Australia articulates, the project would aid clear and mutual communication between these interest groups.

> I think it's us understanding their attitudes towards it and for them to understand our reaction towards it. It's as much about understanding where each other is coming from…we say we have got a big fuel load this year it's been a very big year to keep the fires down and this sort of stuff and there is a lot of nodding and we agree we understand, but we don't really at the end of it understand where they are coming from… fire knows no property boundaries. If people act in a coordinated fashion rather than trying to do it one by one I think [the project] would be a good thing.

Taking this further, individuals from the Aboriginal communities in the region would choose to be involved with the Desert Fire project for tangible and intangible reasons that are not easily separated. It would mean working with other interest groups to better manage country, but it could potentially bring other benefits to the community. The project could be about community development and social justice: empowering and employing people to work on their country thus affording greater access to land that continues to be held under pastoral lease. It could provide further funding to develop the Indigenous ranger programs. This would assist older people to share knowledge about their country with young people, an act that can often only be carried out in situ. This in turn would strengthen the desire to learn other ways of managing the country. The words of an employee of the Central Land Council articulate how the Desert Fire project could facilitate these tangible and intangible project outcomes. He explains that traditional owners

> are beginning to worry a bit about fire management on country… the main thing is they want recognition for their use and ownership of the land they want to be recognised as "rangers", they like that term, they want to wear uniforms they want to have a vehicle, they want jobs, they want training they want money in their pocket they want useful employment on their country.

The potential tangible outcomes of the Desert Fire project as it stands include tapping into wider governance funding structures for monies to further develop ranger programs, conducting research into fire as a management tool on pastoral lands, assisting pastoralist and conservation land managers to put their fire management plans into action and opening up the channels for communication about fire into the future. These tangible outcomes are certainly necessary for the management of fire, but they only address a certain aspect of what it means to work towards sustainable livelihoods in the southern Tanami. Bigger picture strategies for working towards sustainable livelihoods also address intangible social processes. In the context of the Desert Fire project, this relates to the processes of engaging interest groups to overcome conflict relating to fire. As one individual who works closely with Aboriginal people in the region articulates:

> there isn't a plan that is going to make any difference but there is a process and it would be one that is absolutely inclusive […a] participatory process and in that respect it needs to be one that concentrates its resources in bringing people together… get them to talk because the single biggest thing is to get people to understand each other's perspectives and getting people to define their perspectives in a context for an enormous amount of education and extension… there is always room for improvement and a long process of defining how you use fire is as important.

The final analysis of this chapter demonstrates the varieties of environmentalism or varieties of environmental management approaches that typify the environmental management and community development project interface. For example, in Victoria, project members from the local community arena place tangible project outcomes over intangible project outcomes. This could be because they are already empowered to act. In the Northern Territory, it is clear that intangible project processes are regarded as crucial for the tangible project outcomes by a significant number of potential project members from the local community arena in the southern Tanami. This is indicative of the different environmental management and community development issues faced by individuals in the Northern Territory, as compared with those faced by project members from the local community arena in Victoria.

The implications of this analysis show that environmental management at the local community interface is about tangible project outcomes and intangible project process outcomes. When projects are the result of empowered groups of individuals working towards common environmental management goals, it is often easy to separate tangible and intangible outcomes. Such is the situation in the Victorian case study. But when projects are the result of gatekeepers navigating environmental governance landscapes on behalf of others, as is the circumstance in the Northern Territory case study, tangible and intangible outcomes are often closely entwined and interdependent. This results from the fact that the social livelihood issues faced by these individuals are complex. Indeed, conflicts that arise from these social livelihood issues, the causes and ways to approach these causes, may not be understood or identified until the project has begun.

This analysis furthers the discussion started in Chap. 2 that relates to government agencies or groups making decisions about environmental management and community development projects on behalf of needy others. In the instance of the Northern Territory case study where individuals from the local community arena are not able to navigate environmental governance landscapes for the various social livelihood reasons touched upon in Chaps. 5 and 6, a project such as the Desert Fire project would not evolve without the assistance of gatekeepers. The reality is unlike in Victoria where project members from the local community volunteer their time, the Desert Fire project revolves around money. Any work in remote Australia must be well resourced because of the vast distances to travel and the resources necessary to cover running costs. On-ground interest groups do not have the resources or the knowledge to initiate such a project. Problems relating to power, knowledge, social and environment justice arise (discussed in Chap. 2) when decisions are made by gatekeepers on behalf of the needy others. It is at this interface that issues of inequality surface. It is for this reason (as explored further in Chaps. 8 and 9) that I argue any environmental management and community development project is responsible for identifying, exploring, critiquing and acting out the tangible project outcomes and intangible project processes so necessary for the decisions about best practice environmental management at the local interface.

7.4 Conclusion

This chapter showed how the first question of this research enables an exploration of the tensions that exist at the nexus between environmental governance and environmental management. This chapter provided a further exploration into the question: how do knowledges of best practice environmental management move across and between international, national and local scales of environmental governance and community-based environmental management? The investigation considered what constitutes participatory natural resource management at the environmental management and community development project interface. The two empirical case studies provided a lens through which to explore this question. The findings demonstrate that participation is an entangled and complex notion because at any one time it is unclear exactly who is participating with whom. What is clear is that project success is synonymous with community involvement; there are multiple arenas of participation; and there are many varieties of participation active in any environmental management and community development project. In addition the varieties of environmentalism or the varieties of environmental management dictate that project success is not only about tangible project outcomes but also intangible process. For these projects to deliver equitable and sustainable ESD, they must identify, explore, critique and act upon these tangible and intangible outcomes. As such knowledges of best practice environmental management also include knowledge of best practice social process, and these knowledges can only be developed in situ. The evolution of these projects can work to inform best practice environmental management and community development projects in other locales.

References

Cooke B, Kothari U (2001) The case for participation as tyranny. In: Cooke B, Kothari U (eds) Participation: the new tyranny? Zed Books, London, pp 1–15

Guijt I (1996) Participation in natural resource management: blemished past and hopeful future? Paper read at the Making Forest Policy Work conference. Oxford Forestry Institute, Oxford

Pretty J (1995) Participatory learning for sustainable agriculture. World Dev 23(8):1247–1263

Ross H, Buchy M, Proctor W (2002) Laying down the ladder: a typology of public participation in Australian natural resource management. Aust J Environ Manag 9:205–217

Part IV
Knowledge Networks Across the Landscape

Chapter 8
Politics of Knowledge

Abstract The aim of this chapter is to address the second question of this research and to enable an exploration of the tensions that exist at the nexus between environmental governance and environmental management. This chapter (and the next) considers the role of community stakeholder groups and their knowledge in the networks surrounding environmental management and community development. The findings of Chap. 7 demonstrate that project success is synonymous with community involvement. This analysis uses the conceptual framework for cultural hybridity to illuminate that project success of the environmental management and community development projects is dependent upon local community knowledge. This is because local community knowledge is powerful. As demonstrated in this chapter, it is powerful for three main reasons. It is powerful because it is tied to place, it is not just about place but can and does encompass the diverse knowledge cultures identified as necessary for western decision-making systems (identified by Brown, Environ Health 1:20–31, 2001), and it informs perceptions of other knowledge cultures. Therefore, local community knowledge determines whether or not individuals from the local community arena will engage in project work with individuals from other interest groups.

8.1 The Power of Place-Based Knowledge

The research findings reported in Chaps. 6 and 7 demonstrate that knowledge of best practice environmental management moves across and between local spaces of environmental governance and environmental management. The implication of these findings is that the environmental management decisions made by project members from the local community arena in Victoria and the Northern Territory can influence environmental governance and management approaches at various governance scales. As such local community knowledge is powerful. The first analysis of this chapter considers how the place-based characteristics of local community knowledge influence project success.

As discussed in Chap. 7, the success of the Threatened Species project in Victoria would be indicated by the on-ground protection and enhancement of threatened species habitat in the region into the future. Many project members from the government

K. Maclean, *Cultural Hybridity and the Environment*,
DOI 10.1007/978-981-287-323-1_8

arena in Victoria speak about the important role of place-based community knowledge in meeting the aims of the project. The characteristics of local community knowledge are juxtaposed with what is described as the nature of government. Where government roles change and employees are promoted or move offices, the place-based characteristics of local community knowledge mean that it remains tied to place. An employee of the Victorian Government's Department of Sustainability and Environment explains that the community provides *project consistency; their project may have been through two of my predecessors, but still they are consistently doing the same work and getting really good results.* The implication of this is that, as an employee of Parks Victoria explains, project members from the local community arena often have *more information than [the government], so if we don't work with them, we don't get that information.*

Although place-based knowledge is clearly regarded as important for project success by some project members from the government arena, they also acknowledge that by definition it is limited. For example, some individuals from local communities may not be well versed in whole of landscape management approaches. In this way local environmental management approaches may be to the detriment of the wider landscape. A woman who has been involved with the Threatened Species Network for many years explains in relation to community tree planting events:

> it does make [the community] feel good, but it makes you feel even better if you understand why [you are planting trees…. For example there are] huge numbers of trees planted [every year] by perfectly well intentioned groups, <u>in grass lands.</u>

The implications of decisions based exclusively upon place-based knowledge can be very powerful in further compounding environmental management issues. However, as the words and practices of project members from the local community arena in Victoria reveal, place-based knowledge generation is characterised by self-reflection, discussion and some amounts of local experimentation.

People working in the local community arena in Victoria are anxious to develop their place-based knowledge. As a project member who is secretary of her landcare group enthuses, *the more you can learn from other landcare groups, the better.* Another project member speaks about the important role that scientific experts play in informing local management decisions and actions. Her words reflect upon the value of learning from these so-called experts but also how the limitations of place-based knowledge illuminate the limitations of other knowledge cultures. She explains that

> we are certainly interested in learning … knowledge like that gives you power to protect the park […but] because there are a lot of experts coming in, unless we are trained [to develop] a knowledge base in [the local township], once the project is finished, those experts disappear.

The words of the following project member clearly demonstrate the important role that different knowledge cultures play in the ongoing protection of threatened species habitat in Victoria. He explains that

> I'm willing to yield to the scientists on what needs to happen in regards to [threatened species research] and to participate in doing some work according to their [scientific] direction

> [...but] we were able to tell them about the potential threats [to the habitat of the Eltham Copper Butterfly...] they needed to know what was going on here, so we had something to offer them.

The experiences of project members working with the Threatened Species project in Victoria demonstrate firstly that the place-based knowledge of project members from the local community arena is vital for the protection and enhancement of threatened species habitat in the region. Secondly, place-based knowledge taken separately is not enough to meet the aims of the project. Thirdly, the limitations of place-based knowledge illuminate the limitations of other knowledge cultures. For example, it would seem that scientists limit the success of their own work to protect threatened species in the region by failing to develop lasting relationships with members of the local community. These members of the local community could easily monitor the species precisely because they live locally and thus can feed valuable information back to the scientists. In addition, if scientists could further protect threatened species by teaching local people specific research and monitoring methods according to the situation, this might empower local groups to act as the situation dictates. The final quote above demonstrates how place-based knowledge further informed scientists of potential threats to habitat that extended beyond the scope of scientific knowledge of species ecology.

As has been discussed throughout this research thus far, both the impetus of the Desert Knowledge Cooperative Research Centre (DKCRC) and the reality that land in the region is managed by pastoral, conservation and Aboriginal interest groups dictate that local community knowledge is integral to the success of the Desert Fire project. As expressed in Chap. 7, the ramifications of this success are indicative of the ongoing development of sustainable livelihoods in the region and working to overcome conflicts that relate to different land management approaches to fire. The remainder of this section demonstrates how the characteristics and power of place-based knowledge influence the successful management of fire in the region.

Individuals from the pastoral community speak of their knowledge as tied to place. A sophisticated knowledge of place, of past and present seasons and of past fire histories is identified by pastoralists as paramount to the management of fire in the region. A pastoralist explains the importance of this knowledge that is intimately tied to place-based knowledge generated in situ. He explains that *[fire management] is a seasonal thing and everybody operates different... people have different ideas and I think that every place has a different balance of feed.* The choice to use or not use fire as a management tool is equally about knowledge of place and place-based experience of fire. These various knowledges and experiences are demonstrated by the fact that one pastoralist in the region would prefer to exclude fire from his lease; another uses it as the opportunity arises; and another uses it as a general management tool and burns as often as he can, depending upon the weather experienced by his lease.

As touched upon in Chap. 6, Aboriginal knowledge of fire is closely connected to traditional ownership that by definition is tied to place. The words of an employee of the Central Land Council who works closely with Aboriginal interest groups explain *there are people to speak for that country… who are the holders of such [fire] knowledge… and are able to talk about their country in relation to fire management of the country.*

This place-based knowledge is highly valued by managers of the Newhaven reserve. It is considered very important for the sustainable management of fire on the reserve. The words of a manager of Birds Australia based in Melbourne demonstrate how they value this place-based knowledge equally to scientific approaches to fire management. He explains that

> the Aboriginal aspect to fire management in that region is just so important… we as white fellas can sit here and talk as much as we like about our western science but cultural traditional knowledge [of fire is just so important].

As demonstrated above in relation to the place-based knowledge held by project members from the local community arena in Victoria, place-based knowledge of individuals from the local community arena in the Northern Territory is also limited by virtue of being tied to place. There is consensus among project members from the government arena that conservation land managers at Newhaven are limited by their lack of knowledge and resources. The words of a project member who works for the Northern Territory Government Bushfires Council explain that *they don't have a lot of experience in fire… they are prepared to use fire more but it's a big challenge because they are remote and they have many resources out there.*

As indicated above, some pastoralists do not regard fire as a feasible management tool or even as beneficial, let alone integral, to the southern Tanami landscape. One pastoralist believes that the limitations of place-based pastoral knowledge whereby pastoralists do not learn from the experiences of others limit the potential of the pastoral industry and work to further degrade local environments. The place-based knowledge of Aboriginal land managers is also limited by its localness but for different reasons. An employee of the Central Land Council points out the complexity of these limitations:

> people still identify strongly with fire… it is a really important expression of Aboriginal culture, people hold strongly to it but they are not likely to want to be told what to do about it… but at the same time, people don't have that landscape perspective.

Aboriginal people speak also about the fact that their knowledge and practice of fire is now limited by resources. They are only able to use fire on land where they can gain access. As one Aboriginal woman explains,

> in old days people, old people have travelled all over the place and when they see, you know, grass that's big they get a bit tempted to burn it [these days] a lot of people don't have the opportunity and the only time that people can go out on country is when it is organised [by individuals who have access to cars and money for petrol].

As discussed above in relation to the Victorian project, the implications of decisions based exclusively upon place-based knowledge can be very powerful in further compounding environmental management issues. The very fact that individuals from the local community arena in the southern Tanami are interested in speaking about their attitudes and approaches to fire demonstrates their interest in developing their knowledge to improve the management of fire in the southern Tanami region. This is indicative of the dynamic power of place-based knowledge. As the words of two project members from the government arena demonstrate, the success of this project is closely connected to the dynamic and evolving nature of place-based knowledge. Firstly, the project is about *talking to the different partners involved, getting some of their ideas and looking for the commonalities and trying to work from those*. Secondly, because the project is about new knowledge generation about the strategic management of fire across diverse interest groups with diverse place-based knowledges of fire, *once [the many individuals involved in the project] discover something [new] themselves, then it will become part of their ethos*.

The dynamic nature of place-based knowledge is further demonstrated by the attitudes of individuals from the conservation, pastoral and Aboriginal communities. Firstly, as demonstrated in a quote previously shared, the land managers of Newhaven are very interested to learn from traditional owners about, what a manager of Birds Australia based in Melbourne calls, *cultural traditional knowledge of fire*. Secondly, as the subsequent comment reveals, this pastoralist believes that his successful land management has been intimately connected to experimentation with other ideas. He explains that

> you've got to get outside that [comfort] area and challenge yourself as well with other ideas… if you are prepared to do that you can achieve all sorts of results… we've had some failures here like anywhere but also a lot of good results that have come from it.

Thirdly, Aboriginal land managers speak about the evolving nature of their place-based knowledge. For example, in relation to local practices, this Aboriginal elder explains that contemporary application of place-based knowledge of fire is founded upon contestation and debate: many people use fire and *sometimes the women disagree so the men are not able to light that fire*; *they have to be working together to make a better job of it*. Another Aboriginal man involved with the Indigenous ranger program speaks about the ways in which modern technology can assist Aboriginal land managers to engage in fire management on their country. He explains that

> before [we] used to look at smoke and go to bushfire, two days to get there sometimes, now with technology, satellites can spot bushfires, [we] can go to the location with proper protection, hats and so on, and teach young people and teach with the wind and back burn with fire.

The experiences and attitudes of project members and individuals involved with the Desert Fire project in the Northern Territory further establish that the place-based knowledge of individuals from the local community arena is integral to the strategic management of fire in the region. In reality the project exists because of the apparent dissonance between the different knowledges held and practised by the three interest groups living and working in the southern Tanami. For this reason and the fact that these interest groups manage large tracts of the southern Tanami land area, the project is contingent on these place-based knowledges. Further, as discussed in relation to the Victorian project, taken separately, place-based knowledge is not sufficient to meet the aims of the project. Finally, the fact that the project itself is hinged upon developing new approaches to fire management in the region dictates that in order to push the boundaries of the given approaches to fire management in the region, the project must mirror the dynamic and experimental nature of place-based knowledge, to facilitate progressive and locally relevant knowledge generation.

8.2 Local Community Knowledge Encompasses Diverse Knowledge Cultures

In Chap. 1 I introduced Brown's (2001) typology of knowledge cultures in western decision-making systems as the means to unpack the knowledges necessary for equitable and sustainable environmental management in Australia. The second analysis of this chapter engages with this typology to consider the research finding that local community knowledge is powerful because it is not just about place.[1] Put in other words, this analysis demonstrates that local community knowledge encompasses more than simply place-based knowledge. The following discussion reveals in greater detail how project success is contingent on local community knowledge.

As discussed in Sect. 8.1, the place-based knowledge held by project members from the local community arena in Victoria is integral to project success. The project officer points out that the management of threatened species habitat depends upon *better land management decisions into the future*. As such the project must also empower people to develop their knowledge of local threatened species habitats, to realise their own capacity and to voice concern in public forums. The power of this local community knowledge would be determined by the success of project members from the local community arena to be involved in and to inform political forums relating to local environmental governance and management decisions. As such, in addition to place-based knowledge, local community groups will need to have certain sets of specialised, strategic and possibly holistic knowledge to negotiate the futures of threatened species. The words shared in the following analysis show that, although not every individual possesses these kinds of knowledges, local community knowledge is constituted by diverse knowledge cultures identified by Brown (2001) as: individual knowledge, local knowledge described in this research study as place-based knowledge, specialised knowledge, strategic knowledge and holistic knowledge.

Project members from the government arena speak about depending upon and learning from the knowledge of members from the local community arena. For example, an employee of the Victorian Government Department of Sustainability and Environment explains that *the networks we can develop with the community are really important as they teach us a lot and without them we would be buggered*. The local landcare coordinator is quick to acknowledge the role that local community

[1] Chapter 10 takes this analysis further by extending Brown's (2001) typology to conceive of all knowledges as local.

knowledge has in regional, national and international threatened species monitoring programs. He points out that most of the information in flora and fauna databases that informs state and national environmental governance and management of threatened species is underpinned by

> lots of people's volunteer hours [...for example] how would you have an understanding of what is happening to the Australian bird population [without the] tens of thousands of hours that local birdos do?

A further example demonstrates not only the important knowledge that local community groups can share with others but the international nature of this local community knowledge and experience. The bioregional manager speaks about learning from the experiences and shared local community knowledge of conservation movements in Bangladesh about how to improve local strategies to *incorporate local knowledge into decision making*.

These findings demonstrate that the local community knowledge of which these project members from the government arena in Victoria speak is specialised enough to inform scientists working with the Victorian Government in the capacity of flora and fauna managers and decision makers, is rigorous enough to be depended upon as part of regional and national databases maintained by government agencies and is regarded as both specialised and strategic in the way in which it can inform bioregional managers about mechanisms to include local knowledge in decision-making processes.

The way that project members from the local community arena in Victoria describe the diverse aspects of their environmental management and community development work further illuminates the specialised and strategic nature of their knowledge. Project members speak of their roles in the project as encompassing that of educators, of local technical experts, of project managers and of knowledge managers. For example, they work to educate *people about the role of biodiversity*; they source expertise from other local community groups which means that *the field naturalists have been helping quite a few other landcare groups with those technical things that they have the expertise in*; and they speak about learning project management skills by *going out for things like this [project...] we are going to learn a lot from it: how to manage it, how to get commitment and how we market that.* The strategic characteristics of local community knowledge include managing knowledge acquired by external agencies. For example, as this project member articulates, *we know the research was done, but where are the results*? This knowledge brokering is essential for the successful protection and management of threatened species in the region. Another example of the strategic nature of the local community knowledge in Victoria includes holding Victorian Government Departments accountable to planning processes. As this project member explains, managing the boundaries of the local Box-Ironbark Park is essential for the ongoing protection of the Eltham Copper Butterfly habitat: *when the new National Park was declared, [community members of the project] found that they had left a small block of land out of it.*

The knowledge of pastoralists and Aboriginal land managers from the local community arena in the southern Tanami region of the Northern Territory is powerful because it is about more than simply place-based knowledge. It also has specialised and strategic characteristics. For example, pastoralists manage their land according to specialised knowledge of pastoral production. As this project member from the government arena who works for the Bushfires Council explains:

> The most common expression that you will hear from the pastoralist perspective associated with fire and using fire is to control woody weeds [...they also] tend to burn their Spinifex country for the post fire response which may have benefit to their cattle and also to reduce the threat of fires coming out of the Spinifex country... some pastoralists have an almost complete fire exclusion... possibly associated with fear... but other pastoralists you know think of fire as the best tool that they have got on their property.

The use of fire varies from pastoral lease to pastoral lease, but there is no doubt that pastoralists possess specialised knowledge of what it means to manage land for pastoral production. The knowledge of some pastoralist is also very strategic. This is demonstrated by the fact that certain pastoralists may choose to be involved in the Desert Fire project. As discussed in Chap. 1, one impetus for the Desert Fire project is the level of conflict exacerbated by the use of fire in the southern Tanami region. This conflict originates mainly between pastoralists and Aboriginal communities. Pastoralists in the region have different attitudes about overcoming this conflict, and certain individuals display particular strategic knowledge of how to alleviate these fire-related conflicts. One pastoralist explains that Aboriginal use of fire on his lease can be mutually beneficial:

> I don't have to [burn] a lot myself, me mates here do it for me!... I think that is too why we haven't had a lot of big fires because of all their hunting tracks. At night time if the wind isn't blowing they are probably putting all these little fires up... if they started lighting them up in our good grasses it would be [a problem] but while they are just burning on the Spinifex then that doesn't matter.

Another pastoralist speaks of fire as being part of Aboriginal peoples' lives for a long time and that *if you have a complete run in with the black fellas... they will beat you at the time. It's the wrong attitude to have with them and a lot of people still have that attitude on country*. He explains that his strategy is to speak with the elders and the traditional owners of his pastoral lease, to keep them informed of the work he plans to do. He speaks of developing and maintaining mutually beneficial relationships with the Aboriginal people who live near his pastoral lease, such as assisting them to fix damaged car tyres and helping them hunt for kangaroos. He believes that *these little things develop rapport with them that keeps them on side because they can make things very difficult if they want to. And at some places they do*. This same pastoralist speaks of the suspicion that some pastoralists have of government (discussed in detail in Sect. 8.3). He has made a strategic choice to work with government. This is because, as he explains: *we couldn't achieve what we want to achieve on this place unless we involved the government; we haven't got the resources to do the mapping, set up paddock areas, phosphorus soil levels*. As discussed in Chap. 10, this same pastoralist offers his strategic knowledge to suggest strategies to overcome conflict between the government, pastoral, conservation and Aboriginal individuals involved with the Desert Fire project. He suggests that there is always an opportunity to learn from each other. He explains how he learnt some of his specialised knowledge of fire from the Aboriginal people with whom he has worked in his pastoral career thus far. He would like to learn further from Aboriginal land managers: *how they get [the country] to burn when half the time I can't get it to.*

Potential project members from the conservation community speak with much respect about the specialised characteristics of Aboriginal land management knowledge. For example, a local ecologist speaks of the specialised knowledge of Aboriginal women that has assisted with her ecological research. These skills include

> expertise for tracking species, identifying the numbers of predators present as well as their behaviour. For example the women could tell what the cat had done by looking at its tracks: it got a budgie here and a mouse there. Working with the women's daughters who are often bilingual, assists to increase communication.

Another local ecologist reflects on the wisdom of Aboriginal burning regimes. His words show how specialised knowledge of fire and landscape ecology were, and continue to be, closely related to livelihood strategies. He states that Aboriginal people will light the country

> whenever it is ready to burn. If you light it and it keeps going, it's ready to burn… it turns out to be the best way to manage the Spinifex. Burn it when it is ready, don't let it build up [...because then it] becomes a very big fire and it burns all your country and leaves you sitting there in the middle of this black plain with nothing to eat [...in the past] they didn't even have to do it consciously 'cause they walked, they always carried fire sticks because making fire is hard work, so whenever you move someone was carrying the fire stick, when you carry a fire stick coals drop off and starts fires. So you didn't have to do anything, just walk around your country and let it do it itself.

Aboriginal people speak of their knowledge of fire in a way that demonstrates, firstly, the close connection between this knowledge and social, physical and sometimes economic livelihood strategies and, secondly, the unique specialisation of this knowledge. Aboriginal knowledge of fire is an evolving and dynamic practice. It is connected to the past, to place and to action. Knowledge and use of fire is connected to a historical knowledge of the rhythms of the natural environment. This Aboriginal woman explains this specialised knowledge informs land management practices that facilitate hunting and the rejuvenation of the land. She tells how

> in the old days when they used to [burn] it's done in spring. That's when the animals come out, especially the goannas. [Burning] clears the whole land and the first lot of rains to come in and the new growth back into the country.

Another individual speaks of the way that fire was used to bring rain: *people used to light fires when they wanted rain*; *there is a special spinifex to bring rain.*

Contemporary practices incorporate historical, place-based and social knowledges of fire. Individuals continue these practices today in relation to keeping culture alive for ceremony. An Aboriginal woman from the region explains *they use [fire] during men's ceremonies. It symbolises the sons out in the bush, to keep that fire going for them.* They also use it to assist them to continue to live in the region because, as this Aboriginal man explains, *in central Australia fire is really valuable; without fire you starve.* Fire facilitates hunting, as this Aboriginal elder describes *[we burn] so that turkey can land there* and *snakes come out a lot easier too*. Fire is also used by Aboriginal people as a land management tool. This Aboriginal man clarifies that *fire burning is only way to keep country clean, used to get green grass back and to make it easier for animals.*

In relation to the Desert Fire project, Aboriginal people in the region speak about strategies to overcome conflict relating to fire. Most importantly project success depends upon working together to manage conflicts indeed; overcoming conflict is necessary to *work better to look after country.* Individuals speak about the importance of strategically engaging with the project as a way of facilitating cultural burning on parts of their land they have not been able to access for an extended length of time. One man explains how the project could facilitate a link between more traditional approaches to using fire and western approaches. His words highlight contemporary challenges faced by Aboriginal people who feel their generation can see the old ways and also the western ways: *these days in western world now [...we] have to think and live: how to look after country with bushfires or fire, got to look after [the country] in different ways.*

The findings of the second analysis of this chapter demonstrate that the local community knowledge of project members and potential project members from the local community arena in Victoria and the Northern Territory is not just about place. Local community knowledge can also encompass specialised and strategic (following Brown 2001) knowledge cultures. The implications of these findings are twofold. Firstly, local community knowledge is powerful because it includes sophisticated knowledge of place; specialised knowledge of threatened species, of fire, of community development, of awareness raising through education and of project management; and strategic knowledge of facilitation and community politics (explored in Chap. 9). These knowledges are essential for project success in the relevant environmental management and community development projects. Secondly, the fact that local community knowledge is not restricted to place-based knowledge suggests that the knowledge of project members from the government arena is also likely to be composed of diverse knowledge cultures that extend beyond specialised scientific knowledge and strategic knowledge of governance policies and related programs. These implications are explored further in Chap. 10.

8.3 Local Community Knowledge Determines the Success of Environmental Management Projects

The final analysis of this chapter considers how local community knowledge informs perceptions of other knowledge cultures active at the environmental management and community development project interface. The findings show that local community knowledge is powerful because these perceptions determine whether or not project members and individuals from the local community arena will choose to engage in project work with project members from other community groups and the government arena. The findings also demonstrate that the experiences are different for individuals when the environmental management and community development project is based upon overcoming conflict. In such situations these perceptions may in fact be the cause of the conflict.

As explored in Chap. 7, project members from the local community arena in Victoria are empowered to use governance policies and programs to meet their self-determined project ends. They perceive themselves as part of a growing network of individuals working to protect and enhance threatened species habitat in the region. They have good relationships with project members from the government arena. These good relationships are indicative of their perceptions of these project members and the knowledge cultures to which they ascribe. In particular, project members from the local community arena value the localised knowledge of project members from the government arena. However, they are wary of government hierarchy. As a local farmer who is the president of his landcare group explains, *the field officer type people are good because they are actually doing the work … once you get up a couple of rungs [in the government hierarchy] the people are too far removed from what's going on*. This perception is grounded upon experiences of dealing with individuals working in different areas of government. These perceptions are further compounded when, as was indicated by the words of two project members from the local community arena shared in Sects. 8.1 and 8.2, experts who conduct research in the region disappear and take the results of their research with them. The power of the knowledge held by local community members thus influences how they choose to be involved with other individuals into the future.

As the findings shared in Chap. 7 demonstrate, individuals from the local community arena in the Northern Territory may choose to be involved with the Desert Fire project to improve their social, cultural and economic survival. These findings also show that the development and improvement of local livelihoods is closely connected to the development and improvement of relationships between pastoralists, Aborigines and conservation land managers in the region mainly because fire does not stop at land tenure boundaries. These relationships are very much determined by preconceived perceptions of the other. These perceptions are informed by local community knowledge. As such conflicts are often grounded in perceptions of other local knowledge cultures as opposed to the knowledge itself. The findings of this research demonstrate that these perceptions are powerful in two ways. Firstly, they can undervalue the knowledge of the other and, secondly, they can further confound conflicting social relationships. Both aspects can undermine the potential of social relationships developed from a project such as the Desert Fire project to overcome conflict and generate new knowledge about the management of fire across different land tenures in the region. Clearly the inverse is also true. The implications of these findings are twofold and are discussed here.

The power of local community knowledge is grounded upon the fact that the place-based characteristics of local community knowledge include knowledge of local histories and past relationships. The words of a project member from the government arena who works for the Centralian Land Management Association touch upon theses subtleties. She explains that relationships

> go deeper than what an outsider can understand so I don't think that I can properly appreciate where everyone is coming from out there but all I can say is that there are some serious issues there in terms of relationships between Aboriginal people and [one pastoral family] in particular.

As indicated in Chap. 5 and demonstrated in Sect. 8.2, pastoral attitudes to fire in the southern Tanami region vary greatly. In a similar way, perceptions of the value of Aboriginal knowledge of fire in the region also vary. As the words of a pastoralist shared in Sect. 8.2 reveal, some pastoralists believe they can learn from Aboriginal knowledge of fire but others do not. Indeed some believe that the use of fire without a permit in the region should be outlawed as exemplified by the recent review of the Northern Territory *Bushfires Act, 2004*. Some pastoralists make comments one day that contradict previous statements: this is indicative of the complex, emotive and dynamic reality of fire. It also illustrates the situated nature of knowledge whereby the content and way in which information is shared is often context dependent. For example, one pastoralist states that Aboriginal people use fire *because they can*; *if people say it's for hunting and gathering, it's bullshit*; *it's not necessary for them to be following those pursuits today as they have a truck that turns up every week and fills stores up for what they need.* At a later date the same pastoralist speaks about the complexities and importance of understanding how different cultures view fire. He explains that

> for white fellas fire is an issue, they are scared of it, but for black fellas fire has always been there, they have no fear, it is a natural thing. Therefore, it is very difficult to put a white fella's idea to a black fella. For example, the Tanami has been burning for the last 20,000 years so why stop it? It is a tricky situation.

The success of the Desert Fire project is clearly connected to overcoming conflict in the region. By the same token, the success of the project is about overcoming conflict that exists between potential project members from the local community arena and some project members from the government arena. The implications of this are twofold. Firstly, as mentioned previously, local community knowledge is closely connected to local livelihood issues. If projects ignore these issues, they may further compound tensions between the local community and government. As a project member from the government arena who works in natural resource management explains,

> when we design these programs [in terms of what is feasible and viable] we have a theoretical expectation of how those individuals out there can be involved… I don't think enough is taken into account of the social state of the community in that thinking.

These approaches can often work to further develop the culture of suspicion that exists in the region. A pastoralist explains that these suspicions have evolved from a long history of government employees coming in and doing *the wrong thing. They have tried to be little generals in their own little area and alienated a lot of pastoralists*. This culture of suspicion is clearly based upon pastoral perceptions of government: clearly not everyone in government behaves in this way. As this pastoralist articulates,

> if you have got people coming in and [pastoralists] have got total suspicion, they are not going to be free with information. If the pastoralists are not free with information, the researchers are not going to get anything out of it as they can only get out what people put in.

It follows that *if people think that their two bob's worth [of information shared] is not getting anywhere, they will not be actively engaged. He explains that the more comfortable [the pastoralists] feel with [government and researchers], the more their information would be of benefit.*

The implications of the words shared here are twofold. Firstly, they further reveal the power of local community knowledge in influencing project success. This is because local community knowledge informs perceptions of the other. These perceptions may be the result of past experiences such as the culture of suspicion evident between individuals loving and working in the southern Tanami region of the Northern Territory with each other and with government. Or they may be based upon complex and entangled cross-cultural and cross-knowledge culture relationships. They may result from interpersonal relationships and be grounded upon personality conflicts. Whatever the circumstance, the implication is that these perceptions are powerful. They impact upon the future of an environmental management and community development project because at the end of the day the success of these projects depends upon the investment of knowledge, time and resources of all project members or, as is the case with the Desert Fire project, potential project members.

The second implication of this analysis reveals the intrinsic and instrumental values ascribed by individuals to the knowledge of others. The example given above in relation to pastoral suspicion of government shows how such approaches undermine their own work. This further reveals how all knowledge cultures can be limited.

8.4 Conclusion

This chapter showed how the second guiding question of this research enables an exploration of the tensions that exist at the nexus between environmental governance and environmental management. This chapter considered the role of community stakeholder groups and their knowledge in the networks surrounding environmental management and community development. Analysis of the two empirical case studies using the new conceptual framework for cultural hybridity revealed that the success of environmental management and community development projects is dependent upon local community knowledge. This is because, firstly, a sophisticated historical and contemporary knowledge of place is essential for project success. Secondly, the specialised and strategic characteristics of local community knowledge are equally powerful in determining, for example, the ongoing protection of threatened species habitat in Victoria and the management of fire in the Northern Tanami. Thirdly, local community knowledge is integral to project success because it informs perceptions of other knowledge cultures which determines whether individuals will choose to engage with project members from other knowledge cultures.

Reference

Brown VA (2001) Monitoring changing environments in environmental health. Environ Health 1:20–31

Chapter 9
Varieties of Local Knowledge

Abstract The first question of this research is to enable an exploration of the tensions that exist at the nexus between environmental governance and environmental management. This chapter also considers how knowledges of best practice environmental management move across and between international, national and local scales of environmental governance and community-based environmental management. As established in Chap. 6, knowledges of best practice environmental management move through local spaces of environmental governance and community-based environmental *management*. In this chapter, the conceptual framework for cultural hybridity illuminates that these local spaces are comprised of varieties of local knowledge.

The aim of this chapter is to further address the second question of this research and thus to enable an exploration of the tension's that exist at the nexus between environmental governance and environmental management. This chapter also considers the role of community stakeholder groups and their knowledge in the networks surrounding environmental management and community development. Analysis of the two empirical case studies illuminates that the potential of local community knowledge is encapsulated by its power and limitations. These findings expose the combination of knowledge cultures necessary for equitable and sustained environmental management of locally situated projects. As such they reveal the varieties of local knowledge active at the environmental governance and environmental management interface.

9.1 The Potential of Local Community Knowledge

The first analysis of this chapter demonstrates that the potential of local community knowledge is encapsulated by its power and its limitations. The potential of any environmental management and community development project is not only dependent upon acknowledging the limitations of local community knowledge but also it is dependent upon acknowledging the limitations of other knowledge cultures active at this interface. The implications of this are explored in detail below.

As revealed in Chap. 8, the local knowledge held by project members from the local community arena is vital to project success. This is because, as a project

K. Maclean, *Cultural Hybridity and the Environment*,
DOI 10.1007/978-981-287-323-1_9

member from the local community arena in Victoria expresses: *local knowledge is [not] superior to academic knowledge, for example, but without the local knowledge then the academic knowledge is pretty empty and so is political action.* However, as this comment reveals, in the same way that academic knowledge is *pretty empty* without local knowledge, local community knowledge alone is not sufficient to ensure equitable and sustained environmental management at the local project interface. This is because, as expressed in Chap. 2, local community knowledge may not necessarily hold all the answers to localised socio-environmental issues because these issues occur within a national and global setting. The words of a local ecologist from the community arena in the Northern Territory further illuminate the essential role as well as the limitations of local community knowledge cultures in locally situated environmental management and community development projects. In relation to the management of fire in the southern Tanami, he explains that *Aborigines [and pastoralists] are incredibly useful but they are no use if you expect them to be scientists, you've got to know what their limitations are.* A project member from the government arena in Victoria who has been working for Parks Victoria for most of his career speaks candidly of the limitations of government knowledge. He states that *we can only make decisions on what we know the same as the person who introduced rabbits or used DDT.*[1]

The implications of this analysis are many. First, in the same way that local community knowledge is limited by definition, so too are other knowledge cultures active at the environmental management and community development interface. As is demonstrated in Sect. 9.4, equitable and sustained environmental management of the local projects is contingent on first acknowledging the limitations of these knowledge cultures and then celebrating these limitations. Celebrating these limitations is the precursor to developing strategies for knowledge sharing at the local project interface (as discussed in Chap. 10). Second, these findings expose the combination of knowledge cultures that are active and necessary for equitable and sustained environmental management at the local project interface. Third, just as the findings shared in Chap. 8 demonstrated that local community knowledge encompasses diverse knowledge cultures, the knowledge held by project members from the government arena in Victoria and the Northern Territory also encompasses diverse knowledge cultures. In the remainder of this chapter, I take each of these implications in turn and in reverse order, to explore what they mean for a conceptualisation of all knowledge cultures as local.

[1] DDT or dichlorodiphenyltrichloroethane is a compound that was used as an insecticide but is now banned in many countries because of its toxicity to humans and other animals. Rachel Carson's (1962) important work 'Silent Spring' documented the detrimental effect of the (indiscriminate) use of pesticides, including DDT, on the environment. Her book, described as the cornerstone of modern environmentalism, fuelled social discourse around human and environment interactions and shaped the wider environmental movement at the time.

9.2 Place-Based Characteristics of Government Knowledge

The diverse characteristics of local community knowledge explored in Chap. 8 illuminate the fact that knowledge held by project members from the government arena is also complex and diverse. For example, the experiences of the Victorian project officer exemplify the tensions between how local community knowledge is valued as compared with expert knowledge. She feels that her knowledge is more highly valued than that of local community members by virtue of her paid employment. She describes her role as project officer is to encourage local groups to realise the value and power of their own knowledge. She regards *them* as the experts and believes that if she *wasn't getting paid for [her expertise and knowledge but] was just a loud mouth volunteer wanting to be involved in everything, it would be a much different playing field.* Her words and experience demonstrate how easily she could have been cast as a local community volunteer. She was in fact employed by the Catchment Management Authority by virtue of her place-based knowledge, her local community network connections as well as her specialised knowledge of ecology and community development theory and practice. In her own words, before being employed by government, she *was a political campaigner… working for a landcare group on a small project […and before that] a full time volunteer and studying community development.* Her experiences demonstrate that place-based knowledge is not only held by members of the local community arena. Equally, they illustrate how an individual can become an expert simply by virtue of her role.

The words of a project member from the government arena in Victoria who works closely with the local community in matters related to cultural heritage management in the region demonstrate that the success of expert knowledge depends upon place-based knowledge. He explains that *what makes you special after a while is the years and years of experience and mobs and mobs of contacts [that you have developed across the board] and that's what you can't teach anybody*. Secondly, his words demonstrate that his expert knowledge[2] is only as successful as it is locally relevant and appropriate. He explains that

> you have to seek the solution from the community that you are dealing with. I don't go to the community with whom I am working with set ideas. I sit down and I listen and usually I find that if I can engage them in enough discussions they will find a solution for themselves. Sometimes they say: 'oh that's a brilliant solution', and I say: 'well I didn't think of it, it came out of this discussion'. Sometimes it comes out of the most unlikely people.

The work of project members from the government arena in the Northern Territory further illuminates the fact that place-based knowledge of the southern Tanami is not limited to individuals from the local community arena. This place-based knowledge includes knowledge of the fire history of particular tracts of land, knowing the traditional owner of a particular stretch of country and recognising that local experiences are particular to specific places. For example, an active project

[2] Although his knowledge is described as expert for the purposes of this discussion, he does articulate that *I refuse to be an expert… I guess it depends on how you look at yourself in the world.*

member who works for the Bushfires Council speaks of the importance of having an interactive knowledge of past fire events and of seasonal weather conditions. He explains:

> we have had decent rain this year in that area and there has been a fairly quick response to the fuel loads there. The important thing is that the whole concept is to get in and burn before the fuel loads become big continuous bombs again.

An employee of the Centralian Land Management Association speaks about the connection of fire and relationships between interest groups living and working in the southern Tanami region of the Northern Territory.

She explains that

> [overcoming stereotypes is] going to be a major key to solving a lot of the cultural issues and relationships issues between Indigenous and non-indigenous [people]… We are talking about [an area] nearly the size of Victoria so dealing with people's issues and their goals and ambitions, everyone is quite different, there are some common themes but how people get there, they are all quite different.

Her words not only demonstrate her knowledge of place-based social histories, relationships and conflicts but they indicate that other knowledges of fire and of project planning and management will only be as successful as they are locally relevant and appropriate. This is because the goals, ambitions and issues that are closely determined by place and faced by individuals living and working in the region are different.

The implications of the second analysis of this chapter are twofold. Firstly, the words shared here reveal that it is incorrect to speak of local community knowledge as constituting one kind of knowledge and of expert knowledge and government knowledge as constituting other kinds of knowledge as is inferred in the discourse of community natural resource management. This is because each of these groups constitutes various knowledge cultures. Indeed, some individuals from each of these groups have knowledge cultures in common. Secondly, it is clear that despite the diversity of knowledge cultures active in any environmental management and community development project, the success of any given knowledge culture is contingent on local relevance, appropriateness and adaptability.

9.3 Knowledge Cultures Active in Local Environmental Management and Community Development Projects

The third analysis of this chapter engages with Brown's (2001) typology of knowledge cultures in western decision-making systems (presented in Chap. 1). This typology provides a useful way to conceptualise the knowledge cultures that are active and necessary for equitable and sustained environmental management at the local environmental management and community development project interface. Brown and Pitcher (2005: 126) speak of the important and essential role of five different nested knowledge cultures in working towards whole-of-community 'social

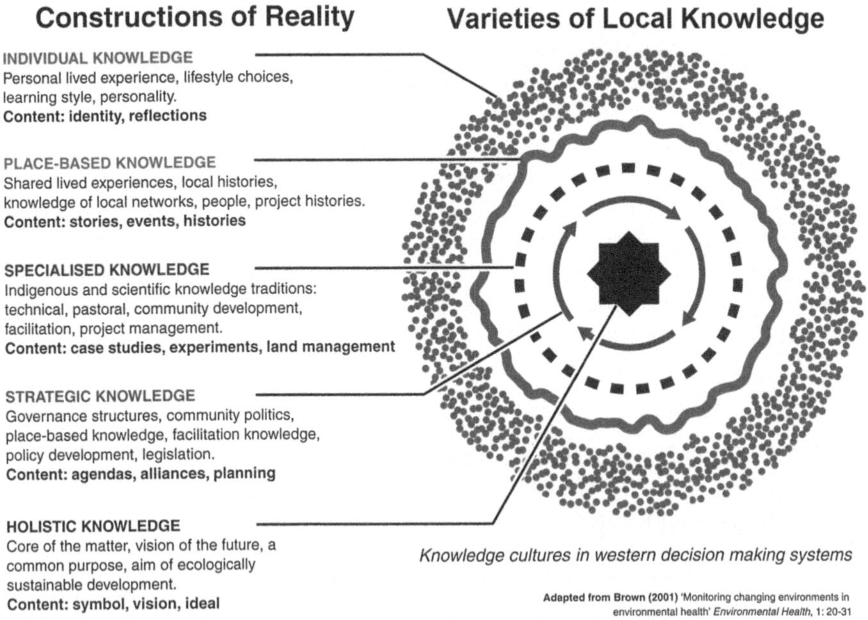

Fig. 9.1 The diversity of knowledge cultures for equitable and successful ESD

learning for sustainability'. They speak of a pattern of reality constructed by the contributions of individuals, the shared experiences of the local community whomsoever this may be, the sum of specialist interpretations, the strategic thinking of local organisations including local government and the holistic perspective offered by the goal and practitioners of sustainability.

In this analysis I extend her typology by exchanging her notion of 'local knowledge' (see Chap. 1) to 'place-based knowledge'. This extension complements the findings presented in Chaps. 6, 7 and 8 that demonstrate the success of any knowledge culture is contingent on its relevance, appropriateness and adaptability to any given locale. As such, the full set of knowledge cultures depicted in Fig. 9.1 is recognised as varieties of local knowledge. These knowledge cultures are not discrete or fixed. An individual's construction of reality and resultant action may be based on one or all of these knowledge cultures. For example, the bioregional manager in Victoria has his own individual knowledge and approach to the world which in turn informs the way in which he engages at the other knowledge interfaces. He has good place-based knowledge in relation to living in the region, working with other individuals in the region, being familiar with local networks and specific projects. He has specialised ecological and community development knowledge. He has strategic government knowledge. As he is responsible for the initiation and development of the whole-of-community Threatened Species project, he has used various knowledge cultures to work towards an innovative holistic knowledge approach to biodiversity management in his local region.

The main point of departure between this figure and Fig. 1.1 (Chap. 1), which depicts Brown's (2001) knowledge typology, is the recognition that all knowledges are tied to place and thus local. In this way, the diagram depicts two layers of meaning. Firstly, it represents the different knowledge cultures active at the two project interfaces. Secondly, it represents the specific places in which these knowledges are enacted. Equitable environmental management and community development projects will recognise these two layers. These projects will result in the practice of cultural hybridity (discussed in Chap. 10). As such, the practice of cultural hybridity will create further knowledge cultures which are not easily predicted but will result from synergies between the knowledge cultures depicted in this diagram (source: extended from Brown 2001).

9.3.1 Knowledge Cultures Explained

9.3.1.1 Individual Knowledge

In a discussion of the value of local knowledge and the local scale to ecologically sustainable development (ESD), the importance of individual knowledge cannot be overemphasised. This is because the way in which we know and act in the world is dependent, in the first instance, on the knowledge that we embody as individuals. This is inherently influenced by other knowledge cultures discussed below, but we cannot deny the reality that knowledge originates and is contained primarily in the head of the individual. Individual knowledge varies across cultures and between genders and age groups and includes personal lived experience, lifestyle choices, learning style and personality.

9.3.1.2 Place-Based Knowledge

The findings reported in Chap. 6 illuminate that projects are tied to place. As such, place-based knowledge is essential for equitable and successful environmental governance and management. Without knowledge of place, any project will fail to be equitable and sustainable. Knowledge of place is not just about knowledge of the biophysical environment. It also includes knowledge of local histories and cultures, local social networks, people and, given the focus of this study, specific environmental management and community development projects. As is detailed in Tables 9.1 and 9.2 that follow, place-based knowledge is not only held by the local community.

Knowledge of local histories includes specialised knowledge of place, for example, local geographic and biophysical environments, as well as cultural sites of significance. It comprises knowledge of environmental histories, such as those to do with changing land management, for example, the declaration of the Box-Ironbark forests and woodlands, parks and reserves in Victoria (see Chap. 5). It also includes knowledge of cultural connections to country and, specifically in relation to the Desert Fire project, knowledge and effects of past events such as bush fire events. Local historical knowledge is also about people, past conflicts and different research traditions. It also relates to local social realities, what are they and what historical and contemporary processes influenced and continue to influence these social realities.

Knowledge of local social networks includes familiarity with localised knowledge networks and the connected inter- and intra-group politics based upon histories and conflicts. It embraces knowledge of localised expert opinion: who is the right person to speak to regarding specific matters. This kind of knowledge includes the ability to tie extra-locale knowledge to a specific place by drawing upon local networks and local expertise. Knowledge of people overlaps somewhat with knowledge of local social networks in relation to knowledge of expert opinion. However, knowing the right person to speak with varies across social and cultural groups. This may include gatekeepers, experts and traditional owners of country. Knowledge of people also relates to knowledge of different cultures, as well as of individual personalities and how best to engage with particular people. It also includes knowledge of local community politics. This last example can also be described as strategic knowledge.

Knowledge of locally situated projects comprises knowledge of past research projects as well as government-funded projects relating to community development and environmental management. This knowledge is also about the successes, failures and potentials of past projects as well as the evolution and history of the specific project(s). Knowledge of locally situated projects embraces knowledge of the networks of other local projects currently underway. This includes knowledge of other projects in the region.

9.3.1.3 Specialised Knowledge

Specialised knowledge is held by many individuals working in the multiple arenas and composing the numerous knowledge networks that make up local environmental management and community development projects. Indeed, there is overlap between place-based knowledge and specialised knowledge. Specialised knowledge includes the Aboriginal knowledge tradition, the scientific knowledge tradition, pastoral knowledge and technical knowledge. It also encompasses knowledge of community development approaches and practices and related facilitation knowledge. It includes specialised historical and cultural knowledge, policy and planning knowledge as well as knowledge of project planning and management. Detailed accounts of these knowledge types follow.

The Aboriginal knowledge tradition comprises knowledge of country, such as in the language of western land management, local geology, geography, biophysical processes, climate and seasons and animal behaviour. It consists of knowledge of place: sites of significance in particular relating to sacred sites, funeral sites and men and women business camps. It includes historical knowledge of people, places and *jurkurrpa*. These practical knowledges could be described as equating with

Aboriginal anthropology and archaeology. Of particular interest to this research is traditional and contemporary knowledge of fire relating to hunting, cleaning the country, when to burn, traditional uses for ceremony and making rain.

The scientific knowledge tradition comprises knowledge generation processes relating to research and development. As relevant to this research study, it includes knowledge of the history and philosophy of the scientific knowledge tradition as well as the applied ecological knowledge of zoology, botany, geology and geography. This knowledge culture embraces both professional and amateur practices. It also comprises fire ecology: the affects of fire on ecosystems, the chemistry of fire, knowledge of what constitutes fuel loads and specific fire behaviours as well as the methods and theories of fire suppression.

Pastoral knowledge is comprised of knowledge of country: local geography, geology, local climates and environmental histories of specific places. In addition, this also comprises knowledge relating to pastoral production: the management of grasses, waters and infrastructure and the management of feral animals and exotic plant species. It includes place-based knowledge of fire management and fire suppression. Technical knowledge consists of knowing how to use geographical information systems and mapping systems, the specific knowledge relating to the use of fire equipment, knowing how to use Internet technology to view fire hotspots and also how to conduct threatened species surveys, to build fences and repair four-wheel-drive vehicles. It also includes specific project management knowledge.

Community development knowledge comprises knowledge of specific theories and approaches to community development including practical tools for participatory democracy such as appreciative enquiry and community juries. It contains knowledge of theories and tools for education and empowerment relating to: capacity realisation, building and maintaining local motivation and related hands-on actions. In practice it includes keeping the community informed of governance structures and process and empowering them to use these structures to their own ends. In this discussion, community development knowledge is premised upon understanding, advocating and celebrating strategies for knowledge sharing between the diverse world views of project members.

Facilitation knowledge consists of knowledge of specific theories and approaches to facilitation, such as collaborative conflict management and values mapping. Central to effective and successful facilitation is the practical knowledge of the politics of working with people and working to broker wider knowledge. Central to effective facilitation is the knowledge and use of appropriate language, including verbal and physical languages as well as conducting facilitation activities in appropriate locations with the right people. Historical and cultural knowledge include knowledge of the disciplines and practices of anthropology, archaeology and history. Understanding cultural interpretations of place is a central tenet of this knowledge.

Knowledge of specific government policies and the process of government planning also fall under specialist knowledge. This knowledge is also central to the knowledge of governance structures as expressed under the following knowledge culture heading: 'strategic knowledge'.

Knowledge of project management and planning comprises knowledge relating to the development and implementation of management plans that are contingent on a knowledge of the processes of equitable community consultation. This also includes the knowledge relating to report writing and accountability of project planning and outcomes. Specific knowledge of governance structures (such as those discussed in Chap. 4) and use of appropriate languages are essential for effective and successful project management. This holds true for the knowledge of how to locate on-ground aspirations, plans and works within bigger picture governance structures. The latter examples are also forms of strategic knowledge.

9.3.1.4 Strategic Knowledge

Engaging with social, environmental and governmental structures strategically is essential in working towards ESD. Indeed, recognising that ESD is as much about people, their personalities, cultures and language as it is about governance process is the first step in genuinely valuing local knowledge for ESD. Strategic knowledge plays a vital role in the development, implementation and process of any environmental management and community development project. There is much overlap between what can be described as strategic with what can be described as specialised and place based. Strategic knowledge encompasses knowledge of governance structures and local community politics. It also includes knowledge of project management and planning, community development and facilitation as well as place-based knowledge.

Knowledge of governance structures comprises historical and contemporary knowledge of legislation and relating policies (see Chap. 4). It also includes the knowledge and ability to create, develop and implement policies and plans such as action and recovery plans. Central to this knowledge type is the ability and knowledge to use the appropriate language to influence, effect and use government structures to meet one's own ends. This is demonstrated by the use of governance structures to attract funding and to hold government accountable to legislation such as the *Environment Protection and Biodiversity Conservation Act, 1999.*

Knowledge of local community politics consists of knowledge of politics of and between different individuals and interest groups. This includes knowing when to align with groups, when to avoid groups and when to remain politically neutral as well as knowing the appropriate language to use when negotiating with other groups. Strategic knowledge is composed of several knowledge cultures already mentioned above. These include project management and planning, community development and facilitation knowledge as well as place-based knowledge.

9.3.1.5 Holistic Knowledge

According to Brown (2001), holistic knowledge pursues the aim of sustainability by working to acknowledge, validate and integrate all the knowledge cultures that are operating at the environmental management and community development interface.

In relation to the two project case studies, it means working from within given government structures to create new visions and goals for equitable ESD. The two project case studies could be described as innovative approaches to this end. Although there is always room for improvement, for adaptive and equitable management of project process, the two approaches could be considered as attempts at more holistic approaches to ESD. I argue that approaches that embrace pluralism, knowledge and the local as places from which to work towards the third cultural space (following Bhahba 1990) are practising holistic knowledge.

The following section introduces matrices of the various knowledge cultures active in the two case study projects (see Tables 9.1 and 9.2). Understanding which knowledge cultures are present at these interfaces is important as a way of conceiving of the value of each knowledge community. It provides a means of conceiving whether any knowledge culture is under-represented and could thus limit project success. In Victoria it is clear that increased specialised knowledge, in particular facilitation, as well as historical and cultural knowledge would assist in improving project success. A reading of the Northern Territory matrix clearly shows that specialised knowledge relating to community development, facilitation, historical and cultural and project management and planning, as well as strategic knowledge of community politics and place-based knowledge are under-represented by the current environmental management and community development project.

Table 9.1 Victorian case study: the knowledge cultures

	Place-based knowledge	Specialised knowledge	Strategic knowledge	Holistic knowledge
Government arena	Project knowledge	Community development knowledge	Knowledge of government structures	TSN project creation
	Some knowledge of people	Facilitation knowledge	Community development knowledge	
	Some knowledge of local networks	Historical and cultural knowledge	Facilitation knowledge	
	Some knowledge of local histories	Project management and planning knowledge		
		Scientific knowledge		
Community arena	Knowledge of local networks	Some knowledge of project management and planning	Knowledge of local community politics	Unknown
	Knowledge of people	Some knowledge of scientific methods	Place-based knowledge	
	Project knowledge			
	Knowledge of local histories			

Table 9.2 Northern Territory case study: the knowledge cultures

	Place-based knowledge	Specialised knowledge	Strategic knowledge	Holistic knowledge
Government community	Some knowledge of local networks	Scientific knowledge	Knowledge of governance structures	The vision and goals of the DKCRC
	Some project knowledge	Technical knowledge	Some place-based knowledge	
		Policy and planning knowledge	Some knowledge of facilitation processes	
		Some knowledge of project management and planning		
		Some knowledge of community development processes		
		Some knowledge of facilitation processes		
		Some knowledge of local histories and cultures		
Aboriginal community	Knowledge of local histories	Indigenous knowledge	Knowledge of local community politics	Unknown
	Knowledge of local networks	Some technical knowledge	Place-based knowledge	
	Knowledge of people	Some knowledge of local histories and cultures		
	Some project knowledge			
Pastoral community	Knowledge of local histories	Pastoral knowledge	Knowledge of local community politics	Unknown
	Knowledge of local networks	Some technical knowledge	Place-based knowledge	
	Knowledge of people			
	Some project knowledge			
Conservation community	Knowledge of local histories	Scientific knowledge	Some knowledge of governance structures	Unknown
	Some knowledge of local networks	Some technical knowledge	Place-based knowledge	
	Some knowledge of people	Some knowledge of community development processes		
	Some project knowledge			

9.4 Celebrating the Limitations of Local Knowledge

The final analysis of this chapter explores how equitable and sustained environmental management is contingent on first acknowledging the limitations of the many knowledge cultures active in the environmental management and community development projects and subsequently celebrating these limitations. This approach complements the edge politics (after Howitt 2001) practised in Chap. 5. The following investigation considers firstly how the extension of Brown's (2001) typology advocated in this chapter allows a reading of the possible commensurability of the knowledge cultures represented in the two project case studies. Secondly, this investigation is countered with a discussion relating to the dangers of further perpetuating the knowledge dichotomies inherent to the metanarrative of ecologically sustainable development.

Despite the various world views exemplified by the knowledge cultures active in the two project case studies, these knowledges can be considered as possibly commensurable because all are necessary for equitable ESD at the environmental management and community development project interface. This book contends that if some of these knowledge cultures are absent, under-represented or undervalued, the resulting project will fail to be equitable. As a project member from the government arena in the Northern Territory who works closely with Aboriginal people articulates, the Desert Fire project will only be successful if it practises *a realistic view of the world or rather a pluralistic view of the world.* The words of a project member from the government arena in Victoria who works closely with local landcare groups echo the importance of acknowledging the many ways of knowing the same world. He critiques the tensions between the way our society values local community knowledge and lived local realities. He articulates that

> our culture doesn't... value other forms of knowing very easily, that might be women's knowledge or Indigenous knowledge or local knowledge or empirical knowledge gained by observation and trial and error [...it isn't validated] until it goes through the process of gaining credentials and a degree of acceptance [...and is] acknowledged by the experts.

The perceptions of these project members complement the discussion in Chap. 2 that presents the case for (ecologically) sustainable development as knowledge. Furthermore, the findings shared previously in this chapter complement the critique developed in Chap. 3 that all knowledge is locally situated. Such a conceptualisation of knowledge allows a reading of the potential commensurability of the many knowledge cultures active at the local environmental management and community development project interface. This reading does not contradict the call by this research to celebrate difference and diversity as important for ESD. Neither does it undervalue the importance of conflict in generating new knowledges and approaches for ESD. Indeed, the process of cultural hybridity (discussed in detail in Chaps. 10 and 11) is ignited by conflict and negotiation. Rather, it provides a means to conceptualise the equal importance and of these diverse knowledge cultures for local environmental management and community development.

Individual knowledge is the basis for any environmental management and community development work. When individuals become empowered to own their knowledge, the potential for equitable and sustained environmental management is enhanced. By definition place-based knowledge is essential for successful environmental management and community development. Specialised knowledge is equally important, and it can either be shared or extrapolated according to the situation. Strategic knowledge is diverse. Although some project members from the local community arena, for example, those working with the Threatened Species project in Victoria, are able to self-mobilise within certain environmental governance landscapes, it is not essential for all individuals from the local community arena to develop this kind of strategic knowledge. In relation to the local realities of many Aboriginal communities, project success may depend upon the important role of a project officer or gatekeeper who can work strategically across all knowledge cultures. Some argue that the more strategic the community is able to be, the more successful and empowered they will also be. Holistic knowledge is equally important to equitable and sustained environmental management and community development because it touches the core of the matter. Developing and maintaining a holistic understanding of the challenges, the goals and potential outputs of any environmental management and community development project is central to working towards equitable and sustainable ESD.

The different knowledge cultures exemplified by the two project case studies and presented in this chapter do not have to be considered in opposition to or contrary to each other. Holistic approaches to environmental management and community development are founded upon social learning strategies. These strategies consider ways to engage equitably with these many knowledge cultures to celebrate diversity and pluralism as the basis of ESD.

9.5 The Dangers of Knowledge Dichotomies

It is clear from the local voices of this research that local community knowledge plays a vital and essential role in the networks surrounding environmental management. For example, in Victoria, project members from the local community arena engage with both government processes and draw on knowledge networks in working to manage and protect threatened species habitat in their region. The local livelihood issues faced by potential project members from the local community arena in the Northern Territory are different to those in Victoria. The local community knowledge held by pastoral, conservation and Aboriginal land managers in the southern Tanami is essential in land management approaches and overcoming conflicts related to fire in the region. Working together with project members from the government arena to manage fire in the southern Tanami is an important step in overcoming conflict which, in turn, is closely connected to the development of sustainable livelihoods in the region.

Conceiving of a world composed of varieties of local knowledge and celebrating these diverse voices is essential in working towards equitable and sustained environmental management. Perpetuating dichotomies that juxtapose scientific knowledge with local knowledge is a very dangerous practice. This is because these dichotomies are hinged upon paternalistic and colonial notions of 'we know better'. This not only breeds suspicion between interest groups, for example, in the pastoral and Aboriginal communities, but also leads to ongoing social and environmental degradation. This is because, as discussed in Chap. 3, local and Indigenous knowledges are not necessarily unscientific (Murdoch and Clark 1994) but neither are they always in harmony with their natural and social environments because some local practices may be environmentally degrading. Equally scientific knowledge is not necessarily asocial, but it does often advocate a technocratic fix that is often devised in isolation from the local situation (Pretty and Scoones 1997).

Narratives and resultant practices that perpetuate the previously mentioned knowledge dichotomies ignore the many variables of knowledge. Firstly, knowledge selection is political. As discussed in Chap. 5, there is difference and diversity across the landscape. As such choosing one form of knowledge generation over another is based upon power rather than an essential objective truth. Secondly, as discussed in Chap. 3, the generation of knowledge is a social process. In all manner of knowledge generation, the collection and analysis of data is dependent upon the individual or group of individuals engaged in the process of knowledge making. All individuals are storytellers. They interpret the biophysical and social worlds in ways characteristic to the social institution to which they belong. As such they perpetuate a given political agenda. For example, some individuals interpret the landscape as a sum of its parts; others interpret the very same landscape as one single entity.

The political nature of knowledge generation begs the question: when does knowledge become skills? The practice of such skills, for example, using equipment to collect data, using the correct words on paper and using the correct tradition in which to communicate, is very much a learnt practice. The example given in Chap. 3 that speaks of the success of proponents of non-science-based knowledge bases using scientific language as a form of currency to acquire government funding highlights the fact that knowledge is about politics rather than purely proving or disproving given truths.

Perpetuating dichotomies that construct local and Indigenous knowledge as panacea to all environment and development problems are equally dangerous in working towards equitable and sustained environmental management. This narrative assumes that local practices will be in accord with the social and environmental principles of ESD. Assuming that the local knows best reinforces colonial narratives of, for example, the romanticised noble savage. In the Northern Territory such a narrative places full responsibility on Indigenous owners to halt the degradation caused by years of colonial use. This degradation has resulted from the overstocking of pastoral stations, the intentional or accidental introduction of feral flora and fauna species into these landscapes as well as the many other landscape changes that have resulted from the changing colonial notions of land management. Equally, it justifies minimal government funding (the Indigenous Protected Area program is working to rectify such practices) because traditional owners are constructed as individuals whose very lives are based upon ethics of stewardship. In reality, many Indigenous land owners are requesting the assistance and calling for increased funding to manage their heavily degraded lands.

From this discussion, it is clear there are many dangers in perpetuating the knowledge dichotomies and resultant hierarchies inherent to the metanarrative of ESD. Conceiving of all knowledge as local provides a means of moving beyond these knowledge dichotomies. Extending Brown's (2001) knowledge typology to conceive of the many knowledge cultures active at the local environmental management and community development interface as local not only supports the voices of this research but complements the applied peoples' geography advocated by this research. Moving beyond the knowledge dichotomies inherent to the metanarrative of ESD is the first step in addressing current levels of environmental and social degradation. The findings and discussion shared in Chap. 10 consider how to operationalise the principles shared in this chapter.

9.6 Conclusion

This chapter showed how the second guiding question of this research enables an exploration of the tensions that exist at the nexus between environmental governance and environmental management. This chapter considered the role of community stakeholder groups and their knowledge in the networks surrounding environmental management and community development. Analysis of the two empirical case studies using the new conceptual framework for cultural hybridity demonstrated the importance and potential of practising an edge politics for equitable and sustained environmental management. This is because the potential of all knowledge cultures in working towards equitable and sustained environmental management and community development is encapsulated by their limitations. These limitations expose the combination of knowledge cultures necessary for successful environmental management of locally situated projects. The findings of this research demonstrate that the success of these knowledges is contingent on their local relevance and adaptability. Extending Brown's (2001) typology of knowledge cultures in western decision-making systems to acknowledge that all knowledges are local provides the means to first unpack the many knowledge cultures active at each project interface; second, to consider the possible commensurability of these knowledge cultures; and, third, to reflect upon the dangers of perpetuating the knowledge dichotomies and hierarchies inherent in the metanarrative of ESD. It also creates the platform from which to consider strategies for knowledge sharing between interest groups engaged in local environmental management and community development projects.

References

Bhabha HK (1990) The third space: interview with Homi Bhabha. In: Rutherford J (ed) Identity: community, culture, difference. Lawrence & Wishart, London, pp 207–221

Brown VA (2001) Monitoring changing environments in environmental health. Environ Health 1:20–31

Brown VA, Pitcher J (2005) Linking community and government: islands and beaches. In: Keen M, Brown VA, Dyball R (eds) Social learning in environmental management towards a sustainable future. Earthscan, London, pp 123–145

Carson RL (1962) Silent spring. Houghton Mifflin, New York

Howitt R (2001) Frontiers, borders, edges: liminal challenges to the hegemony of exclusion. Aust Geogr Stud 39(2):233–245

Murdoch J, Clark J (1994) Sustainable knowledge. Geoforum 25(2):115–132

Pretty J, Scoones I (1997) Institutionalising adaptive planning and local-level concerns: looking to the future. In: Wright S, Nelson N (eds) Power and participatory development. Intermediate Technology Publications, London, pp 157–169

Part V
Strategies for Cultural Hybridity

Chapter 10
Practising Cultural Hybridity for the Third Space

Abstract The aim of this chapter is to address the third question posed by this research (to enable an exploration of the tensions that exist at the nexus between environmental governance and environmental management). How can greater knowledge sharing between the many interest groups involved in environmental management and community development projects be devised? This chapter integrates the epistemological (expressed in the applied peoples' geography) and conceptual (edge politics) tools of the new framework for cultural hybridity with the findings from Chaps. 6, 7, 8 and 9, pertaining to the power of the local to extend the theory that ecologically sustainable development (ESD) is about knowledge (discussed in Chap. 2). The findings and arguments shared in this chapter reveal that equitable and sustainable processes to improve knowledge sharing between interest groups involved in environmental management and community development projects depend upon the practice of cultural hybridity. This chapter demonstrates that the practice of cultural hybridity is threefold. The chapter explores what it means to engage in and actualise the practice of cultural hybridity.

10.1 Processes for an Applied Cultural Hybridity

The arguments advocated in this chapter complement the work of various researchers introduced in Chap. 2 who theorise strategies for overcoming the entrenched dichotomies of the metanarrative of ESD that privilege one knowledge base over another. These researchers speak of 'knowledge in action' discourses (Blaike et al. 1997), the development of 'discourse coalitions' (Hajer 1995), the hybrid nature of 'sustainable knowledge' (Murdoch and Clark 1994), and the importance of 'transepistemic communities' (Knorr-Cetina 1983) in working towards equitable and sustainable development. Of particular interest to this chapter is the work of Bhabha (1990) who speaks of the important practice of cultural hybridity in celebrating difference and diversity. I engage with his arguments to consider how the practice of cultural hybridity can open the opportunity to move beyond the previously mentioned knowledge dichotomies. I work from the stance that

> the importance of hybridity is not to be able to trace two original moments from which the third emerges, rather hybridity… is the 'third space' which enables other positions to

K. Maclean, *Cultural Hybridity and the Environment*,
DOI 10.1007/978-981-287-323-1_10

> emerge. This third space displaces the histories that constitute it, and sets up new structures of authority, new political initiatives. (Bhabha 1990: 211)

In Chap. 9 (Fig. 9.1) I extended Brown's (2001) typology of knowledge cultures in western decision-making systems to complement the epistemology of this research as well as the findings shared in Chaps. 8 and 9 that all knowledge is locally situated and tied to place. This typology enables the theoretical mechanism to identify and unpack the knowledges of best practice environmental management active at the environmental management and community development project interface as well as the knowledge cultures necessary for successful and equitable environmental governance and management. In this chapter I expose how the practice of cultural hybridity not only enables a theoretical strategy to move beyond previously mentioned knowledge dichotomies but also provides the basis for practical strategies for increased knowledge sharing at the local environmental management and community development interface. The following discussion establishes that applied strategies to actualise the practice of cultural hybridity are threefold. These strategies complement the impetus of the research. Engaging in cultural hybridity is firstly, about the ongoing practice of the applied peoples' geography advocated by this research; secondly, conceptualising social processes for planning and implementing projects that complement local voices; and thirdly, cultural hybridity is contingent on creating spaces for negotiation.

10.2 Practising an Applied Peoples' Geography for Cultural Hybridity

The first analysis of this chapter complements the findings from Chaps. 6, 7, 8 and 9 by demonstrating that cultural hybridity is dependent upon the applied peoples' geography and resultant edge politics, practised by this research. This applied peoples' geography provides tools to open up the local spaces of environmental governance and management in ways that are empowering and create the basis for social action (after Harvey 1984). In doing so, it recognises the power of the individual as an agent for social action and change. In a discussion about the essential role and power of the local, one cannot look past the power and potential of the individual in working to move beyond the knowledge dichotomies inherent to the metanarrative of ESD. Indeed, Church (1992) points out that so many of the key social changes throughout history have been down to the inspiration and commitment of just a few people. In the context of an ever-changing political world 'the power of individuals to bring about change is as great or greater than it was when the United Nations was created' (Church 1992: 22). The following discussion illuminates the way that project members from the two project case study describe strategies for increased knowledge sharing at the local environmental management and community development interface can be aligned under four broad principles. These principles complement the research epistemology, reinforce the importance of the applied peoples' geography advocated by this research and exemplify the significance of practising an edge politics for cultural hybridity. Although the four principles are common across the two project case studies, their exact meaning varies according to location.

These principles include:

1. Working to unsettle current epistemology of ecologically sustainable development (or land management)[1]
2. Considering the ingredients necessary for equitable, adaptive and sustained social process
3. Developing planning approaches for equitable environmental management and governance
4. Engaging in activities and techniques for increased knowledge sharing[2]

The remainder of this analysis elucidates what these principles mean for project members in the two empirical case studies in Victoria and the Northern Territory.

10.2.1 Case Study 1: Principles for Protecting and Conserving Threatened Species Habitat in Victoria

Project members involved with the Threatened Species project in Victoria offer three distinct arguments relating to the importance of engaging in processes to unsettle the current epistemology of ESD. Firstly, some project members from the government and the community arenas believe that sustainable environmental governance and management is based upon listening to and valuing all knowledges equally; breaking down knowledge stereotypes of experts and non-experts; and considering local knowledge networks as the locus for collectively finding solutions. Secondly, some project members believe that successful environmental governance and management is about revolutionary learning and action. A project member from the government arena articulates that this learning is dependent upon individual learning. He believes that the individual's approach to the world

> changes when you get pushed into challenging your assumptions… you need something to shake your world view to make you question it and then look for change… that's where change and innovation happens.

Thirdly, some project members from the government arena believe that equitable and holistic environmental governance and management processes must acknowledge the reality that nature is a cultural construct but, in an interrelated way, must

---

[1] This principle forms the philosophical foundations upon which the other principles rest.

[2] Most of the ideas relating to the operationalisation of increased knowledge sharing between groups came from individuals in the Indigenous and pastoral communities. This supports earlier arguments that those living at the local environment and development interface are the ones with the knowledge of how to approach local challenges.

incorporate a sophisticated understanding between spiritual connection to place and resulting environmental governance and management.

Project members identify various ingredients necessary for equitable, adaptive and sustained social process at the local project interface. These ingredients include recognising the role of people, of opportunity costs and of monitoring and evaluation in equitable and successful environmental governance and management. Some project members from the local community arena state that it is essential for government to employ the right people. These people must have good local knowledge and local networks and must be able to liaise and network with diverse individuals and groups. This is important because, as the words of a local landcare president express, *only good communicators will survive*. Other project members explain that these people must also have a flexible, supportive and opportunistic attitude to their work because working with community and other non-government groups requires making the most of opportunities as they arise. On a related point, effective social process is highlighted as important for project success by some project members. This is because equitable environmental governance and management is dependent upon listening to the local as the locus for ESD. Project members point out that these processes must be adaptable and must recognise social diversity as the key to equitable and sustained environmental governance and management. These processes must engage with and value different knowledges as well as recognise and accept the fact that change takes time. Of particular importance is the philosophy of working together rather than against each other. Many project members highlight group psychology, the role of individual personalities, effective communication and the building of trust are central to project success. A final ingredient to facilitate equitable, adaptive and sustained social process is the importance of monitoring and evaluating the social processes of which such projects are composed.

Project members strongly advocate the importance of developing planning approaches for equitable environmental governance and management. Some project members believe that planning approaches must be grounded in bigger picture thinking, they must focus upon the development of strategic and objective approaches, and they must develop an intergroup motherhood statement. Other project members believe that collective learning and knowledge synergies are central to any such planning process. Other ingredients highlighted as essential for equitable and sustained environmental governance and management include clear communication and the development of trust and social capital among individuals from the immediate project community as well as those from wider government and community arenas. Some project members from the local community arena in Victoria articulate the need for clarity of project aims, objectives and work approaches. This includes developing specific work schemas and realising that the specialised knowledge of external experts is often required. Project members believe that ongoing monitoring and evaluation of planning procedures is central to ensuring that the planning process itself is equitable and all-inclusive.

Project members from the government and local community arenas identify specific activities for increased knowledge sharing at the local project interface. These activities include the development of a project management approach that includes frequent committee meetings; the employment of individuals from the local community groups as project officers; as well as identifying who can do what, and thus considering what knowledge is needed to satisfy specific project outcomes. Other identified activities include the ongoing monitoring and evaluation of projects in relation to on-ground tangible project work as well as more intangible social processes and an increase in the number of field trips and field days offered by the project. One project member explains that these days are particularly important because they provide opportunities for place-based learning and knowledge exchange.

In summary, an overwhelming number of project members from the Victorian case study conceive of successful and equitable environmental governance and management as multifaceted. Their words and opinions highlight the fact that project success is dependent upon firstly, achieving practical on-ground project works to protect and enhance threatened species habitat in the region; secondly, recognising the power of the local; and thirdly, developing processes to challenge current environmental governance epistemology and resulting environmental governance practice. A significant number of project members locate knowledge networks, social process and sustained knowledge sharing as central to equitable and successful environmental governance and management at the local project interface in Victoria.

10.2.2 Case Study 2: Principles for Managing Fire in the Southern Tanami, Northern Territory

Project members involved with the Desert Fire project in the Northern Territory speak about the various benefits the project could bring to the southern Tanami region. There are also various opinions about what a strategy to manage fire in the region should encompass. For example, a manager of Birds Australia based in Melbourne believes the strategy should be a tangible document developed in consultation with all interest groups. There should be consensus about *the objectives and methods and then there should be a series of actions. This could end up being a booklet with series of maps, fires zones, people saying we are going to do this in this zone*. A pastoralist from the region advocates that the strategy should be a living document: *once a book was put out then it is up to the [Bushfires Council] to have regular meetings*. An employee from the Central Land Council who works closely with Aboriginal people in the region believes that fire management cannot be contained in a book. He explains:

> there isn't a plan that is going to make any difference but there is a process and it would be one that is absolutely inclusive [...a] participatory process and in that respect it needs to be one that concentrates its resources in bringing people together, to understand each other's perspectives, there is always room for improvement and a long process of defining how you use fire is as important.

The voices of these project members illuminate that a fire management strategy means different things to different people. As is elucidated in the following discussion, project members describe several strategies that inform the previously mentioned principles for increased knowledge sharing at the local environmental management and community development interface. Satisfying all four principles will eventuate in equitable and sustained environmental governance and management in the southern Tanami.

Some project members speak about the importance of working to unsettle current approaches to land management. In this context it means valuing knowledge equally. As an employee of the Central Land Council articulates, in relation to Indigenous knowledge of fire:

> you can say to people: look in your community you have got some amazing knowledge about burning and how to manage country and fire, this group of western scientists over here would like to know about it and they would like you to show them how to use it.

Valuing local pastoral knowledge is equally important because, in the words of this pastoralist, *most of the pastoralists have got knowledge, all sorts of knowledge, from fire to drought. They have got to put that knowledge forward as everyone's area is slightly different.* On a related point, to some project members, working to unsettle current approaches to land management means living outside the paradigm. This pastoralist enthuses that

> you've got to get outside that [personal comfort] area and challenge yourself as well as other ideas, to see if something is going to work, if you are prepared to do that you can achieve all sorts of results.

Working to unsettle current approaches to land management is also about moving to the middle ground. The words of a local ecologist highlight the importance of this. He explains that

> Of course there is a middle ground… but the trouble is that we [whitefellas] are not prepared to change… there are two different cultures… overlapping this much and we are saying you mob have got to move, we are not going to move an inch. Even if we moved a little bit it would make it easier but we are not prepared to.

Living outside the paradigm and moving to the middle ground means acknowledging the existence and limitations of stereotyping people. For example, it is important to move beyond stereotypes of Indigenous peoples. The same local ecologist explains the importance of getting *rid of the noble savage myth for a start because that is a huge impediment.* It is also important to unsettle stereotypes of pastoralists. For example, as a project member from the government arena who works closely with pastoralists articulates, contrary to popular belief *the great thing about [the pastoral] industry here is that most people are organic but don't go to the level of getting certified.*

Working to unsettle current approaches to land management also means considering local contradictions. The words of a pastoralist from the region touch upon this dynamic:

> we are talking about stopping black fellas in inappropriate lighting of fires, but we are still actually burning. So I had one old fella, when I asked him why he burnt, say that I was burning that fire last week, so why shouldn't he?

Working to unsettle current approaches to land management also means working with, rather than being paralysed by, local realities. As a non-Indigenous pastoral manager of an Aboriginal pastoral enterprise states *[Aboriginal] people want to work, maybe not every day, maybe only one day in 6 months, but they want to so surely it's a great labour force of willing people.*

Project members identify various ingredients that are necessary for equitable, adaptive and sustained social process. These include adequate, responsible and ethical government employment practices, for example, Aboriginal and pastoral individuals should be paid for their knowledge and expertise. Some individuals believe that this would not only send the message to these interest groups that their knowledge is genuinely valued by government and scientists but it would also assist in moving beyond the culture of suspicion that exists between pastoralists, Aboriginal people and employees of government agencies, that often lead to communication breakdown and conflict. This is particularly important because, as this pastoralist points out, *the government and research agencies need to realise that they only get out what local people are prepared to put in.*

Some project members involved with the Desert Fire project believe that engaging with and developing planning approaches for equitable environmental governance and management is central to both overcoming conflict relating to fire in the region and the success of the project. An Aboriginal woman from the region states that the different groups have got to talk to each other and listen to each other because *if they did come together they could get a bit of an idea of why the other one is doing what they are doing*. Planning approaches are particularly important considering that working together to overcome conflict is pivotal to better fire management in the region. As this Aboriginal elder points out *sometimes the women disagree so then men are not able to light that fire, they have to be working together to make a better job of it.*

Some project members speak of the potential of planning approaches to assist the different interest groups in finding common ground and goals. The words of this Aboriginal woman articulate how planning processes have the potential to facilitate innovation. She explains: *maybe get the pastoralists to talk and say their bit and get our fellas [traditional owners] to say what they think and see what they come up with.*

Many project members working at the environmental management and community development interface in the Northern Territory identify the need to engage in activities and techniques for increased knowledge sharing. It is interesting to note that most ideas shared in the following discussion come from pastoralist and Aboriginal project members. These activities include discussions of the importance of people, place, tools and techniques for increased knowledge sharing between interest groups working to manage fire in the region. Pastoralists and Aboriginal people recognise the need to bring people together from far and wide to talk about the use of fire in the region. One pastoralist points out that such meetings must happen several times because once is not enough to galvanise relationships, develop approaches to fire management and open the channels for equitable knowledge sharing between all interest groups. It is essential to get the *right* people together at these meetings. An Aboriginal woman from the region emphasises the importance of speaking to the right traditional owners. This not only relates to their right to speak for that country but also their ability to inform the wider community about the meeting and to encourage the right people to attend.

Project members from both the pastoral and Aboriginal communities acknowledge that in order for the different interest groups to come together, indeed to *sit together*, meetings must be held away from the politics of the community and the politics of land tenure. Meetings must be held on neutral ground *where people can concentrate*. These project members identify specific tools and techniques to facilitate discussion which would involve, as this Aboriginal woman articulates, *getting people to talk their bit*: *[traditional owners] are happy to listen and to talk*. These tools and techniques include the presence of interpreters and interactive materials such as videos and books with pictures.[3] In addition there should be mixed methods of engagement: the meetings should get the *[Aboriginal] rangers out burning and then talking about fire*. A pastoralist points out the need for a good facilitator because *you can't have [pastoralists] being a bit outspoken, they have got to hold their tongue a little bit*. Another project member who works closely with the pastoral industry speaks about the importance of engaging in values mapping activities. She explains that *we need to think of the way to move forward [beyond conflicts over fire], so we need to map areas of value, to identify areas that people want to protect*.

Project members living and working in the southern Tanami have excellent suggestions for practical approaches to begin planning for the management of fire in the region. In order for these approaches and strategies to be equitable and successful, they must not embody specific power inequalities. For example, the use of maps and satellite images are incredibly helpful in both sharing fire management technology but also indicating the bigger picture issues of widespread fires in the region. However, it is important that these maps do not give the wrong messages. For example, maps can be *very accusatory [they can] tell one kind of story. We need the map to be neutral and then see if these fires are an issue for people [in the region]*.

Equally, although overcoming conflict and improving communication between interest groups are central to the successful and equitable management of fire in the region, it is also important to respect the wishes of different project members. For example, as project members from the pastoral and Aboriginal interest groups point out, the different interest groups can work together but do not necessarily need to be together. This relates both in terms of accommodation when interest groups may come together for meetings or work purposes. As a pastoralist *explains [Aboriginal people] like to go and camp by themselves and we like to camp by ourselves and I respect that... I don't believe in trying to mix groups and all this great social thing [multiculturalism] that Australia believes in*. This is also reflected in personal relationships. As this Aboriginal man articulates *even though we fight we can work together to look after country*.

---

[3] Two such books were used as communication facilitation tools during the first stage of the Desert Fire project.

In addition to the activities and processes detailed above, some project members speak about the role of public awareness raising. One Aboriginal woman believes there could be signs advising people not to use fire *along areas where pastoral leases are. [Aboriginal people travelling through] would see those signs and take note of them.* These signs should also explain why it is important to be careful with fire. The signs should be instructive and clear but not unwelcoming. For example, an Aboriginal man suggests that signs could show the threatened species in the region and be *in the language of the other people [there are many tourists that pass through the area] like the French, the Germans, the Japanese, this will make them happy and they will be happy to be on that land.*

In summary, as has been demonstrated by the local voices of the Desert Fire project case study, environmental governance and management in the southern Tanami region is clearly about more than simply developing and applying a practical fire management strategy. The findings of this analysis highlight the fact that successful environmental management in the region is contingent upon acknowledging the complex and sometimes contradictory approaches to land management in the Northern Territory. It is dependent upon valuing local knowledge and working towards equitable, adaptive and sustained social networking. It is also about working within the social realities of the region to develop novel, innovative and all-inclusive approaches to knowledge sharing and on-ground land management approaches.

The first strategy advocated by this analysis is grounded in the practice of the applied peoples' geography for cultural hybridity. Practising this geography acknowledges the power of the local in environmental governance and management. The four derived principles that have resulted from an analysis of this geography describe specific fundamental elements that are central to increasing knowledge sharing at the local environmental management and community development interface. These elements expose the reality that achieving success at the local environmental management and community development interface is multifaceted and complex. It is equally about achieving practical on-ground works and developing strategies that complement local social realities for improved knowledge sharing between interest groups.

The four principles derived by this analysis constitute the first strategy necessary for the practice of cultural hybridity. However, taken in isolation, they do not provide the means to actualise the potential for cultural hybridity. They do provide, however, the basis for a project planning and implementation process that embraces and celebrates diversity. Such a process aligns with theoretical methodologies that celebrate difference, social learning and conflict as catalysts for overcoming the many challenges of environmental governance and management. Section 10.3 draws upon the social learning and community development literatures (see Chap. 2) to introduce ways to conceptualise processes to enact the four principles derived in this analysis. The analysis of the following discussion provides a second strategy to actualise the potential of cultural hybridity for environmental management and community development.

10.3 Conceptualising Processes for Cultural Hybridity

The second analysis of this chapter considers ways to conceptualise project planning and implementation approaches that embrace the four broad principles derived in the previous discussion. This analysis engages with three models[4] from the social learning and community development literatures and the five metaphors for Yolngu[5] learning (Marika-Mununggiritj and Christie 1995) to assist in conceptualising the planning and learning processes necessary for equitable and successful environmental management and community development at the local project interface. The models and metaphors are useful for two reasons. Firstly, they are a useful tool to demonstrate the importance of conceptualising the stages and cycles necessary for the practice of cultural hybridity. Secondly, an analysis of these stages illuminates ways to actualise the four principles derived in the previous analysis. Important to note here is that the five Yolngu metaphors for learning originate in Yolngu country, northeast Arnhem land in far north Australia. As such, these metaphors are derived from place-based Yolngu knowledge and experience and are connected to Yolngu country. It would be more appropriate to use learning metaphors derived by local actors from the two case study projects. However, as such metaphors of learning do not yet exist, this study draws on these five Yolngu metaphors of learning to provide another way to conceptualise the learning process.

There is a wealth of literature advocating that successful planning for environmental governance and management is about social learning, relationship building, ownership and improved social and political acceptability (McCool and Guthrie 2001).[6] The actual process itself can be as important, if not more so, than the outcome. The role and power of the planning process cannot be overemphasised. This is because both the way in which planning is conceived and practised can either embody the process of working to unsettle the epistemology of ESD (this equates with principle 1 derived above) or it can work to reinforce the power inequalities of the current metanarrative of ESD. Equally, the planning process can be inclusive of the identified ingredients for equitable, adaptive and sustained social process (this equates with principles 2 and 3 derived above). Alternatively, by denying these ingredients, the planning process can continue to ignore local voices and local realities and thereby perpetuate prescriptive approaches to environmental management and community development that are almost guaranteed to fail for the many reasons extolled in the research thus far. The three models presented in this chapter embody particular approaches to social learning and project management.

[4] Although it may seem contradictory to this research epistemology to speak of models, it is possible to ground localised social learning and adaptive management in models that have open and dynamic learning, local knowledge, flexibility and adaptability as their core concepts.

[5] The Yolngu people are an Indigenous group from north east Arnhem land in far north Australia. Their language is Yolngu Matha.

[6] These attributes reflect those articulated by individuals working at the local environmental management and community development project interface.

Figure 10.1 demonstrates the importance of acknowledging the power of these models, if engaged with exclusively, to value intangible process outcomes on the one hand and tangible project outcomes on the other hand. As shown in Fig. 10.1, all these models exist along a continuum of social process. This continuum has epistemology as the core concept at one end and community development practice as the core concept at the other. As discussed in Chaps. 7 and 8, the success of the environmental management and community development projects in Victoria and the Northern Territory is based upon both tangible project outcomes and intangible process outcomes. These models can be helpful to facilitate particular ways to conceptualise project planning and implementation processes that integrate the many aspects of such projects.

The Co-learning Cycle (Keen and Mahanty 2005: 106) depicted in Fig. 10.1 engages with the philosophy and practice of social learning. This model is useful in considering the essential and ongoing co-learning necessary for equitable and successful environmental governance and management at the environmental management and community development interface. The decision-making cycle (Aslin and Brown 2004: 11) model also calls for ongoing learning processes. It speaks about practical ways and tools to engage at each stage of the learning and decision-making cycle. Both these models are informed by the adaptive management and social learning literatures. Equally useful is the project management cycle (Piper 2005). This model has evolved from community development literatures and experiences. This model is based upon project management and thus tends to describe distinct and, it could be argued, prescriptive stages of community engagement that do not recognise the need for ongoing learning and adaptive process throughout. As such this model exemplifies how specific conceptions of power can be embodied in planning and project management processes. However, this model is still a useful tool to highlight the stages of any project.

The Yolngu metaphors for learning are not expressed or fixed within a model. Rather they are encapsulated in five words: *galtha*, *dhin'thun*, *lundu-nha:ma*, *dhudakthun* and *gatjpu'yun* (Marika-Mununggiritj and Christie 1995). The notion of *galtha* goes beyond the models presented above by speaking of a connecting spot or the importance of a unique place and time to learning. *Galtha* is 'the spot where people make solid contact with the earth, they have been brought together from different places, and now they are having a discussion together to agree on a plan of action' (Marika-Mununggiritj and Christie 1995: 60). *Dhin'thun* speaks of research in relation to the specific methods used to discover information about the past which in turn inform the way in which decisions made during the process of *galtha* are pursued and followed up. *Lundu-nha:ma* literally means to '"see the journey" taken by our ancestors, and this involves identifying the land and the people we have interacted with through the years, their motivations, their loyalties, their ideas, and everything else which has made them great' (Marika-Mununggiritj and Christie 1995: 61). *Dhudakthun* speaks about the importance of 'learning to love and understand our homeland and the ancestors who have provided it for us, so as to create ourselves reworking the truths we have learned from the land and the elders into a celebration of who we are and where we are going in the modern world'

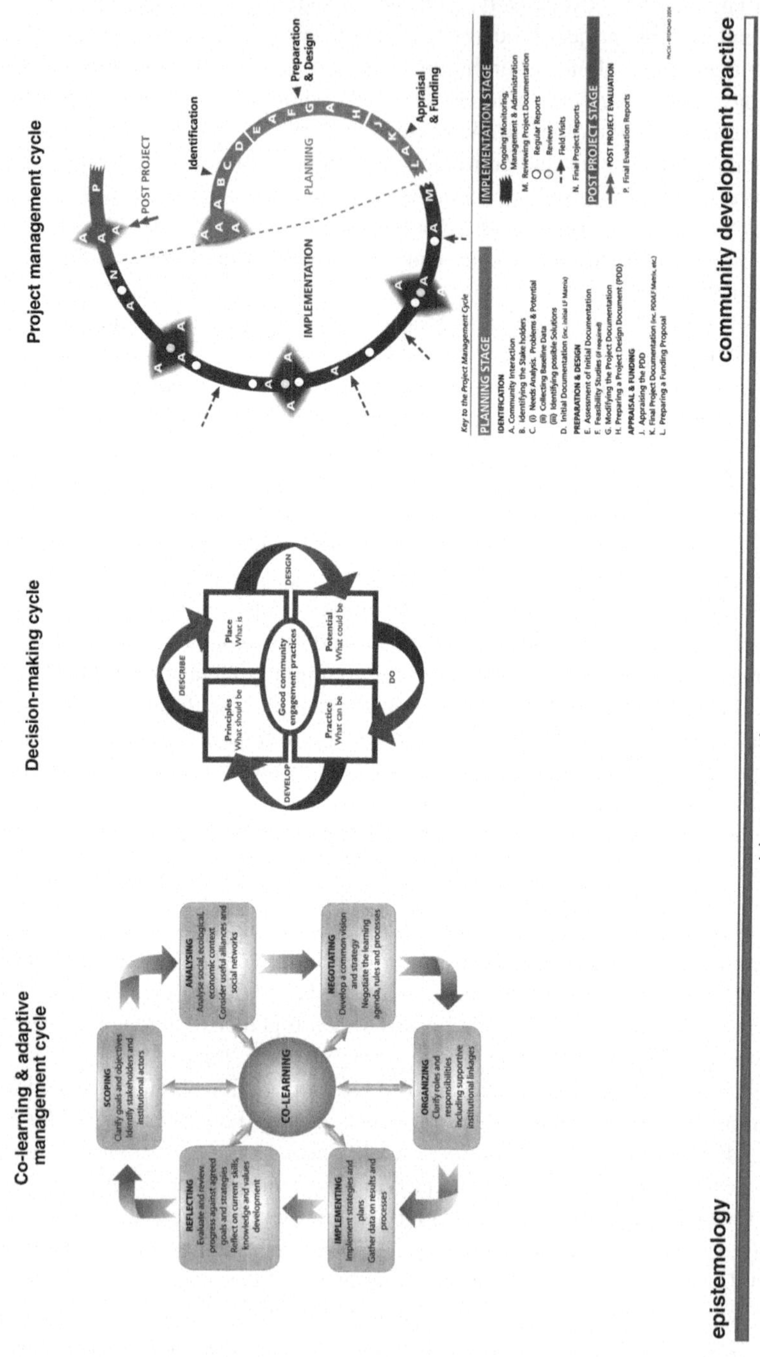

Fig. 10.1 A continuum of learning cycle models (Sources L–R: Keen and Mahanty (2005: 106), Aslin and Brown (2004: 11), and Piper (2005))

(Marika-Mununggiritj and Christie 1995: 61). *Gatjpu'yun* means 'that we are excited and hopeful and confident for the future. We know what we are looking for. It is not a discovery we are looking for, but the knowledge and skills to be true Yolngu in the modern world' (Marika-Mununggiritj and Christie 1995: 62).

Taken separately or together, these models and metaphors give practical ways of conceptualising the planning and the project management processes necessary for equitable and successful environmental governance and management of environmental management and community development projects. Table 10.1 demonstrates how the four principles derived in Sect. 10.2 align with various stages of the social learning and project management cycles depicted in Fig. 10.1 and with the Yolgnu metaphors of learning described above. Engaging with these models and metaphors enables a foundation from which to conceptualise the processes necessary to actualise cultural hybridity. The first column reintroduces the four principles derived above; the second and third columns include the two specific social learning models relating to co-learning and adaptive management (Keen and Mahanty 2005) and decision making (Aslin and Brown 2004); the fourth column is based upon the project management cycle (Piper 2005); and the final column includes the Yolngu metaphors for learning (Marika-Mununggiritj and Christie 1995). As depicted in Table 10.1, these learning metaphors are not limited to any one stage of the learning cycle: they occur throughout.

Table 10.1 aligns the four derived principles with the social learning and community development models presented in Fig. 10.1 and the Yolngu metaphors for learning. Drawn by author from L–R: Keen and Mahanty (2005: 106), Aslin and Brown (2004: 11) and Piper (2005) and Marika-Mununggiritj and Christie (1995).

In summary, there are various ways to conceptualise, order and understand the tangible project outcomes and the intangible process outcomes of any environmental management and community development project. As articulated in Fig. 10.1

Table 10.1 The learning cycle matrix

Four principles	Co-learning and adaptive management	Decision-making cycle	Project management cycle	Yolngu metaphors for learning
Unsettling; ingredients	Scoping; analysing	Describe; place	Identification	*Gatha*
Ingredients; planning	Negotiating; organising	Design; potential	Preparation and design	*Dhin'thun*
Activities	Implementing	Do; practice	Implementation	*Ludu-nha:ma*
Ingredients; planning; activities	Reflecting	Develop; principles	Post project evaluation	*Dhudakthun*

and Table 10.1, these outcomes are entwined with the different stages and cycles of social learning, project management and with the five Yolngu metaphors for learning. The analysis presented in this section illuminates the fact that actualising the potential for cultural hybridity is closely connected to learning cycles. The second strategy advocated by this chapter points to the importance of conceptualising processes to actualise the potential of cultural hybridity. Engaging with specific planning and project management models provides the tools to conceptualise such processes. A holistic and flexible conceptualisation for cultural hybridity acknowledges that at any one time various aspects of the learning process may be occurring. Equally, this learning process is necessary for an all-inclusive, evolving and locally owned environmental management and community development project planning and implementation processes.

10.4 Creating Spaces for Cultural Hybridity

The third analysis of this chapter demonstrates how integrating the strategies presented in Sects. 10.2 and 10.3 further facilitate the potential for cultural hybridity. Taken together, the strategies advocated in Sects. 10.2 and 10.3 provide practical approaches for actualising local knowledge synergies within environmental management and community development projects. In this final section of the chapter, I argue that achieving approaches that listen to the local voices and engage in planning and learning processes for equitable and successful governance and management also require the creation of spaces for negotiation. The impetus for creative spaces, places and processes for cultural hybridity is the final strategy advocated in this chapter. The strategy presented in this section integrates the research epistemology as expressed through the applied peoples' geography and the edge politics practised throughout the findings from Chaps. 6, 7, 8 and 9 pertaining to the power of the local and the two strategies advocated above with practical tools from the participatory community development literature to extend the notion that the practice of cultural hybridity is about creating spaces for negotiation.

Working towards greater interfacing between individuals and the interest groups they make up involves reaching a creative space where individuals are able to perceive other ways of knowing, other spaces of power, are able to conceive of reality as messy and power as entangled.[7] This creative space celebrates hybridity by welcoming the practice of objectivity that privileges contestation, deconstruction, passionate construction, webbed connections and hope, for transformation of systems of knowledge and ways of seeing (Haraway 1991). This space also paves the way for the Bhabha's (1990) third cultural space and allows individuals to consider what lies between spaces of knowing the world and social process. The negotiation of this space involves rich and diverse social learning. It is very personal and very

[7] The critique practised thus far in this book opens up such a creative space.

individual. The reality is people must be ready and even perhaps searching for a way to live outside their *personal comfort area* or paradigm or wishing to *shake-up their world view*. This can perhaps be facilitated from within an open learning environment such as that expressed in Sect. 10.3. Creatively negotiating spaces for cultural hybridity demands several practical and tangible factors.

Firstly, inspiring a creative intellectual space from which the individual is able to consider other ways of knowing the world as equally valid and important is fundamental to creating spaces for cultural hybridity. In practice this means valuing local knowledge, developing the power of the individual, celebrating diversity and conflict and creating an open and challenging learning environment. Secondly, genuinely negotiating spaces for cultural hybridity depends upon place. The project planning process, negotiation between interest groups, potential collaborative conflict management and so on must be actively engaged in at a neutral place. This place must be devoid of implicit or explicit power relations that reinforce any one narrative or discourse. Engaging with all interest groups to decide upon a creative place is part of the process.

Thirdly, negotiating creative spaces for cultural hybridity is dependent upon the development of sustained and adaptive processes and practices. As such all individuals and interest groups need to move beyond previously held preconceptions of the other. They must genuinely listen to what others are saying. This kind of listening creates a forum in which all individuals feel confident to express their ideas, knowing they are really being heard. There are various tools and methods that can assist creative listening.[8] Fourthly, creative listening depends upon clear and comprehensible communication. Individuals must be clear on what they are trying to communicate; they then need to use appropriate language, symbols and approaches to convey their meaning. This may involve cross-cultural communication that does not reinforce any one narrative. There are various tools and methods that can assist creative communication.

Finally, creating spaces for negotiation that engage in the practice of cultural hybridity for a third cultural space is very complex and difficult. Reality dictates such an equitable and genuine process will take time. Such a process is unique to any given situation. In practise a creative process is developed and owned by all those who choose to be involved. The goals, objectives, outcomes and criteria of the process are clearly understood and articulated by all those involved. The process and the on-ground works is monitored, evaluated and learnt from (see Table 10.2 for a simplified summary of the aims and purpose of each of these factors).

The learning cycle and project management models introduced in Sect. 10.3 can assist in the development of such a creative process. There is a wealth of communication and planning strategies in the community development practice literature that can provide specific participatory learning and action tools to further engage project members in the planning and implementation of such creative processes (e.g., IIED 1988–2006; Pretty et al. 1995; Allen and Kilvington 2001a, b;

---

[8] The tools and methods exist in the community development literatures.

Table 10.2 Mutually contingent factors for creating spaces of negotiation

Aim	Purpose
Creative space	A creative intellectual space means celebrating diversity, difference and conflict *Creating an open and challenging learning environment requires*
Creative place	Engaging all interest groups to decide upon a creative and neutral place for negotiations and decision making *Equally*
Creative listening	Developing sustained and adaptive processes for cultural hybridity demands a forum in which all individuals feel confident to express their ideas, knowing they are really being heard *This also depends upon*
Creative communication	Clear, dynamic and interactive communication *Cultural hybridity is situated in*
Creative, adaptive process	A creative process that is developed and owned by all those who choose to be involved. The goals, objectives and outcomes of the process are clearly understood and articulated by all those involved

Chambers 2002; Walsh and Mitchell 2002; Lambertet al. 2003; Eamer 2004; Claremont and Davies 2005). There are also planning approaches, such as the logical framework approach (see Piper 2005), that can assist in framing such creative processes.

10.5 Conclusion

This chapter showed how the third guiding question of this research enables an exploration of the tensions that exist at the nexus between environmental governance and environmental management. This chapter considered how greater knowledge sharing between the many interest groups involved in environmental management and community development projects can be devised. Equitable and sustainable processes to improve knowledge sharing between interest groups involved in environmental management and community development projects depend upon the practice of cultural hybridity. Engendering this practice is contingent upon three strategies. Firstly, practising an applied peoples' geography for cultural hybridity further acknowledges the power of the local in environmental governance and management by celebrating the power and potential of the individual as an agent for social change. The four derived principles for improved knowledge sharing at the local interface are evidence of this power and potential. The second strategy advocated by this chapter pertains to the importance of conceptualising processes for cultural hybridity. This strategy engages with social learning and community development models as well as, for example, the five Yolngu metaphors for learning to articulate the stages and cycles of project planning, implementation and learning processes. These stages and cycles clearly correspond to the four derived principles previously mentioned. The final strategy advocated by this chapter recognises the importance of the five factors essential to creating spaces for negotiation between the many interest groups involved in environmental management and community development projects. This final strategy integrates the research epistemology, the four principles derived in the first strategy and the project planning, implementation and learning processes argued for in the second strategy. Taken together these three strategies provide the impetus, the process and the space necessary to move beyond knowledge dichotomies inherent to the metanarrative of ESD. These strategies have the potential to engage Bhabha's (1990) third cultural space for equitable and sustained environmental governance and management into the future.

References

Allen W, Kilvington M (2001a) Building effective teams for resource use efficiency. Manaaki Whenua Landcare Research, Lincoln

Allen W, Kilvington M (2001b) ISKM (Integrated Systems for Knowledge Management), Manaaki Whenua Landcare Research. www.landcareresearch.co.nz. 12 Aug 2006

Aslin HJ, Brown VA (2004) Towards whole of community engagement: a practical toolkit. Murray-Darling Basin Commission, Canberra

Bhabha HK (1990) The third space: interview with Homi Bhabha. In: Rutherford J (ed) Identity: community, culture, difference. Lawrence & Wishart, London, pp 207–221

Blaike P, Brown K, Stocking M, Tang L, Dixon P, Sillitoe P (1997) Knowledge in action: local knowledge as a development resource and barriers to its incorporation in natural resource research and development. Agr Syst 55(2):217–237

Brown VA (2001) Monitoring changing environments in environmental health. Environ Health 1:20–31

Chambers R (2002) Participatory workshops: a sourcebook of 21 sets of ideas and activities. Institute of Development Studies, Brighton

Church C (1992) Living in a time of change. In: UNCED (United Nations Conference on Environment and Development) (ed) Earth summit'92. The United Nations conference on environment and development: Rio de Janeiro. The Regency Press, London, pp 22–28

Claremont R, Davies L (2005) Collaborative conflict management. Lansdowne, Sydney

Eamer J (2004) Keep it simple and be relevant: the first nine years of the arctic borderlands ecological knowledge co-op. Environment Canada, Whitehorse

Hajer M (1995) The politics of environmental discourse: ecological modernization and the policy process. Clarendon, Oxford

Haraway D (1991) Simians, cyborgs and women. Routledge, London

Harvey D (1984) On the history and present condition of geography: an historical materialist manifesto. Prof Geogr 36(1):1–11

IIED (International Institute for Environment and Development) (1988–2006) Rapid rural appraisal notes 1–21 & participatory learning and action notes 22–53. International Institute for Environment and Development. www.iied.org. 12 Aug 2006

Keen M, Mahanty S (2005) Collaborative learning: bridging scales and interests. In: Keen M, Brown VA, Dyball R (eds) Social learning in environmental management. Towards a sustainable future. Earthscan, London, pp 104–122

Knorr-Cetina KD (1983) The ethnographic study of scientific work: towards a constructivist interpretation of science. In: Knorr-Cetina KD, Mulkay M (eds) Science observed. Sage Publications, London, pp 115–140

Lambert J, Elix J, Priest B (2003) Values mapping: a flexible tool for building sustainability partnerships. Community Solutions. www.communitysolutions.com.au. 17 July 2006
Marika-Mununggiritj R, Christie MJ (1995) Yolngu metaphors for learning. Int J Sociol Lang 113:59–62
McCool SF, Guthrie K (2001) Mapping the dimensions of successful public participation in messy natural resource management situations. Soc Nat Resour 14:309–323
Murdoch J, Clark J (1994) Sustainable knowledge. Geoforum 25(2):115–132
Piper C (2005) Participatory project management workshop. TorqAid, Melbourne
Pretty JN, Guijt I, Thompson J, Scoones I (1995) A trainer's guide for participatory learning and action. International Institute for Environment and Development, London
Walsh F, Mitchell P (eds) (2002) Planning for country. Cross-cultural approaches to decision-making on aboriginal lands. Jukurrpa Books, IAD Press, Alice Springs

Chapter 11
Working Together to Better Manage the Country

Abstract The challenge of this book has been to engage with the metanarrative of ESD to consider theoretical and practical mechanisms to overcome the intra-generational inequalities inherent to this metanarrative, and resulting institutionalised practice. The aim of the book has been to consider ways to move beyond the dichotomies of exploitation inherent in this metanarrative. This chapter illuminates the theoretical and empirical significance of this research for contemporary research and practice in the field of environment and development. The following section presents the conclusions of the research: the role that the new conceptual framework for cultural hybridity has for theoretical debate and practical on-ground action. These conclusions synthesise the claims made by the new framework with empirical reflection for social action. Working towards cultural hybridity depends upon both theoretical tools and practical strategies. The theoretical tools provide the basis and impetus for social action. The practical strategies provide ideas for social action and represent the praxis between theory and action/practice. The chapter ends with a discussion that imagines the role and design of formal government institutions, on-ground projects and the individual or the self for social action to enable cultural hybridity.

11.1 Conceptual Strategies for Cultural Hybridity

This research provides a conceptual framework to enable the move beyond dichotomies inherent to the curr ent metanarrative of ESD, towards the practice and process of cultural hybridity. As has been shown throughout this book, the framework consists of an applied peoples' geography (after Harvey 1984), and an 'edge politics' (after Howitt 2001), three guiding questions to critique the politics of any environmental management and community development project as the way to open the space for cultural hybridity, and a suite of strategies to provide a way to enable cultural hybridity in different contexts with different players.

The applied peoples' geography that is advocated by and practised in this book provides the means to consider the theoretical complexities of environmental governance and management. Unpacking these complexities is the first step in the process towards cultural hybridity. The applied peoples' geography advocated in

K. Maclean, *Cultural Hybridity and the Environment*,
DOI 10.1007/978-981-287-323-1_11

this book recognises knowledge as situated (see, e.g., Haraway 1991; Watson-Verran and Turnbull 1995) and networked across time and space (see, e.g., Massey 1991, 1993; Waston-Verran and Turnbull 1995; Escobar 2001); power as entangled (see Foucault 1980; Sharp et al. 2000); governance scale as relational and networked (see, e.g., Lefebvre 1991; Smith 1992; Delaney and Leitner 1997; Howitt 1998); and nature as socially constructed (see, e.g., Cronon 1996; Willems-Braun 1997; Castree 2001; Castree and Braun 2001). Practising this geography provides a way to open up the multiple, entangled and networked spaces of environmental governance and management to consider the nexus between global spaces of environment and development and local spaces of environmental management and community development. This geography provides a foundation for the social action necessary to overcome the dichotomies that are inherent to the metanarrative of ESD, and move towards processes of cultural hybridity that are advocated in this book as fundament to alleviate current levels of environmental and social degradation. The edge politics (after Howitt 2001), advocated in this book, provides the means to actualise the conceptual (and theoretical) ideas of the applied peoples' geography. This practical exercise provides a way to unpack the tensions between government rhetoric at the environment and development interface at the global and national scale and the livelihood realities of individuals working to manage the environment at the local scale (the environmental management and community development interface). Understanding the complexities of the political, cultural, knowledge and social landscapes at any environmental management and community development interface demonstrates that equitable and sustained environmental governance and management must recognise local specificity (Maclean 2009; cf Howitt et al. 2013). Institutions that celebrate local diversity enable the adaptive management process that is necessary for resilient, equitable and sustained ESD in any nation.

The three guiding questions posed and answered in Parts III, IV and V show how important it is to critique the politics of any environmental management and community development project. The critique that combines the applied peoples' geography with the edge politics can open the space for cultural hybridity and provide the space to consider strategies to enable cultural hybridity in different contexts with different players.

The extension of Brown's (2001) typology of knowledge cultures in western decision-making processes to recognise that all knowledge is locally situated and connected to place provides the means to consider the complexity of entangled knowledge cultures and knowledge networks of which environmental management and community development projects are composed. Accordingly, it sheds light on the many and diverse varieties of local knowledge necessary for equitable and sustained ESD in any nation. This mechanism highlights the power, value and limitations of these knowledge cultures. In doing so it provides a practical mechanism to overcome theoretical debates that position these knowledges as incommensurable and therefore irreconcilable.

The practising of strategies that celebrate cultural hybridity provides practical mechanisms to move beyond dichotomies of exploitation. This is because 'the process of cultural hybridity gives rise to something different, something new and unrecognizable, a new area of negotiation of meaning and representation' (Bhabha 1990:211). This book advocates that practical strategies that deliver both tangible project outcomes and engage with intangible project processes will result in improved knowledge sharing within environmental management and community development projects. These strategies create the foundation for the alleviation of current levels of environmental and social degradation in any nation. Such strategies and projects enable engagement with the third cultural space. This is because these strategies and projects are premised upon working together to better manage the country.

11.2 Practical Strategies for Cultural Hybridity

Such strategies are significant for the process and pursuit of ESD because they provide the opportunity to imagine what ethical institutions for social action and change should comprise. Given the political and social instability of global politics and the ecological and social uncertainty of responses to these politics, predicting the future is impossible. Following the work of those who advocate the practice of adaptive management (e.g., Dovers 2003; Dovers and Wild River 2003; Sayer and Campbell 2004), social learning (for example, Parson and Clark 1995; McCool and Guthrie 2001; Fien and Skoien 2002; Schusler et al. 2003; Keen and Mahanty 2005) and given the reality of the lived local realities of individuals at any environmental management and community development interface, I call for institutions and processes that celebrate diversity as the basis for resilient and sustainable ecological, cultural and social landscapes across any nation. Institutions and processes that are premised upon adaptive management and thereby genuinely listen to local experiences and engage proactively with processes of monitoring and evaluation and social learning should dictate the future of environmental governance planning and practice.

Diversity can be celebrated and realised through the management and facilitation of an extensive network of environmental management and community development projects. Institutional culture is central to facilitating adaptive management. A greater number of individuals with knowledge and experience of what it means to engage actively in adaptive management must be employed to work within these institutions. The knowledge, experience and skills of these kinds of managers would complement that of local community facilitators.

As the following words of a project member from the government arena in Victoria clearly elucidate, ethical institutions for equitable and sustained environmental governance and management should actively involve people and actively support social process and the creation of effective networks. He states that environmental governance and management is

> about linking local government, the Catchment Management Authority, the local community, and the Department of Sustainability and Environment. Those sorts of connections are critical to having natural resource management work. It works beyond the level of the project: it creates networks and partnerships that are very powerful and if they are not there nothing works.

His words also hint at the reality that equitable and sustained social processes for environmental governance and management involve three separate but mutually contingent arenas: formal government institutions, on-ground projects and the individual or the self. In the following discussion, I imagine the role and the approach of each of these arenas in working towards equitable and sustained environmental governance and management. I begin with formal government institutions.

11.2.1 Imagining Formal Institutions for Social Action

Formal government institutions that are committed to equitable and sustained ESD should be founded upon the reality that environmental governance and management is about diverse knowledge cultures including the specialised knowledge of scientists, Indigenous people and pastoralists and the strategic knowledge of government officers and project managers. The synergies that result from the sharing of these diverse knowledge cultures have real potential in alleviating current levels of social and environmental degradation in any nation. These synergies reflect the reality that knowledge is always evolving, that all individuals are makers of knowledge and all individuals are political agents who have the potential to be agents for social change. These government institutions would also recognise that, just as knowledge is always evolving, so too is the goal of ESD. In this way ESD is as much about ongoing social process as it is about achieving a particular goal. Furthermore, decision making for ESD is not contingent on a single answer or the search for a particular set of truths rather it is grounded upon negotiation and locally appropriate approaches. These formal government institutions would reflect the reality of lived local experience that demonstrate how each place in the landscape and each environmental management and community development project is the product of geographic places and unique networks comprising people and their knowledge cultures. As such the institutions would represent the collection of localities of which the landscape is comprised. The institutions would recognise that these many places and localities that exist within different government jurisdictions (e.g. federal, state or territory) are connected together by networks, and not hierarchy. Furthermore, the culture of these institutions would recognise that formal institutions are not about a group of people working with a specific budget in a building in any other city, but they constitute groups and individuals networked across the landscape.

The main role of these institutions would be to manage and facilitate these networks in a way that creates spaces for local negotiation relating to best practice localised environmental management. These creative spaces would provide the potential for cultural hybridity. The best way to facilitate these creative spaces is through environmental management and community development projects. The management of these networks would connect localised networks to the bigger picture of regional, national and international environmental governance and management, and thus they would meet the goals and imperatives of national strategies and legislation and international conventions and laws. The facilitation of these networks includes the implementation of national and international strategies, conventions and laws in ways that do not limit or contradict the power of localised networks. Implementation would include relevant jurisdictional structures (e.g. one at a federal government, state and or territory arena) to coordinate funding, provide the vehicle for partnerships, collaboration and networking between different interest groups and knowledge cultures and encourage networking. Implementation would also include iterative learning processes such as realistic and feasible monitoring and evaluation whereby the bigger picture government institution genuinely listens and learns from localised experiences. In this way these institutions would be more creative, engaging and productive in governing the environment than institutions whose main goal is to ensure that designated monies are hitting the ground. By example, these institutions would be about creating hope for the future.

The approaches that these institutions would take to manage and facilitate the said networks are multiple. The management of these networks would be conducted by regional bodies. Each network, project and individual is fundamental to equitable and sustained environmental governance and management in any nation and this would be managed locally via institutions that are connected to a larger network of similar institutions nationally. The form of these regional institutions could vary according to the capacity and requirements of each region. This would reflect the unique reality of place-based environmental governance and management, but it would also acknowledge that without intra-generational equity, inter-generation equity for ESD is not possible. As such these regional bodies would be locally appropriate but also equitable. This would not limit the networks rather it would create an interface where these networks and resulting projects and processes could be managed. For example, in a land area that has a sparse but often centralised population that includes Indigenous groups that hold native title over land, a regional body could be designated according to land tenure type or Indigenous language groups. In areas that are relatively more populated with a uniform spread across the landscape, regional bodies may align with designated catchments. In all circumstances, these regions would be well funded to not only manage the networks and provide funding for projects but to also develop monitoring and evaluation processes that would be a cornerstone driving each institutional body. The culture of these institutions and practices would be one of creativity and imagination precisely because it is impossible to predict what will happen at the project interface. Any other institutional culture would contradict the potential to create spaces for negotiation for environmental governance and management both at the project interface and within the institution.

These institutions would facilitate these networks via environmental management and community development projects. This would be a means of celebrating and realising the diversity discussed above. These projects would be enabled through funding. Funding accountability would not be dictated to by traditional western time frames, for example, to be used within a given financial year, but would be determined by locally relevant and appropriate approaches. It would be managed through regional bodies. Project proposals would be facilitated by individuals who are employed by these institutions for their knowledge of community as well as their knowledge of facilitation and cross-knowledge-culture communication. Preferably these individuals would be from the local region and would possess a bigger picture knowledge of environmental governance and management across the region and in the relevant country. Part of their role would be to work with local groups to realise their own potential and power: to realise that the local is global. These facilitators would be able to draw upon and work to build larger networks of individuals with varying knowledges (place-based, specialised, strategic, holistic) and skills. However, it is important to note that personality is fundamental to success in this role. The role of personal attributes is discussed below in relation to the individual or the self as arena for social action.

These networks would be regarded as key to the success of the projects to deliver knowledge synergies for ESD. Institutions and individuals within such institutions need to focus on brokering networks and knowledge sharing across localities with the aim of developing environmental management and community development projects. The success of project proposals would be determined by the extent to which the projects work to facilitate network building across diverse knowledge cultures. For example, how many potential interest groups and knowledge cultures would be involved, would this project build upon existing networks and broker new ones? Integral to this process is the recognition that potential project members must not be forced into a mould whereby the success of project applications is contingent on the use of a mainstream language such as science. In a similar way, it is important that the project proposal facilitators do not consider themselves as experts in each knowledge culture. This is because the projects are about facilitating knowledge sharing and synergies across different knowledge cultures. These projects are imagined by this research as the main arena in which diverse knowledge cultures have the potential to create innovative and locally appropriate strategies for environmental management and community development. These strategies and potential knowledge synergies create the potential for the practice of cultural hybridity argued by the research as fundamental in working to alleviate current levels of social and environmental degradation in any nation.

11.2.2 Imagining Projects for Social Action

As has been demonstrated by this research, the environmental management and community development project arena is the nexus where environment and development policies meet environmental management and community development practice. Localised environmental management projects are thus integral to the alleviation of current levels of social and environmental degradation. The project arena draws together all that which the formal government institutions facilitate. The role of the project arena is thus as the locus for diverse knowledge networks to create the space for cultural hybridity and the creation of new knowledge. It is at this arena that tangible project outcomes and intangible social process outcomes are negotiated. Also, it is at this arena where knowledge sharing for cultural hybridity has the most exciting and immediate potential. The approaches taken at this arena to fulfil the project role would and must be multiple. Firstly, it is essential that individuals working at the project interface appreciate that the local is global. It is also essential that individuals working at the local project arena have a sophisticated understanding of the varieties of participation active at this interface. Not only would an awareness of this work to break down 'us and them' dichotomies between government, the local community and experts, but it would also acknowledge the important role of gatekeepers in navigating environmental governance structures on behalf of certain groups of individuals. Secondly, it is at the project arena that all individuals must develop an understanding of the complexities of knowledge. This includes the value, power and limitations of local knowledge. Such an awareness would demonstrate the essential role of the five knowledge cultures (as advocated by Brown 2001) in working towards equitable and successful ESD at the local interface. Developing a sophisticated and critical understanding of the equal role of all knowledge cultures at the environment and development interface would create the opportunity to engage with ideas of a third cultural space. Thirdly, working with individuals at the local project arena to conceive of a third cultural space, particularly in contexts of conflict, would create the space where theoretical postulating collides with practical process.

This book demonstrates with the two empirical case studies that at the project arena, intangible processes are as important for environmental governance and management as tangible project outcomes. Given, for example, the urgency of species extinctions and the social livelihood issues of Indigenous people who are culturally, socially and economically connected to the management of fire, engaging in lengthy social processes may seem futile. These processes are essential, however, to alleviate current levels of environmental and social degradation. At the project interface engaging in planning processes that provide strategies for successful knowledge sharing to both deliver tangible project outcomes as well as intangible process outcomes is integral in working towards ESD. These strategies are based on planning, practising and engaging in project work on the ground.

11.2.3 Imagining the Self as an Arena for Social Action

Ethical institutions for equitable and sustained environmental governance and management are comprised of people, social process and networks. The institutional arena is about managing and facilitating networks and the project arena is about negotiating social processes at the locus where these networks intersect. Both discussions have alluded to the important role of the individual or the self in these networks and social processes. This discussion explicitly expresses the role of the individual as an arena of social action.

Formal institutions and projects are comprised of individuals. The role of these individuals is to make decision about best practice environmental governance and management. These individuals exercise various amounts of power according to their knowledge and their role within a given institution or project. This power is not a static or limited entity but rather as Foucault (1980:98) expresses:

> [p]ower is employed and exercised through a net-like organisation. And not only do individuals circulate between its threads; they are always in a position of simultaneously undergoing and exercising this power... individuals are the vehicles of power, not its points of application.

The role of the individual or the self as an arena for social action cannot be under emphasised: it is the individual who is the political agent for social change and social learning. This is because, as has been demonstrated throughout this research, the local is political. As Brown (2001) states, knowledge originates in the head of the individual and the process of creating spaces for cultural hybridity must also begin in the head of the individual. The first step in working towards greater knowledge sharing for environmental management and community development at the local project arena is about individuals reaching a creative intellectual space where they are able to perceive other ways of knowing, other spaces of power, and are able to conceive of reality as messy and power as entangled (cf Foucault 1980). This creative intellectual space celebrates hybridity by welcoming the practice of objectivity that privileges contestation, deconstruction, passionate construction, webbed connections and hope, for transformation of systems of knowledge and ways of seeing (Haraway 1991). The negotiation of this space involves rich and diverse social learning that is very personal and very individual. The individual must be ready and even perhaps searching for a way to live outside their *personal comfort area* (Case Study 2: community member) or paradigm or wishing to *shake-up their world view* (Case study 1: government representative). Thus, it follows that the individual or self must be imagined as a fundamental arena for social action.

Just as the individual is the foundational arena for social action so too is this arena the basic unit of diversity. Celebrating diversity and difference among individuals is fundamental to successfully realise the power of diverse project arenas as the basis for future equitable and sustained environmental governance and management. Therefore, the approaches that individuals take in working towards equitable and sustained environmental governance and management must reflect the reality of interpersonal diversity. Individual approaches will vary according to life history, personality, knowledge base and whether the individual aligns the self with the formal institutional arena or the on-ground project arena. In both of these arenas, the individual or the self has the potential to imagine spaces of hope for sustained and equitable environmental governance and management into the future. The individual can take responsibility for working with others to create these spaces. The individual can work to create locally appropriate spaces that work within local community and interpersonal politics and acknowledge local limitations. The individual can realise the importance of interpersonal relationships, the role of personality and group psychology in creating these spaces. Fundamental to the role of the individual as arena for social action is an awareness of others, of other ways of knowing, communicating and listening. Clearly not all individuals will be capable of or interested in their potential role as an arena for social action. However, for those individuals who are interested in this role, these approaches are integral for

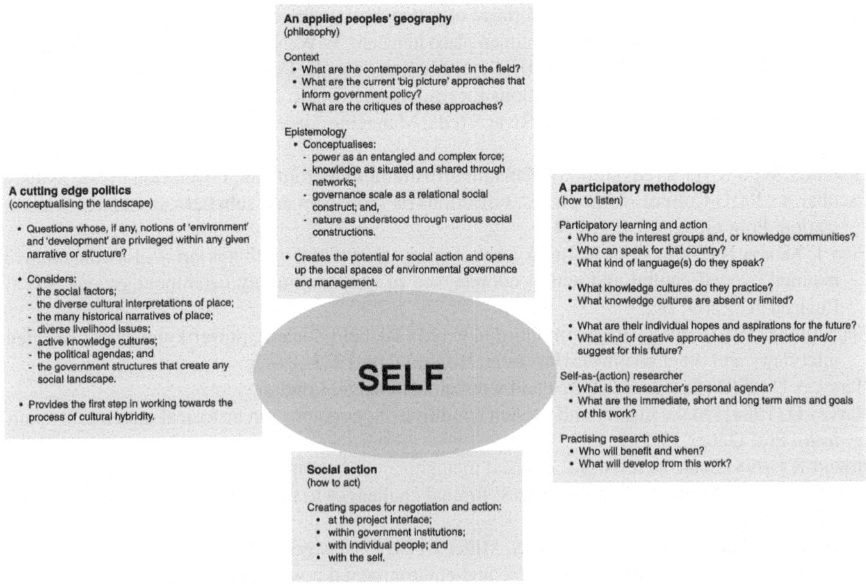

Fig. 11.1 Toolbox of the self as an arena of social action

working towards and engaging in processes of ESD. These individuals have an important role to play in facilitating the development of networks and knowledge sharing and synergies between the many interest groups involved in environmental governance and management.

This book advocates a new conceptual framework for cultural hybridity. This framework celebrates local diversity as the basis for equitable and sustained ESD. It provides the theoretical tools of an applied peoples' geography and practical conceptual tools of an edge politics, as well as practical strategies to enable processes for cultural hybridity – tools to create spaces for negotiation at the environmental management and community development interface (see Fig. 11.1 for a diagrammatic account of this toolbox). By example, the book demonstrates theoretical and applied strategies whereby the individual can begin to perceive the self as an arena for social action. Thus, we come full circle in this new conceptual framework for cultural hybridity.

References

Bhabha HK (1990) The third space: interview with Homi Bhabha. In: Rutherford J (ed) Identity: community, culture, difference. Lawrence & Wishart, London, pp 207–221

Brown VA (2001) Monitoring changing environments in environmental health. Environ Health 1:20–31

Castree N (2001) Marxism, capitalism, and the production of nature. In: Castree N, Braun B (eds) Social nature: theory practice and politics. Blackwell, Oxford, pp 189–207

Castree N, Braun B (eds) (2001) Social nature: theory, practice and politics. Blackwell, Oxford

Cronon W (1996) The trouble with wilderness, or getting back to the wrong nature. In: Cronon W (ed) Uncommon ground: rethinking the human place in nature. W.W. Norton & Company, London
Delaney D, Leitner H (1997) The political construction of scale. Polit Geogr 16(2):93–97
Dovers S (2003) Processes and institutions for resource and environmental management: why and how to analyse. In: Dovers S, Wild River S (eds) Managing Australia's environment. Federation, Sydney, pp 3–14
Dovers S, Wild River S (eds) (2003) Managing Australia's environment. Federation Press, Sydney
Escobar A (2001) Culture sits in places: reflections on globalism and subaltern strategies of localization. Polit Geogr 20:139–174
Fien J, Skoien P (2002) "I'm learning…how you go about stirring things up – in a consultative manner": social capital and action competence in two community catchment groups. Local Environ 7(3):269–282
Foucault M (1980) Two lectures. In: Gordon C (ed) Michel Foucault: power/knowledge: selected interviews and other writings. Harvester, Brighton, pp 1972–1977
Haraway D (1991) Simians, cyborgs and women. Routledge, London
Harvey D (1984) On the history and present condition of geography: an historical materialist manifesto. Prof Geogr 36(1):1–11
Howitt R (1998) Scale as relations: musical metaphors of geographical scale. Area 30(1):49–58
Howitt R (2001) Frontiers, borders, edges: liminal challenges to the hegemony of exclusion. Aust Geogr Stud 39(2):233–245
Howitt R, Lunkapis G, Suchet-Pearson S, Miller F (2013) New geographies of coexistence: reconsidering cultural interfaces in resource and environmental governance. Asia Pacific Viewpoint 54(2):123–125. doi:10.1111/apv.12013
Keen M, Mahanty S (2005) Collaborative learning: bridging scales and interests. In: Keen M, Brown VA, Dyball R (eds) Social learning in environmental management. Towards a sustainable future. Earthscan, London, pp 104–122
Lefebvre H (1991) The production of space (trans: Nicholson-Smith D). Blackwell, Oxford/Cambridge MA
Maclean K (2009) Reconceptualising desert landscapes: unpacking historical narratives and contemporary realities for sustainable livelihood development in Central Australia. GeoJournal 74(5):451–463
Massey D (1991) A global sense of place. Marxism Today, 24–29 June
Massey D (1993) Power-geometry and a progressive sense of place. In: Bird J, Curtis B, Putnam T, Robertson G, Tickner L (eds) Mapping the futures: local cultures, global change. Routledge, London, pp 59–69
McCool SF, Guthrie K (2001) Mapping the dimensions of successful public participation in messy natural resource management situations. Soc Nat Resour 14:309–323
Parson EA, Clark WC (1995) Sustainable development as social learning: theoretical perspectives and practical challenges for the design of a research program. In: Gunderson L, Holling CS, Light S (eds) Barriers and bridges to the renewal of ecosystems and institutions. Columbia University Press, New York, pp 428–460
Sayer J, Campbell B (2004) The science of sustainable development: local livelihoods and the global environment. Cambridge University Press, Cambridge
Schusler TM, Decker DJ, Pfeffer MJ (2003) Social learning for collaborative natural resource management. Soc Nat Resour 15:309–326
Sharp J, Routledge P, Philo C, Paddison R (2000) Entanglements of power: geographies of domination/resistance. In: Sharp J, Routledge P, Philo C, Paddison R (eds) Entanglements of power: geographies of domination/resistance. Routledge, London, pp 1–42
Smith N (1992) Geography, difference and the politics of scale. In: Doherty J, Graham E, Mallek M (eds) Postmodernism and the social sciences. Macmillan, London, pp 57–79
Watson-Verran H, Turnbull D (1995) Science and other indigenous knowledge systems. In: Jasanoff S, Markle GE, Petersen JC, Pinch T (eds) Handbook of science and technology studies. Sage, Thousand Oaks, pp 115–139
Willems-Braun B (1997) Buried epistemologies: the politics of nature in (post) colonial British Colombia. Ann Assoc Am Geogr 87(1):3–31

Glossary and Terms

Best practice environmental management Best practice environmental management implies a particular set of truths or processes upon which the environmental should be management. Such a notion is paternalistic and in direct contradiction to the epistemology and aim of this research study. I reclaim this term to consider the variety of different approaches to environmental management that are practised by different groups at the local environmental management and community development project interface. Throughout the book, I argue that genuine 'best practice environmental management' would result from synergies between these situated knowledges. This would create an iterative approach to localised environmental management.

Caring for country A term used to describe the philosophy of Indigenous land management practices. The Northern Land Council explains that 'Aboriginal people have a special relationship to land that is different to the majority of non-Aboriginals. It is not a commodity to be bought and sold' (NLC 2003: 1).

Friends Groups Groups of volunteers who work in conjunction with government agencies such as Parks Victoria, in managing parks and reserves around Australia.

Gatekeeper This term is used frequently in the qualitative social science literatures. It describes individuals who provide or prohibit the means to access certain groups of individuals. As such the term is also loaded with negative patriarchal connotations, particularly in relation to Indigenous peoples. I proactively reclaim this term to suggest the important role of particular individuals in facilitating the potential for equitable knowledge exchange between different cultural groups who otherwise would not have access to each other.

Jurkurrpa Jukurrpa means Dreaming, Story or Law in some central Australian languages. It is 'the basis for Warlpiri Law and custom; the period during which the Warlpiri social, moral and physical universe was created, which has an ongoing reality through the continuity of the practice that constitute Warlpiri culture' (Vaarzon-Morel 1995: 111).

K. Maclean, *Cultural Hybridity and the Environment*,
DOI 10.1007/978-981-287-323-1

Polyvocality This term literally means 'many voices'. In this context, it affirms the need to move beyond positivist social research practice that is grounded within the scientific tradition to recognise and embrace diversity.

Post-colonial The post-colonial literature is extensive and grounded upon diverse experiences that differ from nation to nation (e.g. see Ashcroft et al. 1995). As such this term has different connotations for different nations and for different groups of peoples within those nations. Willems-Braun (1997) states that there cannot be a global theory of colonial culture, only localised theories and historically specific accounts that provide insight into varied articulations of colonialist and counter colonial representations and practices. Australia could be described as a young nation grappling with what it means to move beyond the post-colonial. Australia could also be described as a nation whose colonial heritage persists in contemporary times, particularly in relation to Indigenous land rights, social status and so on. When I use this term, I refer to a body of literature that both critiques colonialism and considers what it means to move beyond colonialism.

Traditional owner This refers to Indigenous people who have traditional ownership over an area of country and thus have the cultural right and authority to speak for that country.

Warlpiri Warlpiri is a central Australian language that is spoken by approximately 3,000 people as their first language. The traditional lands of these speakers cover a relatively extensive area to the north-west of Alice Springs (CLC 2006: 1).

Yolngu Yolngu people live in northeast Arnhem Land, Northern Territory. Their language is Yolngu Matha.

Index

K. Maclean, *Cultural Hybridity and the Environment*,
DOI 10.1007/978-981-287-323-1

The manufacturer's authorised representative in the EU is Springer Nature Customer Service Centre GmbH, Europaplatz 3, 69115 Heidelberg, Germany. If you have any concerns regarding our products, please contact ProductSafety@springernature.com

Printed and bound by CPI Group (UK) Ltd, Croydon, CR0 4YY
22/09/2026
02220945-0004